LOOKING OUTWARD

BOOKS BY ADLAI E. STEVENSON

Major Campaign Speeches, 1952

Call to Greatness

What I Think

The New America

Friends and Enemies

Putting First Things First

Looking Outward

LOOKING OUTWARD

Years of Crisis at the United Nations

Adlai E. Stevenson

Edited, with commentary, by

ROBERT L. AND SELMA SCHIFFER

Preface by

PRESIDENT JOHN F. KENNEDY

HARPER & ROW, PUBLISHERS

New York, Evanston, and London

109017

LIBRARY OF CONGRESS CATALOG CARD NUMBER: 63-16520

*To Eleanor Roosevelt, whose heart and strength united
men and nations*

CONTENTS

❦ vii

Contents

Contents

PREFACE

✌ ✌ *This collection of speeches and papers offers a valuable* tour *d'horizon of contemporary American foreign policy in all of its scope and variety. In particular, this work will give its readers a fresh and full understanding of the reasons why the United States supports the United Nations and why that institution so well serves our national interest.*

Many crises have threatened the peace of the world since Adlai Stevenson became the United States Ambassador to the United Nations. The force, eloquence and courage with which he has advanced the American viewpoint have played no small part in helping to confine those crises to the council chambers where they belong. Looking Outward *is, in consequence, no academic or textbook exposition of our foreign policy in the United Nations. It is rather a running discourse on some of the most electric events of our time. It is thought generated on the spot, not hindsight called up in tranquility; it is the voice of Ambassador Stevenson, quickened by crisis. That, of course, is the heart of the UN's existence—to provide a forum in which the clash of ideas in healthy debate will supplant the clash of arms in deadly combat. That it may do so with steadily mounting success is our hope in this age when man's capacity to wreak destruction still overshadows his ability to reach the stars.*

Our belief in the indispensability of the United Nations does not, of course, mean that we are in total agreement with every decision the United Nations might take. What it does mean is that we are a nation of laws—and that we respect the law of nations. So it follows that we invest the highest hope in the organization which encourages

✌ xi

all nations, large and small, to walk the same path of justice and progress we ourselves have chosen in our own history. In supporting the United Nations, we not only support aims and ideals inscribed in our own Constitution, but we work to convert the high goals of our own foreign policy into living reality: the achievement of a world community of independent states living together in free association, in liberty and in peace.

I was present as a member of the press when the United Nations was organized in San Francisco in 1945. Governor Stevenson was there too for the Department of State, although he wasn't making as many speeches as he does now. Nor was I—but we have both made up for our silence in the years since.

During his presidential campaigns Governor Stevenson raised the level of our national political dialogue. As our representative in the United Nations, he has similarly raised the level of the international political dialogue. The proof lies in the pages which follow.

John F. Kennedy

EDITORS' NOTE

❦ ❦ Putting together a volume of speeches and writings of Adlai Stevenson poses a vast dilemma for any editor: What do you leave out? With misgivings, therefore, and with apologies for any omissions, we assume full responsibility for selecting, arranging and editing the material, and for the explanatory notes with which we have, in part, attempted to sketch in some background for his utterances.

Every crisis of the period covered by this volume could not be included. But these pages are a substantial record of his first two and a half memorable years as the United States' Permanent Representative to the United Nations.

It was necessary, of course, to eliminate purely ephemeral matters, discussions of procedural questions and parenthetical issues raised in parliamentary interruptions that had little bearing on substance. Other than these, his views appear here as he voiced them.

With reference to the arrangement, we have—with one or two exceptions—divided the material between his statements in the United Nations and outside. We did this for two reasons: Not only do his statements in the United Nations reflect official United States policy, but by grouping them together we feel they offer a form of stockholders' report on America's representation in the councils of the United Nations during this period. They also provide essential background for those speeches away from the UN in which Governor Stevenson discusses a wide range of the problems that beset the United States and the world.

And we have also included a limited selection touching on no problems, but which appear here for their sheer delight.

We are grateful to Governor Stevenson for his cooperation in this undertaking.

R. L. S. and S. S.

INTRODUCTION

✿ ✿ In this book are selections by the editors from my speeches and writings during the past two and a half years—since President Kennedy appointed me Permanent Representative to the United Nations. Generally speaking, the words of any public man tend to be more transient than permanent, and so I am flattered that the publishers felt that these views of mine merited the relative respect of a book.

I am glad they did, too, because most of the selections relate to the United Nations. And the United Nations is your business as well as mine. Since becoming United States Ambassador to the United Nations, I have concluded, sadly, that some Americans know too much, but far more know too little about the organization: too much, as Dean Rusk has said, to give it the continuing attention it deserves, too little to understand its vital importance in the conduct of our foreign relations.

Today we are deciding whether the family of man shall live as in the past—in anarchy and violence—or build a new, decent world community with freedom as its political habit, and peace as its goal. Has mankind ever been faced with a more fateful decision?

We have been the victims of the past; we don't intend to be the servants of the future. So we Americans are deeply committed to living in a free and peaceful world. In this convulsive atomic age the only way to *live* is to live in peace. And because the Charter of the United Nations is both the vision of this new world and the road map, we are resolved, by necessity and desire, to make the United Nations system work.

Perhaps this book should have been entitled "The UN Revisited," because, as a member of the United States Delegation, I was one of the jubilant midwives at its birth at San Francisco and one of its anxious nurses during its infancy in London and New York.

A rhyme comes back to me from those long-gone days in London when the nations first met to try out their fragile new experiment:

> I live in a sea of words
> Where the nouns and the adjectives flow;
> Where the verbs speak of actions that never take place,
> And the sentences come and go.

I thought then if they did not overload it with too many tasks, which they did, they would surely tear it apart with dissension, which they almost did, or they would drown it in words. (Why do so many people feel that to be immortal a speech must be eternal?) Returning after fifteen years I found the United Nations more overloaded, more riven by dissension, still suffocated with rhetoric, but—miraculously —mature, strong and vibrant with hope.

At a dinner in London during those early days we all made little speeches expressing satisfaction with "our baby's" progress. The Soviet Delegate's brief and acid contribution was: "When does baby get teeth?" Well, baby has teeth. The UN was tougher than the faint hearts predicted and evil hearts hoped. It has survived a brutal adolescence with all manner of assaults and misfortunes—like the Korean war, one hundred Soviet vetoes, the three-headed-monster theory of executive management called the "troika," Dag Hammar-skjöld's sudden death, and imminent bankruptcy. Meanwhile, it has performed some prodigious feats of peace keeping and nation building—in Iran, Kashmir, Palestine, Suez, the Congo. And one must not overlook the humanitarian work for refugees and children, or the economic assistance to less developed countries everywhere.

The membership now numbers 111 nations, with more to come. The agenda at the General Assembly each autumn numbers 100 items or more, filling the alphabet from atomic energy to Zanzibar. Somehow the United States seems to be involved in every one. Take 100 agenda items and multiply them by 111 nations and you end up with a figure of more than 11,000. Eleven thousand decisions to be made. The task of the United States Mission to the United Nations is simple: merely to make sure that those 11,000 decisions are compatible with the national interest—while everyone else is trying to make sure that they are compatible with *their* national interests.

The crises are incessant; so is the travel back and forth between New York and Washington; the cables and reports from every quarter of the globe come in daily torrents; so does the mail; the conferences and meetings and politicking are unending; so are the speeches that have to be written, the visitors that have to be seen, and the luncheons, receptions and dinners that have to be attended. And they say I have diplomatic immunity! Add to all this the everlasting combat with the Russians and you may understand why there are times when I yearn for the peace and quiet of a political campaign and a rally in Madison Square Garden!

Is it all worthwhile? Of course it is—if peace is worthwhile. Making peace is not merely a matter of nations looking at each other, but of their looking together in the same direction. Each peaceful gesture, each little thing, each humble effort at pacification, accomplished at any level, brings peace closer. The journey of a thousand leagues begins with a single step. We must never neglect any work of peace that is within our reach, however small. We have constantly to carry on, or re-begin, the work of building the institutions and practices of a nonviolent world, keeping always in mind, beyond the setbacks and disappointments, our *own* vision of a peaceful future for men.

Military power and alliances may deter war, but are not likely to develop the means or procedures for peaceful settlement or containment of vital differences among states. And surely the most rewarding task of civilized man today is that of reconciling different points of view, of accommodating national positions, of producing a consensus from a workable design for a meeting of the minds—for looking not at each other but in the same direction.

Will the Russians ever "look in the same direction"? Czarist history is no more encouraging than Soviet history. But a partial nuclear test treaty has been concluded at long last—the identical treaty we proposed in the United Nations in October 1962. It is not a reduction of arms; it does not even halt the growth of arsenals. But it is a first big step forward.

This agreement was possible only because Premier Khrushchev wanted it. One can but hope that it points toward a progressive relaxation of tension.

And a relaxation of tension is what the United Nations daily attempts to do. It can't, of course, restrain a great power against its will. But it can do the next best thing: it can and has intervened to prevent a direct confrontation by the great powers, and it can mobilize the mighty moral weight of world opinion—which no ambitious state however large can lightly ignore. And, as we daily witness, wild winds of change are rattling the gates, inside and out, that have so long imprisoned the strong and gifted Russian people.

If Communism is a problem for the United Nations, the United Nations is also a problem for Communism. For the United Nations is basically a community of tolerance and a community of tolerance is a terrible frustration for the totalitarian mind.

But it is not without frustrations for all the rest of us, too. For if we condemn Communism, as we must, for its contempt for political dignity, we must condemn as unrelentingly lapses in social dignity, our own included. And what nation, shackled by its history, can yet claim the beatific state of universal love and brotherhood? I have Harlan Cleveland, Assistant Secretary of State, to thank for reminding me of G. K. Chesterton's satirical verses about "The World State":

> Oh, how I love humanity,
>   With love so pure and pringlish,
> And how I hate the horrid French,
>   Who never will be English.
> The international idea,
>   The largest and the clearest,
> Is welding all the nations now,
>   Except the one that's nearest.

>   This compromise has long been known,
>   This scheme of partial pardons,
>   In ethical societies
>   And small suburban gardens,
>   The villas and the chapels where
>   I learned, with little labor,
>   The way to love my fellow man
>   And hate my next-door neighbor!

But, acknowledging the mote in our eye, we Americans can be proud that the ideals of the United Nations spring chiefly from our own tradition—the same belief in the equality of all men, before God and before the law, on which the American experiment was founded. Today what was once a Western ethic, even a white man's ethic, has become virtually universal. Peoples long divided by race and political subjugation, with all the lingering resentments that flow from that condition, now meet in a community of equals at the United Nations. And that sense of community, of interdependence, of common peril and hope, fragile though it may be, weighs heavily in the scales of peace in this dangerous world.

Perhaps Pope John XXIII may have had something like this in mind when he wrote in "Pacem in Terris":

It is our earnest wish that the United Nations—in its structure and in its means—may become ever more equal to the magnitude and nobility of its tasks, and that the day may come when every human being will find therein an effective safeguard for the rights which are inalienably his as a human being.

In a world made one by science and threatened by universal destruction, some personal rights—above all the right to life and security—can no longer be safeguarded by the individual national government. World society has to achieve the minimum institutions of order, and the only embryo of such an order is the United Nations system.

Though, as I say in this book, it still exercises minimal authority, the United Nations does represent the will of most governments to recognize more than national interests; it has policing power, an international court, functional agencies for health, agriculture, labor, education. Day by day it attempts to conciliate, mediate, discuss, compromise, or, if need be, simply delay the conflicts which play, like earthquake tremors, across the frail political crust of our society.

That it does cannot be overestimated. For—to preview some of the words on ensuing pages—on this shrunken globe men can no longer live as strangers. We can war against each other as hostile neighbors, as we are determined not to do; we can co-exist in frigid isolation, as we are doing. But finally we will have to learn to live together in the world as we do in the community, to respect each other's differences, to heal each other's wounds, to promote each other's progress, and to benefit from each other's knowledge.

However dark the prospects, however intractable the opposition, however devious and mendacious the diplomacy of our opponents, we ourselves have to carry so clear and intense a picture of our common humanity that we see the brother beneath the adversary, and seize every opportunity to break through to his reason and conscience, and, indeed, enlightened self-interest.

I have tried to give voice to these views of the tough and fascinating game of multilateral diplomacy in many ways for many years, as some of the following pages will attest. I can but hope that those kind enough to find something of value in what I have said will react like some scientists when an important breakthrough was announced. According to the news report, "a wave of guarded enthusiasm swept through the audience."

These writings will not have been in vain if they sweep you with "a wave of guarded enthusiasm" for the United Nations.

Adlai E. Stevenson

New York
July 30, 1963

PART I

PRINCIPLES
AND
PROBLEMS

THE PRINCIPLES THAT
GUIDE US

❦ ❦ *Adlai Stevenson's first official appearance at the United Nations since 1947 took place at a meeting of the Security Council on February 1, 1961. It was the occasion for a warm round of congratulatory speeches welcoming the most eminent statesman who had ever taken a permanent seat at the Council's horseshoe-shaped table. In his reply, Governor Stevenson set forth "certain principles" that would guide the United States in its approach to the crises of our day. Although brief, it sums up a personal philosophy and a creed for the United Nations that are evident throughout these pages.*

I have sometimes said that flattery is all right, Mr. President, if you don't inhale. Well, you have made it very hard for me not to inhale, thanks to a charity and kindness which have touched me so deeply. In the days—and perhaps nights—ahead of us, I shall always remember with gratitude this hour; and may all of our wishes be as good for all of the peoples of the world as your kind words have been good for me today.

As perhaps you know, I had a part in the birth of the United Nations in San Francisco in 1945, and in its early walks as an infant in London and then in New York in 1946 and 1947. And now I am pleased to be sharing in the problems of its adolescence.

The problems of adolescence are often those of young love. I be-

Statement to the Security Council, February 1, 1961.
❦ 3

lieve this is true in all countries. Would that *all* of our problems in this Council were the same.

And though *some* may not be amiable, I hope that we may deal with even the thorniest of them in an atmosphere of tolerance and of good will.

We are, to use the French phrase, the Nations United. Let us *be* united—united in a patient and persevering attempt to find the things we can agree upon and to build upon them a structure of understanding and cooperation against which whatever storms may be ahead shall beat in vain.

To one who has been long absent from these councils, it is striking and heartening that the United Nations has not only survived the turmoil and the conflict of the years, but has grown wiser, stronger and an ever more potent factor in the shaping of world events.

We of the United States wish the United Nations to be still more potent, for the grave dangers of this nuclear age demand much more unity among the nations. The common yearning of all men, expressed in the Charter, is to achieve freedom from war, poverty, disease, ignorance and oppression. That is what binds us all together. Our security, no less than our salvation, is the ability of nations and governments to see through the clouds of conflict and discern the truth about our common interests—and then, boldly and in concert, to act. Only the actions of states, both large and small, can impart vigor to this organization and can redeem the pledges of the Charter.

The United Nations is a sensitive measure of the tremors which shake the community of nations—tremors which have built up to dangerous levels. But we are not helpless spectators. The tremors are man-made and man can still them.

To help the organization meet the task before it, we of the United States—believing as we do that the times are too dangerous for anything except the truth—will be guided by certain principles:

First, we know the great importance which the newer and less developed nations attach to the United Nations. In their search for peace, for mutual tolerance, for economic development, for dignity and self-respect, our interest is theirs. We don't seek military allies among them, nor do we wish to impose our system or our philosophy upon them—indeed, we cannot; freedom cannot be imposed on anyone. Our concern for these nations is that they should be truly independent members of the peaceful community of nations.

As the oldest anticolonial power, the United States is in favor of freedom and of self-determination for all peoples. We rejoice in the rapid and peaceful revolution which has brought into being and into our midst at the United Nations so many new sovereignties. Our great desire is that this transition should proceed peacefully and in good order, with the least possible suffering, bitterness and new conflicts. We applaud what has been done to bring about this orderly transition, both by the emerging nations and by their former rulers. And we applaud the efforts of this Council to assist the orderly transition in the Congo through the Secretary General.

Equally important, if not more so, is the work which this organization can do to further economic development, without which political independence cannot long be sustained. The United States attaches the highest importance to improving the conditions of life of the peoples in the newly emerging countries. In that work the United Nations has already proved its effectiveness as a source of technical assistance, of expert knowledge about capital investment, and of administrative personnel to help those who are determined to help themselves. And all without any political condition or any ulterior motive. So we shall vigorously support the work of the United Nations in the field of economic betterment.

We shall also do all in our power to use the United Nations as "a center for harmonizing the actions of nations." We believe the United Nations is an opportunity for preventive diplomacy which can identify and solve potential disputes before they reach the acute stage sometimes induced by the glare of publicity.

The United States Government is giving its most earnest attention to the impasse over disarmament. We know, as President Kennedy has said, that "the instruments of war have far outpaced the instruments of peace." We know that progress toward disarmament becomes daily more imperative and we are ceaselessly aware of the vital interest in this problem which is felt by all of the members of the United Nations.

May I also say that if the United Nations is to continue to function, two things are essential. It must be properly financed and the integrity of the office of the Secretary General and of the Secretariat must be preserved. We hope all members from every region will join in fulfilling these indispensable minimum conditions.

Finally, with such a fateful agenda, it is more than ever important that, in these councils, we avoid useless recrimination. Free debate is an essential part of the United Nations process. But let us not demean free debate.

The new President of the United States has said that he regards the United Nations "as an instrument to end the cold war instead of an arena in which to fight it." We hope that all of the governments here represented will share his view, and that our deliberations in this Council may be uniformly directed toward the calm and constructive solution of the problems that confront us. May peace among the nations begin with peace among the members of the Council.

We are the Security Council, my colleagues, and it should be to us that the peoples of the world look for the security they so desperately long for. It should be to us that they look for leadership—for strong, sober, constructive leadership. And if they don't look to us with confidence, it is our fault.

So I wholeheartedly pledge myself to the high and the challenging task of cooperating with you in our common endeavor to provide the leadership the world is asking of us. I devoutly hope and pray that we may fulfill this solemn obligation.

PART II

THE CRISES

A TIME FOR ACTION:

THE DEVELOPING CRISIS IN THE CONGO

❦ ❦ *Governor Stevenson had barely occupied his seat in the Security Council when the first crisis was upon him—the Congo. It was also the first of countless times in the next two years, and more, when he saw the Congo threaten to erupt into a major East-West confrontation; the first of his many sharp exchanges with Ambassador Zorin, then the Soviet representative, and the subject of his first major United Nations address on a substantive issue, one that defined the position of the new United States Administration on the complex Congo problem. Figuring prominently in his remarks was a reply to a Russian statement (carried in that morning's newspapers) and a Soviet proposal that, among other things, would have discontinued the United Nations operation in the Congo and dismissed the late Secretary General, Dag Hammarskjöld. The Soviet proposal was ultimately defeated. It received one affirmative vote.*

This is the first occasion for the United States, under the leadership of President Kennedy, to speak formally in the Security Council on a question of substance.

It is a moment of grave crisis in the brief and tragic history of the Congo and a moment of equally grave crisis for the United Nations itself. I had hoped it would be otherwise.

Within recent days we have seen the successive withdrawal of two national units of the United Nations Forces, the violent death

From a statement to the Security Council, February 15, 1961.

❦ 9

of former Prime Minister Patrice Lumumba, the reported recognition of the Gizenga regime in Stanleyville by the United Arab Republic and a threat by the U.S.S.R. to provide unilateral assistance outside the United Nations. What we decide here in the next few days may, we believe, determine whether the United Nations will be able in the future to carry on its essential task of preserving the peace and protecting small nations.

This is a time for urgent and constructive action. In the midst of passions, it is a time when the Security Council must be calm. In the midst of efforts to destroy the United Nations action in the Congo, it is a time when we must persevere in the interests not only of the Congo, but of all of us, large and small.

The choice, as always, is a choice we make as members of the United Nations. Either we will follow a path toward a constructive and workable solution or we will follow a path of negative recrimination and self-interest.

As a new arrival listening and talking to delegates, I have wondered sometimes in the past few days if everyone is actually thinking about the Congo—a new republic struggling to be born—or if the Congo has been obscured by passions and prejudices about the doctors—Kasavubu, Lumumba, Gizenga and Tshombe. Opinion seems to be polarizing about them, not about the patient. So it is more important than ever to rally strong support to the United Nations in order to save the patient.

As I said, I had hoped that my first formal remarks to the Security Council on the vexed problems of the Congo could have been directed solely to constructive suggestions which would be helpful to the Congolese people. Instead, I find myself compelled to comment on a statement and a proposed resolution by the Soviet Union, published in this morning's newspapers, which are virtually a declaration of war on the United Nations and on the principle of international action on behalf of peace.

Permit me to analyze what, stripped of intemperate rhetoric, the Soviet Union proposes. It is nothing less than the abandonment of the United Nations' effort for peace in the Congo and a surrender of the United Nations to chaos and to civil war.

But—to digress for a moment—the statement and the resolution also say many things we are glad to hear, things which support positions that my country has always maintained. On colonialism, for one, my country fought colonialism in 1776 (when, if I may say so, the ancestors of the authors of the Soviet proposals had scarcely stirred beneath their bondage). And we have fought it ever since. My countrymen died to end colonialism in the Philippines, and they have assisted the Philippine people to attain their present high destiny of complete independence. And my countrymen have died to end colonialism in Cuba, though some Cubans seem to have forgotten it.

We rejoice, too, to hear the Soviets denounce political assassinations with such vehemence. In this country it has always been condemned, whether committed by Congolese, by colonialists or by Communists. For we condemn any violation of human rights, any death without due process of law, whether of African politician, Hungarian patriot or Tibetan nationalist. The United States stands squarely for the rights of man, individual man, man himself, as against any tyranny, whether it be the tyranny of colonialism or the tyranny of dictatorship or the tyranny of the majority.

We also note the Soviets' demand that Belgian foreign military and paramilitary aid be withdrawn. We, the United States, insist that all foreign military aid, from whatever source and to whatever end, be removed from the Congo, and that no such aid be permitted to interfere with the free and independent working out by the Congolese people themselves of their own political destiny. We mean this and we intend to keep on meaning it. And we mean it with particular reference to the threat—which we hope we misinterpret—by the Soviet Government that—and I quote—"it is ready to render all possible assistance and support" to a so-called Congolese government in Stanleyville which has no legal status.

The injunction of the General Assembly resolution adopted with the support of all members of the United Nations, except the Soviet bloc, against any unilateral military aid whatever, whether direct or indirect, should be adhered to fully by all United Nations members. This applies to those Belgians who are providing military advice and assistance to the Congo. It applies equally against military assistance to the forces in Orientale.*

The United States, for its part, does not intend to sit by if others consciously and deliberately seek to exacerbate the present situation. We are prepared to use all of our influence, if other members of the United Nations do likewise, to prevent such assistance from coming to the Congo, no matter from what quarter it comes.

So, Mr. President, we rejoice that the Soviet Union shares the distaste of the United States for colonialism and joins with us in condemning political assassination and foreign interference in the Congo.

I pass lightly over the Soviet Government's petulant attack on Secretary General Dag Hammarskjöld and his great office. He needs no defense from me nor does the institution. His record is an open book, a book which all peace-loving peoples recognize as the record of a dedicated international civil servant whose only loyalty is to international justice and international peace. Let the Soviet Government, if it wishes, pretend that he does not exist; it will find that he is far from a disembodied ghost; and it will find that peace-loving states will continue to support his patient search for the right road to security and peace in the Congo and for all peoples. The United Nations may have made mistakes in the Congo, as who has not, but nothing justifies an intemperate and unjustifiable attack on the integrity of the office of Secretary General.

We know that the United Nations has been denounced with vehemence by Kasavubu, by Gizenga and by Tshombe. Well, they also attack each other with equal vehemence. Could there be better testimony of impartiality? I would recall, if I may, that the Christian Scriptures say, "Woe unto you, when all men speak well of you!" Neither the United Nations nor the Secretary General seems likely to suffer from the affliction of universal approval.

We regret that the Soviet Government has not as yet seen fit to cooperate with states which truly seek peace in attempting to work out constructive steps for the solution of the agonizing problems the Congolese people are now facing. Instead, the Soviet Government pro-

* Stanleyville is the capital of Orientale Province.

poses the complete abandonment of the United Nations operation in the Congo. And in one month!

What does this mean? It means, my colleagues, not only the abandonment of the Congo to chaos and to civil war—to, if you please, the cold war—it means abandonment of the principle of the United Nations itself.

Does any one doubt it would mean chaos? Does this Council, the *Security* Council, favor abandoning security for insecurity and anarchy?

Do we want to withdraw the only elements that stand foursquare against civil and tribal war? Does the Soviet Government really want Africans to kill Africans? The United States does not, and it devoutly hopes that the Soviet Government does not, too, and that it will join the United States and other peace-loving states in supporting and strengthening the only force that can prevent Congolese civil war— the United Nations.

And now the cold war. Does the Soviet Government really want to chill what should be warm and temperate in Africa with the icy blasts of power politics? The United States does not. Its only interest in the Congo is to support the Congolese people in their struggle for real independence, free from any foreign domination from *any* source.

The United States deplores any war, cold or otherwise. Its only desire is to live in peace and freedom and to let all other peoples live in peace and freedom. It will resist with all of its power all assaults on its own peace and freedom, and it proposes to join with all other peace-loving peoples in resisting, in the cooperative framework of the United Nations, all assaults on the peace and freedom of other peoples.

In that spirit we declare that, so far as we are concerned, Africa shall never be the scene of any war, cold or hot. But we also declare that Africa for the Africans *means* Africa for the Africans, and not Africa as a hunting ground for alien ambitions. And we pledge our full and unstinted support against any attempt by anyone to interfere with the full and free development by Africans of their own independent African future.

We believe that the only way to keep the cold war *out* of the

Congo is to keep the United Nations *in* the Congo, and we call on the Soviet Union to join us in thus ensuring the free and untrammeled exercise by the Congolese people of their right to independence and to democracy.

But the position apparently taken by the Soviet Government involves more than the unhappy and despicable fate of three Congolese politicians.* It involves the future of the fourteen million Congolese people. They are the ones with whom we are concerned.

We deplore the past and we condemn those responsible for it, no matter who they may be. But we submit that it is the future that is all-important now, and that the best efforts of this Council should be concentrated on the future security of the Congo and, indeed, on the future security of *all* peoples.

For it is the security of *all* peoples which is threatened by the statement and by the proposal of the Soviet Government.

Let me make my meaning abundantly and completely clear. The United States Government believes—and profoundly believes—that the single best and only hope of the peoples of the world for peace and security lies in the United Nations. It lies in international cooperation, in the integrity of an international body rising above international rivalries into the clearer air of international morality and international justice.

The United Nations has not achieved perfection, nor has the United States, and they probably never will. The United States, like the United Nations, is composed of humans; it has made mistakes, it probably always will make mistakes; it has never pleased all people, it cannot please all people; in its desire and wholehearted determination to do justice it may offend one group of states in 1952, another in 1956, and perhaps still another in 1961. But always the United States has tried, and we believe it will always try, to apply even-handedly the rules of justice and equity that should govern us all.

Are we callously to cast aside the one and only instrument that men have developed to safeguard their peace and security? Are we to abandon the jungles of the Congo to the jungles of internecine warfare and internal rivalry?

* Patrice Lumumba and two associates who were assassinated.

The issue, then, is simply this: Shall the United Nations survive? Shall the attempt to bring about peace by the concerted power of international understanding be discarded? Shall any pretense of an international order, of international law, be swept aside? Shall conflicts of naked power, awful in their potential, be permitted to rage in Africa or elsewhere, unchecked by international cooperation or authority?

These are questions which call for an answer, not so much by the great powers as by the smaller ones and the newer ones. My own country, as it happens, is in the fortunate position of being able to look out for itself and for its interests, and look out it will. But it is for the vast majority of states that the United Nations has vital meaning and is of vital necessity. I call on those states to rise in defense of the integrity of the institution which is for them the only assurance of their freedom and their liberty, and the only assurance for all of us of peace in the years to come.

And I also call upon the Soviet Union to reconsider its position. My government is earnestly determined to cooperate with all governments in an attempt to improve international relationships and to further friendships among peoples, and it has welcomed evidences of cooperation toward that end by the Soviet Government. Let those evidences be buttressed by concrete steps by the Soviet Government looking toward constructive solution of the difficult problems that confront us all. Let us join in condemning the past, but let us join in facing the future with calm determination to support steadfastly and strengthen sturdily the United Nations, the last best hope of us all.

Now let me turn to what can be done to arrest the sad deterioration that has taken place in that divided country—the Congo. There are certain fundamental principles which have had, and will continue to have, the full support of the American people and of the United States Government. These principles, we believe, are apparent to all.

In the first place, the unity, the territorial integrity, the political independence of the Congo must be preserved. I am sure the United Kingdom will not object if I repeat that the United States was one of the first anticolonialists, and that during the 186 years since we have stood steadfastly for the right of peoples to determine their own destiny. And the United States desires nothing for the Congo but its complete freedom from outside domination and nothing for its people but the same independent freedom which we wanted for ourselves so long ago.

Much as the United States was once beset by internal dissensions, so the Congo, since its independence, has been beset by secessionist movements—in the Katanga and in Orientale Province, too. So far as we are concerned, however, the borders of the Congo today are identical with the original borders of July 1, 1960, and the United States is ready to join with other states which support the integrity of the Congo to maintain this principle within the framework of the United Nations.

Second, the Congo must not become a battleground—cold or hot—for the big powers. In keeping with this belief, when the United States was first requested to provide troops for the Congo, we told the Congolese Government to appeal to the United Nations.

And in contrast to others, we have never at any time provided to anyone in the Congo a single tank, a single gun, a single soldier, a single piece of equipment that could be used for military purposes. We have, instead, responded to every request made to us by the United Nations promptly and vigorously and so that the entire control over our assistance passed from our hands to those of the UN.

Third, we support the United Nations action in the Congo to the fullest measure of our power. For—and I repeat—the best way to keep the cold war and the hot war out of Africa and the Congo is to keep the United Nations in. To those members who are still contemplating withdrawal, I suggest a long, hard, careful look at what might happen if the United Nations Force collapses, or if the United Nations mission fails because of lack of support from its members.

Finally, we believe that the Congolese people must be allowed to develop their own political settlement by peaceful means free from violence and external interference. The Congo's political problems must, in the last analysis, be worked out by the Congolese themselves. The United Nations can assist in this effort—by helping create peace and stability and also by extending its good offices as, indeed, it has done. But only a settlement commanding the support of the Congolese people will long endure.

On these principles—the maintenance of territorial integrity and political independence, the isolation of the Congolese from big-power and small-power interference, continued vigorous United Nations assistance, and the settlement of internal political controversies by peaceful means—on these principles rests, in our opinion, the only possibility for a solution. And if the United Nations does not take effective action immediately, not only may conflict break forth in full fury in the Congo, but the hopes of African unity may be destroyed for many years to come by the divisions which will be produced among African nations.

This is the measure of the gravity of our crisis, and we call upon all members around this table to face soberly and solemnly these realities. We are prepared to meet in the Council by night and by day until we can reach consensus and agreement. The occasion for—the time for— effective action in the Congo is now. We must seize it and we must seize it quickly.

A TIME TO BUILD:
THE END OF THE CRISIS IN THE CONGO

❧ ❧ *Russian efforts to undermine the United Nations in the Congo failed; but the crisis continued as mineral-rich Katanga virtually seceded from the Congo. How the United Nations finally met that threat and hopefully set the Congo on the road to unity is analyzed in the following article written by Governor Stevenson and published extensively. Although not an official paper, the article—which also answered critics of the United Nations action—stated the United States position in giving its full support to what Governor Stevenson described as "a victory for the rule of law and peace."*

The entry of the United Nations forces into the Katanga mining center of Kolwezi without a shot having been fired has concluded, as near as we can tell at this point, the military phase of the long story of the war-torn Congo.

A time to build is now at hand. But before we turn our attention to the vast reconstruction job, I think it would be well for me to answer some of the many questions I have been asked about what the United Nations is doing in the Congo to begin with, and why the United States has given its full support to the United Nations effort.

First, to review a bit of history, the problem of the Congo was brought to the United Nations in July, 1960, shortly after the former Belgian territory achieved its independence—somewhat abruptly, I

From an article for North American Newspaper Alliance, January 27, 1963.
❧ 18

would say, in comparison with other African states.

Belgian forces, until then responsible for maintaining the law, were withdrawing, and within a matter of a few days the young republic was in a state of extreme disorder. Troops rebelled. There was looting, rioting, killing; civil war threatened, and the Belgians began to fly troops back to protect their citizens still in the Congo.

It was feared from the outset that this chaotic situation would invite Communist intervention. And, shortly, Communist military equipment and so-called technicians did, indeed, appear on the scene; but the Central Government, wary of the reasons for such "aid," ordered the "technicians" out of the Congo.

President Eisenhower, with these facts before him, had three possible courses of action when Congolese leaders asked for American assistance. One was to refuse the appeal of the Congo for help, leaving it to wallow in bloodshed and strife until an interested power might choose to move in and pick up the remaining pieces.

The second was to send American troops as requested, a move that might have led to military intervention by other great powers with other objectives.

The third—and the course the President took—was to propose that the United Nations was the best instrument available to restore and maintain law and order, and to prevent unilateral intervention from outside. In that way, the Congolese people themselves could settle their internal problems in their own way.

That was the policy of President Eisenhower, and that is the policy President Kennedy has steadfastly supported.

The object of the United States in supporting the United Nations during this long and trying period has been to advance American policy in Africa, a policy designed to aid in the development of truly independent, cooperating, progressive nations that stand firmly against chaos and subversion regardless of source. And, let me emphasize, this is our policy not only for Africa, but for the rest of the world.

It seems to me, therefore, the policy objectives of both the United States and the United Nations in the Congo coincided exactly. Americans should understand this very real fact, and those who opposed the United Nations operation should also search their hearts and ask themselves: Would they have preferred to use American soldiers to maintain order while the Congolese settled their political troubles?

Another one of the questions most frequently asked has to do with the legal justification for the United Nations action in the Congo,' and if that action sets a precedent giving the UN the right to interfere in the internal affairs of other countries, our own, for instance. The answer is simple. No!

The United Nations is forbidden by its Charter from intervening in the domestic jurisdiction of any state. It is in the Congo in response to a direct request of the legitimate government of the Congo. The United Nations did not "intervene"; it accepted an invitation. And the right to accept the Congolese Government's invitation is clearly specified in the Charter, which states that the first purpose of the United Nations is "to maintain international peace and security, and to that end, to take effective collective measures for the prevention and removal of threats to the peace. . . ."

Furthermore, the Charter not only confers on the Security Council "primary responsibility for the maintenance of international peace and security"; it gives it authority to take such "provisional measures" as it considers necessary to prevent a dangerous situation from getting worse—in other words, to prevent a *threat* to the peace from becoming a *breach* of the peace.

A recent majority opinion of the International Court of Justice on an issue related to the Congo holds that the Security Council's action "was clearly adopted with a view to maintaining international peace and security," and added that "it must lie within the power of the Security Council to police a situation even though it does not resort to enforcement action against a state." The majority of the World Court, therefore, found that international law has been observed and the United Nations has acted within the bounds of its Charter.

Let me also clarify some confusion about the United Nations peace-keeping forces in the Congo.

When the Security Council first asked the Secretary General to organize a peace-keeping mission in the Congo, he indicated that the selection of personnel would be such "as to avoid complications because of the nationalities used." This excluded "recourse to troops from any of the permanent members of the Security Council."

At the same time, my predecessor as Ambassador to the United Nations, Henry Cabot Lodge, announced that the United States would respond to any reasonable request by the United Nations in the fields of transport and communications.

Within twenty-four hours after the Secretary General's call, the first troops, from Tunisia, were on the scene, and the second unit, a Swedish contingent, was on its way. It was a movement made possible by what has now become the largest international airlift in history, carried out for the United Nations—with remarkable efficiency and a perfect safety record, I am proud to say—by the United States Air Force.

Not a single American soldier has been involved in combat in the Congo peace-keeping operation. And, of course, not one has been wounded or killed.

Twenty-one other nations from all over the world, however, contributed eighteen thousand troops to the successful United Nations effort.

A special word should be said for India. Not only did it provide invaluable forces, including the brilliant commander of the United Nations field operation, but it kept them in the Congo in spite of the immense problems it faced at home as a result of the wanton Communist Chinese invasion of its borders.

Let me now turn to a question about the right of Katanga, or any province in the Congo, to secede. It is a matter of record that several provinces attempted to break away from the Central Government, notably Orientale Province and Kasai. But the Central Government, with the help of the United Nations, was able to put down these attempts to destroy its territorial integrity.

The so-called "secession" of Katanga, the last in the series to be dealt with by the United Nations, was actually a sudden proclamation of Tshombe's in the midst of the civil disorder that broke out shortly after the Congo's independence was declared. But his action was never confirmed or approved by the people of Katanga, or by a plenary session of the Katanga Provincial Legislature.

The number of casualties in the Congo civil war, in Katanga, among Katangans, probably exceeds those of any other province in the Congo. Thousands of Balubakats have been killed. And thousands more fled their homes and sought the protection of the United Nations in camps in Elisabethville, in order to escape molestation by Tshombe's armed forces.

The truth is that during most of 1961 and 1962 Tshombe was not in effective control of most of Katanga, and his power was largely confined to the mining area of South Katanga.

Actually, there was no valid question of self-determination in the case of Katanga at any time. A unified Congo was worked out months and months before independence at a round table in Brussels by the tribal and provincial leaders of the Congo with Tshombe participating and with his acquiescence. He voted for and signed the Fundamental Law that was then adopted to govern the country. The decision was reached by free choice.

Tshombe, however, was able to pay his administrators, his army, his foreign political advisers, his mercenary officers and his far-flung public relations experts from taxes owed to the Congo's Central Government, but which were diverted to the government of the Katanga. Obviously, the withholding of these funds badly impaired the attempts of the Central Government to function in the manner required as the legally constituted government of the Congo.

As we look back now, there is little doubt, I think, that left to themselves, free of outside pressure, the Congolese people might long ago have resolved their internal problems and saved us all a great amount of money and even more trouble.

Finally, many people have written to me asking: Why couldn't the United Nations achieve its goals without the use of force?

The United Nations was authorized to use force by the Security Council if it became necessary, in the last resort, to defend itself. And force would not have been necessary if Tshombe had at any time maintained the commitments he had made and if the United Nations forces had not been attacked, as they were.

I would sum up in this way. The end of Tshombe's attempted secession is welcomed by all who really wish well for the Congo and for Africa as a whole. The goal of the United Nations has been to help establish conditions under which the Congolese people themselves can peacefully work out their own future.

This was impossible, however, as long as the Congo was threatened with dismemberment, chaos, civil war and foreign intervention. And for this reason the Eisenhower Administration and the Kennedy Administration vigorously supported the efforts of the United Nations to maintain law and order and to reunify the Congo under incredibly difficult circumstances and amid much vocal and influential opposition.

The United Nations, I think, has carried through successfully the most complex, the most dangerous peace mission of its history. Civil war has been averted and so has the danger of a great-power confrontation, with all of its ominous implications, in the heart of Africa.

But the work and the responsibility of the United Nations are not finished now that the military phase is over. The building phase has only begun and it is our hope, the hope of all who have faith in the United Nations, that the Congo will rise from the struggle as a stable and progressive nation guided by the principles and aspirations of the United Nations Charter.

And when the job is finished, I think history will record the wisdom of the United Nations action in the Congo. For it resulted, I would emphasize, not in victory for the United Nations—the United Nations seeks no victories—but in a victory for the rule of law and of peace.

HE BELONGS TO ALL MANKIND:

THE DEATH OF DAG HAMMARSKJÖLD

❦ ❦ *The Congo was directly responsible for still another crisis, one that posed a direct threat to the United Nations "as a potent factor in the shaping of world events." The Soviet Union, thwarted in its effort to gain a foothold in Central Africa by Dag Hammarskjöld's determination to carry out the UN's mandate to restore order and peace and to preserve the integrity of the newly independent Congo, at first tried to effect his dismissal. When that move failed, it "boycotted" him, much as it had the United Nations' first Secretary General, Trygve Lie, when he, too, had upheld the concept of his office. Mr. Hammarskjöld, quietly and with dignity, continued his duties—with the backing of the entire organization, minus, of course, the Soviet bloc. It was this devotion to duty that cost Mr. Hammarskjöld his life, in an airplane crash in Central Africa on September 18, 1961. In his moving eulogies to his friend of many years (in the Sixteenth General Assembly the day after it opened, and at Uppsala, Sweden, where he represented the United States at the state funeral) Governor Stevenson conveyed the sense of shock and genuine grief felt by all Americans—and did not disguise his own.*

Statement to the General Assembly, September 20, 1961.

❦ 24

It is my task to express on behalf of the people and government of the United States our profound sorrow and our deep distress at the tragic death of our Secretary General, Dag Hammarskjöld. In his passing the community of nations has lost one of the greatest servants it ever had, a brilliant mind and a brave and compassionate spirit.

I doubt if any living man has done more to further the search for a world in which men solve their problems by peaceful means and not by force than this gallant friend of us all. Indeed, he gave his life in a mission of peace, a mission to persuade men to lay down their arms that reason might prevail over force.

Dag Hammarskjöld was the embodiment of the international civil servant that the Secretary General of the United Nations should ideally and always be. He was resolutely impartial, resolutely even-handed and resolutely firm in carrying out the mandates with which he was entrusted. He never swerved from what he conceived to be his duty to the United Nations and to the cause of peace, and he never wavered under irresponsible invective and unjust criticism.

Mr. Hammarskjöld's skill as a diplomatist was admired in every chancellory of the world, and it was attested to many times when leaders who could not bring themselves to confide in each other were glad to confide in him.

But closer to his heart than the urgent tasks of diplomacy, and more enduring in its value for humanity, is the ideal to whose realization he contributed so greatly in his capacity as head of the Secretariat. That ideal has become an increasing reality. For its sake a great price has already been paid. The ideal of an international civil service whose members are available in fair weather and foul to do the work of the community and, if need be, to uphold it with their lives. Since the founding of the United Nations thirty-four United Nations officials and Secretariat members have given their lives in the line of their international duty. Mr. Hammarksjöld and the five Secretariat members who died with him are the latest names on this roll of honor.

Every nation has its heroes, but what these people died for, and what thousands of their colleagues still labor for today, is something more universal, something which transcends all national and regional interests and all ideologies of power and conquest—the world community of nations.

The future of that community is in great measure in our hands to build or to destroy, to uphold or to neglect. Today it is only half-formed. It is beset with danger and with forbidding problems. But it is the hope of man. It has need of the best energies and the finest talents which we, its members, can put at its service.

Dag Hammarskjöld once said, at a moment of crisis in his life and that of the United Nations, "The man does not count, the institution does." Yet institutions are made to serve man, and it is from the greatest men that they derive their character and their strength. The memory of this one man—humane, cultured, judicious, possessed of a poetic and philosophic vision, free of passion other than a passion for the rule of reason and decency, modest and brave—this memory will always be with us as a reminder of the best that the United Nations can be, and of the qualities which it demands of us.

Mr. President, I should like to suggest to my fellow delegates that a suitable memorial be provided as a permanent tangible tribute to Mr. Hammarskjöld and to the ideals which he served so nobly, preferably a living memorial to advance the work for peace and international understanding which was his life.

I make this suggestion in the knowledge that no memorial, no tribute can ever be adequate. Dag Hammarskjöld's true memorial will be the great new institution in the family of man which it is our duty to build and to nourish.

There is a poem by the great Indian poet Rabindranath Tagore which contains these lyric lines:

> Listen to the rumbling of the clouds, O heart of mine.
> Be brave, break through and leave for the unknown.

We are indebted to Mr. James Reston of the *New York Times* for reminding us this morning of what Mr. Hammarskjöld's response was when these words of Tagore were quoted to him. He said, "I think that these lines express in a very noble way the attitude we must take to this venture called the United Nations. We may listen to the rumbling of the clouds, but we can never afford to lose that kind of confidence in ourselves and in the wisdom of man which makes us brave enough to break through and leave, always leave for the unknown."

Mr. President, Dag Hammarskjöld has left for the unknown—bravely and in the cause of us all.

UPPSALA WAS THE WORLD TODAY

None of us will forget the ceremony in that ancient and splendid cathedral, which has witnessed so much of the grandeur and glory of Swedish history; the solemn walk through the streets of that lovely old town lined with thousands of silent, reverent people, Dag's fellow townsmen; the scene in the cemetery beneath the tall, swaying elms, and more of that exquisite choral singing in the twilight.

Today, with the soft touch of autumn on the Swedish landscape, we have felt sorrow and joy in abounding measure—the sorrow of our loss and the joy of the eternal, everlasting spirit.

It was fitting that today the nations among whom he mediated with such skill and devotion should have gathered at his grave to pay a last tribute to Dag Hammarskjöld.

But the outpouring of grief was not just in Uppsala; it was everywhere. For when he died, people young and old cried in New York, people who never knew or saw him. I saw it with my own eyes, and what was true in New York was true on all the streets of the world. Uppsala was the world today, for he was a hero of the community of man, and he is gone when we needed him most.

It would be good for the world to remember of him that his great strength was not demonstrative or overbearing, but quiet and profound. He wrote: "We all have within us a center of stillness surrounded by silence." His was no mere mind of stratagems and devices.

From an address following the funeral service for Dag Hammarskjöld, Stockholm, Sweden, September 29, 1961.

He was possessed of poetic and philosophic vision. I think he believed with Socrates that the quality of courage is not just the readiness to stand and fight and die, but rather is rooted in the philosopher's quest of good and evil.

The quest will go on—and let us build for him, and for all the brave souls who have died in this cause, the only monument worthy of them —the family of man and its capital, its citadel, the United Nations.

ONE CANNOT ASK MORE OF ANY MAN:
THE ELECTION OF U THANT

❦ ❦ The death of Mr. Hammarskjöld touched off new Soviet efforts to weaken the office of Secretary General, and in short order the "troika" was again parked before the United Nations. As outlined a year earlier by Premier Khrushchev, it called for splintering the office into three segments, representing—according to the Soviets—"the Socialist countries, the countries belonging to the Western military blocs and the neutralist states." This proposal to extend the Soviet veto to the Secretary General, however, was supported only by the Soviet bloc, and after seven weeks of negotiations Governor Stevenson was able to announce: "There will be no 'troika' and no veto in the Secretariat." Ambassador U Thant of Burma was unanimously named Acting Secretary General, and a year later, after another Soviet attempt to revive the "troika," the word "acting" was removed from his title. Governor Stevenson, who had paid tribute to U Thant a year earlier, did so again with unconcealed pleasure.

On this rostrum a little more than a year ago I said we could rejoice that there was available to us a diplomat of such character, ability and experience that he could command the unanimous support and confidence of this world organization. I am happy to repeat these words today.

Statement to the General Assembly, November 30, 1962.

❦ 30

Those of us who attended the funeral of Dag Hammarskjöld in the ancient cathedral of Uppsala will never forget him, or the dignity and strength he gave to his office. None of us may forget Dag Hammarskjöld and all he stood for. We are blessed indeed, therefore, that the man we have chosen to succeed him carries on his proud tradition.

U Thant has been in office now for little more than a year, and we have rich evidence of the skill, the patience, the energy, the intelligence with which he has met his formidable and trying responsibilities.

U Thant, as an international civil servant, has been devoted to the common good of all people. That so many nations have faith in him is testimony to his strength of mind, his clarity of purpose and, not least, his firm belief in the Charter and in the independence and integrity of the office he holds.

A man does not grow overnight. U Thant, as Secretary General of the United Nations, reflects, I believe, the principles and aspirations of a life's work devoted to the cause of peace and understanding among all peoples.

This Assembly, by its action now in naming U Thant as Secretary General, well serves itself and the world. It demonstrates again its determination to be a true parliament of man, faithful only to the law of the Charter and its great goal of ridding the world of "the scourge of war." The full record of this Seventeenth Session of the General Assembly still remains to be written; but nothing we do in the remaining weeks will surpass the importance of this moment to the United Nations as an organization.

I say this with full awareness of the critical issues that confront us. For by reaffirming the integrity of the office of Secretary General we have reaffirmed our belief in the United Nations as a viable force in the affairs of men.

This is not the time to talk of the issues that divided some of us in our concept of the office of Secretary General. It is the time to emphasize, as it shall always be the time to emphasize, that this organization must grow and flourish. It can do so only if it retains its strength and influence, and the confidence of the peoples and governments of the world.

That is why the United States has opposed any action that would have compromised the exclusively international character of the responsibilities of the Secretary General and the Secretariat. In all the history of international organization—in the history of internationalism —no more precious flower has grown than the truly international Secretariat. And I am confident that, in the tenure of U Thant, that flower will not wither.

For all nations, large and small, can now take heart in the knowledge that we have a Secretary General armed with his full powers under the Charter. They can now take heart in the knowledge that they have given continued force and meaning to that vital provision of the Charter that debars "instructions from any government" to the Secretary General and his staff.

And they can now take heart in the knowledge that they have given their full support to the maintenance of a Secretariat recruited on a wide geographical basis and representing "the highest standards of efficiency, competence and integrity."

These are firm foundations, and today we have chosen not to undermine them, but to build higher on them, secure in the conviction that they will hold fast.

As I contemplate the problems confronting U Thant, I wonder if we should not congratulate ourselves rather than him. I would also, as a friend, offer my own good wishes to U Thant as he now continues his work to help ease the critical issues of our day. The wisdom and serenity that are but part of the ancient heritage of his country will, I am sure, be a source of strength and stability in meeting his heavy responsibilities in the coming years, even as they have already in the one just past.

Abraham Lincoln once said: "Let us have faith that right makes might; and in that faith let us to the end, dare do our duty as we understand it."

U Thant has shown he has that faith. One cannot ask more of any man.

NUCLEAR DEATH DANCE:
THE NEED FOR A TEST BAN TREATY

𝕧 𝕧 *It should be recalled that in the 1956 Presidential campaign Governor Stevenson, the Democratic candidate, advocated a ban on testing to stop the further development of nuclear weapons. Five years later, on August 31, 1961, he was profoundly shocked by the Soviet Union's sudden resumption of nuclear tests. "Once again," he said, "the iron fist of the Soviet Union has crushed the hopes of peace-loving peoples." Two months later, with a feeling and conviction seldom heard in the United Nations, he urged an immediate test ban treaty. The "Indian Resolution" he refers to was drafted by Krishna Menon and called not for a treaty but a voluntary moratorium without safeguards. It was passed over United States opposition. But the General Assembly also gave its support to a joint American-British resolution calling for a resumption of the Geneva negotiations for a treaty with effective controls, and it asked the Soviet Union not to explode its vaunted 100-megaton "super" bomb. The plea was ignored. At the next Assembly session, Governor Stevenson authored a United States proposal for a "limited ban" on all but underground testing. At first rejected by the Soviet Union, the "limited ban" became the basis for the nuclear test treaty signed eight months later.*

An emergency confronts this committee and the world! The Soviet Union is now nearing the conclusion of a massive series of nuclear

Statement to the Political Committee, October 19, 1961.

𝕧 33

weapon tests. Unless something is done quickly, the Soviet testing will necessarily result in further testing by my country and perhaps by others.

There is still time to halt this drift toward the further refinement and multiplication of these weapons. Perhaps this will be the last clear chance to reverse this tragic trend. For if testing is stopped, the terrible pace of technological progress will be decisively retarded. A ban on tests is, of course, only the first step; and the control and destruction of nuclear and thermonuclear weapons is the ultimate goal. But it is an indispensable first step.

Accordingly, I must inform the committee that the United States is obliged in self-protection to reserve the right to make preparations to test in the atmosphere, as well as underground.

But the United States stands ready to resume negotiations for a treaty tomorrow. We will devote all our energies to the quickest possible conclusion of these negotiations, either here or in Geneva. If the Soviet Union will do the same and stop its tests, there is no reason why a treaty with effective controls cannot be signed in thirty days and this suicidal business ended before it ends us.

But, I repeat, unless a treaty can be signed, and signed promptly, the United States has no choice but to prepare and take the action necessary to protect its own security and that of the world community.

I trust that this expression of hope for the triumph of reason will convey some measure of the depth of our feeling about the subject and of our desire to do our share to save the human race from a greater menace than the plagues which once ravaged Europe. We believe we have done our share, and more, ever since the United States proposals of 1946. I remind you that if those proposals had been accepted by the Soviet Union, no state would now have nuclear weapons; and we would not now be in such a perilous crisis.

I have claimed the privilege of making this declaration for the United States because few delegates, I dare say, feel more deeply about this matter than I do, in part, perhaps, because I proposed that nuclear tests be stopped almost six years ago—and lost a great many votes in the 1956 Presidential election as a result! Had the nuclear powers agreed even then, think how much safer and healthier the world would be today.

I pray we do not lose still another chance to meet the challenge of our times and stop this dance of death.

I confess a feeling of futility when I consider the immensity of the problems which confront us and the feebleness of our efforts to deal properly with them. We have lived for sixteen years in the Atomic Age. During these years we have ingeniously and steadily improved man's capacity to blow up the planet. But we have done little to improve man's control over the means of his own destruction. Instead, we have worried and wrangled and talked and trifled while time trickles away, and the hands of the clock creep toward midnight.

I would not imply that the problems of control are easy. Just as the nuclear bomb itself lays open the inner mysteries of science, so the attempt to control the nuclear bomb cuts to the core of our political ideas and mechanisms. As the bomb itself represented a revolution in science, so the control of the bomb may in the end mean a revolution in politics.

But we must not let the very immensity of the problem dwarf our minds and our calculations. We must act—and we must take hold of the problem where we can. One obvious way is to tackle the question of nuclear testing.

No one would argue that the abolition of testing would itself solve all our problems. It would mean only a small beginning in the assault on the evil, ancient institution of war. But, in a world of no beginnings, a small beginning shines forth like the morning sun on the distant horizon. We have talked long enough about the horror which hangs over us. Now is the time for us to get down to business —to fight this horror, not with soft words and wistful hopes, but with the hard weapon of effective international arrangements.

This view shapes our attitude toward the Indian resolution. As I have said, we share the hatred of the sponsors for the whole wretched business of nuclear testing. We are just as determined to stop the spread of such weapons to countries not now possessing them, the contamination of the atmosphere and the bellowing threat of nuclear war. We want to stop these things dead before they stop us—dead!

The world now knows from bitter experience that an uninspected moratorium will not secure the results which the sponsors of the resolution seek. For almost three years, representatives of the Soviet Union, the United Kingdom and the United States met at Geneva to work out a plan to bring nuclear testing to a definitive end. Significant progress was made. The conference adopted a preamble, seventeen articles and two annexes of a draft treaty.

When President Kennedy took office, he ordered an immediate review of United States policy in order to overcome the remaining obstacles to a final agreement. At Geneva, the United States and the United Kingdom submitted comprehensive treaty proposals aimed at ending the fear of nuclear tests and radioactive fallout through a pledge by all signatory nations to cease all tests of nuclear weapons, a pledge backed and secured by effective international inspection.

But the representatives of the Soviet Union reacted very oddly to this generous and determined attempt to reach an agreement. They rejected positions they had already accepted. They renounced agreements they had already made. The whole world familiar with this subject wondered at this Soviet performance. Experts pondered their tea leaves and produced laborious speculation to explain the Soviet change of heart. Alas, we understand today the brutal simplicity of the reasoning behind the Soviet reversal.

We now know that the Soviet representatives at Geneva had long since ceased to negotiate in good faith. We now know that, while Mr. Tsarapkin was delaying action at Geneva, the Soviet scientists and engineers and generals were secretly laying plans for the resumption of nuclear testing—and worse than that, for the resumption of testing in the atmosphere.

Let us make no mistake about it. You cannot decide to resume testing on Monday and actually resume on Tuesday. A sequence of tests of the sort with which the Soviet Union is currently edifying the world requires many, many months of preparation.

In an open society, like ours in the United States, such preparation simply could not be undertaken in secrecy. But in a closed society, like the Soviet Union, almost anything can be done without publicity or disclosure.

And so, while the Soviet representatives condemned nuclear testing at Geneva, the Soviet Government prepared for nuclear tests in Russia. Then they announced their decision to resume testing just two days before the unaligned nations gathered at Belgrade. With no apparent motives except intimidation and terror, Chairman Khrushchev boasted about his 100-megaton bombs.

Today, seven weeks after the Soviet Union began to test nuclear weapons again, and after it had tested more than a score, the Soviet Union has finally told its own people that its nuclear explosions are actually under way. Cushioning the shock, the Soviet leaders announced the *end* of the current series instead of the *beginning*. And Mr. Khrushchev has decided to bring the Soviet program to a crashing conclusion with a 50-megaton bomb.

Are we supposed to be grateful that Chairman Khrushchev has decided not to reach at a single leap his announced goal of the 100-megaton bomb?

As everyone knows, there is no military purpose whatever in such gigantic weapons. For years the United States has been able to build such weapons. But we are not interested in the business of intimidation or bigger blasts.

Now, in a single instant, the Soviet Union intends to poison the atmosphere by creating more radioactivity than that produced by any series since 1945. It may interest the members of this committee to know that from this one test, the 30-60 degree North Latitude band of the world where 80 percent of all of the people of the world live can expect to receive two-thirds as much new fallout as was produced by *all* of the fallout produced by *all* of the tests since 1945. Why must they insist on exploding a 50-megaton bomb? It is not a military necessity.

And no doubt, when the present series of tests reaches its cataclysmic conclusion, the Soviet Union will piously join in the movement for an uninspected moratorium.

Let us be absolutely clear what another such moratorium means. It is clear that it serves neither the cause of peace nor of international collaboration, nor of confidence among nations. We were all in this trap before. We cannot afford to enter it again, and the United States will not.

We do not believe that nuclear testing will ever be abolished by exorcism. It will be abolished only by action. So I plead with the members of this Assembly, which has been called the *conscience* of the world, to demand—not more words, but more deeds.

Standing alone, a treaty banning nuclear weapons would be an immense leap forward toward sanity. It would be a tangible gain for humanity. It would slow down the arms race. It would eliminate all danger from poisonous materials cast off by nuclear explosions in the atmosphere. It would check the multiplication of new types of nuclear weapons and discourage their spread to additional nations, thereby reducing the hazard of accidental war. Above all, it would mark a great adventure in international collaboration for peace.

Out of our experience with a test ban treaty can come a mutual confidence, the tested procedures and the concerted policies which will enable the world to mount a wider and deeper attack on war itself. If nations can set up a collective system which abolishes nuclear tests, surely they can hope to set up a collective system which abolishes all the diverse and manifest weapons of self-destruction.

The world is asking for bread. Another moratorium resolution would offer it not even a stone. The United States stands ready today, as we have stood ready for many months, to sign a treaty outlawing nuclear tests. As I have said, until such a treaty is signed, we have no choice as a responsible nation but to reserve our freedom of action.

So, at the risk of repetition, let me state again the position of the United States. The current Soviet nuclear test series is approaching its announced conclusion. While thorough analysis of the Soviet tests will require some time, it is already completely clear that they will intensify competition in the development of more and more deadly nuclear weapons. Thus these tests have increased the possibility of ultimate disaster for all of mankind.

There is only one safe and sure way to stop nuclear tests, and to stop them quickly. That is to conclude a treaty prohibiting all nuclear weapons tests under effective controls.

In the last three years the negotiations at Geneva made significant progress toward such a treaty. The United States is still willing and eager to resume these negotiations. If in this fateful moment all three countries involved will really devote their skills and ingenuity to achieve agreement, not evasion, deceit and equivocation, there is, I say, no reason why a nuclear test ban treaty with effective controls cannot be signed within thirty days.

United States negotiators are ready to sit down at the table with Soviet and British representatives for this purpose. But until there is a treaty and tests can be stopped, the United States must prepare to take all steps necessary to protect its own security.

An uninspected moratorium will only lead the world once again into the morass of confusion and deceit. A test ban treaty is the path to peace.

If the Soviet Union really wants to stop nuclear testing, we challenge it to join us now in signing a test ban treaty.

THE FIRST BUSINESS OF
THIS DANGEROUS WORLD:
DISARMAMENT

❦ ❦ *President Kennedy, appearing before the Sixteenth General Assembly in September 1961, challenged the Soviet Union "not to an arms race, but to a peace race." A comprehensive program for general and complete disarmament under international control within the framework of the United Nations was then presented by the United States. The Soviet Union, which previously had accepted a set of principles to guide disarmament negotiations, however, refused to go through with its agreement; it also raised obstacles to a forum for the negotiations. These were the factors at play when Governor Stevenson made the following statement stressing the need for immediate action. Shortly before the session ended, the Soviet Union joined with the United States in sponsoring a resolution that reactivated the Geneva disarmament talks.*

War is one of the oldest institutions. It is deeply imbedded in the traditions, the folkways, the literature, even the values of almost all countries. It has engaged countless talented men and produced countless national heroes. At the same time, civilized men and women for centuries past have abhorred the immorality of organized killing of men by men.

From a statement to the Political Committee, November 15, 1961.
❦ 40

Yet, let us confess at once, to our common shame, that this deep sense of revulsion has not averted wars, nor shortened one by a day.

While I do not say that all wars have been started for unworthy purposes, let us also confess, morality to the side, that almost all past wars have served to promote what was conceived to be the national or princely or religious interests of those who fought them—or at least those who won them.

For in past wars, there have been winners as well as losers, the victors and the vanquished, the decorated and the dead. In the end, valuable real estate and other riches have changed hands. Thrones have been won, regimes transferred, rule extended, religions and ideologies imposed, empires gained and lost, aggressions halted or advanced.

Thus wars in the past have sometimes been a means of settling international disputes, of changing political control, of inducing social transformation and even of stimulating science and technology.

And I suppose that on moral grounds it is only a difference of degree whether millions are killed or only thousands, whether the victims include children in the debris of a big city building or only young men lying on a battlefield in the countryside.

Nor has war been a very efficient way of settling disputes. Yesterday's enemies are today's friends. First, the victor pays for destruction of his enemy, then for reconstruction of his friend.

But war in the future would differ fundamentally from war in the past, not in degree but in kind. It is this which seems so difficult to grasp. Thermonuclear war cannot serve anyone's national interest—no matter how moral or immoral that interest may be, no matter how just or unjust, no matter how noble or ignoble, regardless of the nation's ideology, faith or social system.

It is no satisfaction to suggest that the issue of morality in war thus has become academic. Yet this is the fact and perhaps it will serve to clarify the dialogue of war and peace. For we can now free our collective conscience of nice ethical distinctions, and face the stark, amoral fact that war has ceased to be practical, that no nation can contemplate resort to modern war except in defense against intolerable exaction or aggression. Therefore we must abolish war to save our collective skins. For as long as this nuclear death dance continues, millions—tens of millions—perhaps hundreds of millions —are living on borrowed time.

I suggested that war is such an ancient institution, so deeply entrenched in tradition, that it requires a strenuous intellectual effort to imagine a world free from war. So it does. But I submit that the alternative effort is to imagine a world at the end of another war; when great areas and great places have been turned into radioactive wasteland; when millions upon millions of people are already dead, while debris from those great mushroom clouds drifts ghoulishly over the living; when great parts of our institutions, ideologies, faiths and beliefs, even our art and literature, lie smashed in the smoke and rubble of material destruction.

I submit that however difficult the vision of a world *without war* may be, it is not only a happier, but an easier vision to imagine than one of a world *after war*. In any event, we must choose between them.

The United States has a proud record in the effort to do away with armaments. We supported the two Hague Conferences. We took the lead in naval disarmament after World War I. We did our utmost to make the comprehensive Disarmament Conference of 1932 a success. And after World War II, we stripped our armed forces to the bone, in the hope and belief that we had made some progress toward a peaceful world.

Disarmament was one of the first orders of business for the United Nations. At the first meeting of this Assembly, the United States Delegation, of which I was a member, made a proposal as revolutionary as the scientific discovery which prompted it.

At that time we proposed to destroy the few atomic weapons which the United States alone possessed, to outlaw forever the manufacture of such weapons, to place the development of atomic energy in all its forms under the full control of the United Nations and to turn over to this organization all facilities and all information bearing on atomic science and technology; all this to prevent an atomic arms race.

The world does not need to be reminded here of the tragic consequences of the rejection of that initiative of a decade and a half ago. Since then there has been a long series of commissions, committees, subcommittees and conferences, inside the United Nations and out, which have tried to deal with the question of general disarmament and first steps toward it.

After the Soviet Delegation walked out of the Ten-Power General Disarmament talks in June, 1960, our main hopes were focused on the Three-Power negotiations at Geneva for a treaty to ban the testing of atomic weapons.

After two and a half years of patient negotiations, in the course of which significant progress was made, the United States and Britain tabled a comprehensive treaty which they had every reason to believe would meet the remaining points of difference with the Soviet Union. The United States and Britain were prepared to sign such a treaty at once—and still are.

Then on the last day of last August came the shocking news that the Soviet Union would break the moratorium which it had advocated and vowed never to break. The United States and Britain immediately offered to agree with the Soviet Union to ban at once all tests in the atmosphere without inspection, to spare mankind the hazards of radioactive fallout. We regret that, like the Baruch Plan proposals in 1946, this offer was also rejected by the Soviet Union.

Since that time the Soviet Union has carried on a series of nuclear weapons tests with unprecedented pollution of the atmosphere. It was climaxed by the explosion of history's most appalling weapon, a super-bomb of more than fifty megatons, or more than fifty million tons of TNT. This weapon's destructive power exceeds any known military requirements. So its principal purpose is to serve the political strategy of terror.

This action was taken in disregard of pleas from governments and peoples all over the non-Communist world—and, finally, in defiance of an unprecedented resolution of the United Nations General Assembly supported by eighty-seven nations.

To all our pleas, the Soviet Union, for months past, has invariably replied that it will agree to a ban on nuclear tests only as part of an agreement for general and complete disarmament. By insisting on this link between an issue which we had nearly resolved and the difficult issue of disarmament, the Soviet Union has tightened the knot and made it harder than ever to untie.

So let me point out at once to the distinguished representative of the Soviet Union that it is his country alone which insists on making a genuine and effective test ban dependent on the achievement of general disarmament. And because it does so insist, the Soviet Union, as we now move into the debate on general and complete disarmament, becomes *doubly* answerable to world opinion. The world will look to it in this debate to answer not one but two burning questions: Do you or don't you want disarmament? And, once again, do you or don't you want an end to nuclear weapons, in fact or just in rhetoric?

There is this much connection between the two subjects: The advance in weapons technology as a result of tests must ultimately increase our common peril. It is a measure of the tragic failure of all our efforts to reach disarmament agreements. And it is a compelling challenge to my government to try again, to make a fresh start, to insist with the utmost urgency that the weapons which have made war an obsolete institution be laid aside quickly before others are forced in self-defense to carry this insensate race yet another stage toward ultimate folly.

No doubt there are those who will ask how we can dare realistically to speak of disarmament today, when the winds of conflict blow all about us. There are those who will ask whether this is mere wishful thinking, whether this is more than escapism.

To that we would reply: Escapism, no—escape, yes. For a man *must* escape—not in wishful dreams, but in hard reality. We *must* escape from this spiral of fear, from the outmoded illusion that lasting security for peoples can be found by balancing out the wildly destructive power in the hands of their governments.

As President Kennedy said to the General Assembly:

> Today, every inhabitant of this planet must contemplate the day when it no longer may be habitable. Every man, woman and child lives under a nuclear sword of Damocles, hanging by the slenderest of threads, capable

of being cut at any moment by accident, miscalculation, or madness. The weapons of war must be abolished before they abolish us.

He also outlined the United States' conception of what is needed to create a world without war. It is a view which embraces first steps, subsequent steps and the ultimate goal at the end of the road. And it goes far beyond the technical steps in arms reduction. It requires the reservation of outer space for peaceful uses. It includes international programs for economic and social progress. And it insists especially upon the essential need to build up the machinery of peace while we tear down the machinery of war, that these must go hand-in-hand, that these, indeed, must be but two parts of a single program.

For in a world without arms military power would be taken out of the hands of nations; but other forms of power would remain, and mostly in the hands of the same states which are the most powerful military states today.

Conflicting ideologies would still be with us.

Political struggles would still take place.

Social systems would still be subject to disruptive pressures from within and without.

Economic strength would still be a factor in, and an instrument of, national foreign policies.

And the world would still be the scene of peaceful transformations, for it cannot and should not remain static.

Let us be clear about all this:

Disarmament alone will not purify the human race of the last vestiges of greed, ambition and brutality, of false pride and the love of power. Nor will it cleanse every last national leader of the least impulse to international lawlessness. No sane and honest man can pretend to foresee such a paradise on earth—even an earth without arms. But it would be a safer earth, where the contest and conflict could be waged in peace.

Obviously, then, disarmament will not usher in utopia. But it will prevent the wanton wastage of life and the wholesale destruction of material resources. And it will free the energies of man to engage in beneficent pursuits. How much could be done to improve the conditions of man—his education, his health, his nutrition and his housing—even if a small portion of the funds and the ingenuity of man now devoted to improving the art of killing were transferred to improving the art of living! .

Who would keep the peace in a disarmed world? How would our disputes get settled when arms have been taken away?

If we can answer these questions, we are much nearer to a solution of the problem of disarmament. For these are questions that open up the unexplored ground between first steps toward disarmament and the vision at the end of the road. And the vision of a world free from war will remain a utopian illusion until means for keeping the peace lend it reality.

It therefore seems clear to me that the only way to general and complete disarmament lies along two parallel paths which must be traveled together. One leads to the absence of arms, the other to the presence of adequate machinery for keeping the peace. As we destroy an obsolete institution for the settlement of disputes, we must create new institutions for the settlement of disputes—and simultaneously.

Let me repeat for emphasis. We do not hold the vision of a world without conflict. We do hold the vision of a world without war, and this inevitably requires an alternative system for coping with conflict. We cannot have one without the other. But if we travel the two roads together—if we build as we destroy—we can solve the vast technical problems here involved.

Let me come now to the United States proposals for dismantling the towering and costly machinery of war.

To begin with, the United States emphatically embraces the commitment to general and complete disarmament. We proclaim the goal—without reservation—and in the shortest possible span of time. And we take this terminology to mean exactly what it says— the general and complete disarmament of all national forces capable of international aggression, and the safe disposal of all their arms.

The United States proposal is, indeed, a radical one.

It calls for large reductions of armaments even in the first stages, both conventional and nuclear armaments.

It calls for an end to production of fissionable materials for weapons purposes, and the transfer of such materials from existing stocks for nonweapons use.

The program calls for a stop in the further development of independent national nuclear capabilities.

It calls for the destruction or conversion to peaceful uses of strategic nuclear weapons delivery vehicles.

It calls for an end to the production of such delivery vehicles.

It calls for the abolition of chemical, biological and radioactive weapons.

In short, the United States program calls for the total elimination of national capacity to make international war. And to ensure that all these steps are actually carried out by each side every step of the way, the plan calls for the creation of an International Disarmament Organization within the framework of the United Nations.

If the United States program is comprehensive, it also is flexible. It does not pretend to be the final word, nor would we wish it to be. We expect it to be examined exhaustively, to be altered and to be improved. It certainly is not perfect, but it can stand up to close scrutiny, for it has been prepared at great pains and in good faith. It is presented in dead earnest, and in the conviction that propaganda on the subject of disarmament is a cynical and cruel mockery of man's deepest hope.

At one point and one point alone, however, the United States is, and will remain, inflexible. This is on the familiar question of verification, on the indispensable need for the world to know that disarmament agreements are, in fact, being carried out. Because of the confusion that persists on this point, I must dwell upon it for a moment.

First of all, verification must be understood not as a technical point but as a fundamental principle, as the essential condition for any significant progress in disarmament, as its *sine qua non*. To pretend that there is enough confidence between the major armed powers to accept disarmament without verification is to deny the existence of the arms race itself. For the arms race is nothing if not living proof of the absence of mutual trust, and confidence has been rudely shaken by recent events.

I will say quite bluntly that mistrust exists on our side—and how could it be otherwise? The hostility of Soviet leaders toward my country, its institutions and its way of life is proclaimed, documented and demonstrated in a thousand ways. Yet we earnestly seek agreement with them, through diplomatic methods and through agreements recorded in words and deeds. So we may be excused, it seems to me, if we are wary of agreements deeply involving our national security with a nation whose recent leader wrote this: "Good words are a mask for the concealment of bad deeds. Sincere diplomacy is no more possible than dry water or iron wood."

These are the words of the late Marshal Stalin. I am aware that his former absolute authority has been subject to a certain re-evaluation recently. But the present Premier of the Soviet Union who served Stalin so loyally still proclaims his indebtedness to Lenin. And after the Treaty of Brest-Litovsk, Lenin said this: "We must demobilize the army as quickly as possible, because it is a sick organ; meanwhile we will assist the Finnish Revolution. Yes, of course we are violating the treaty; we have violated it thirty or forty times."

More recently we have seen wholesale violation of agreements pledging self-determination to the peoples of Eastern Europe—not to mention so contemporary an event as the erection of a wall through the middle of a city in violation of a postwar agreement.

I do not mention these matters to belabor the dead, nor to rub salt in wounds both old and fresh, nor to becloud the disarmament problem with irrelevant questions. They are not irrelevant, because there can be no disarmament without agreement, and because clear warnings and harsh experience have taught us to insist upon independent and international verification of agreements with the Soviet Union.

Our deepest hope, our most fervent prayer, is for proof that this acquired lack of trust will no longer be justified. Meanwhile, we do not ask that those who are suspicious of us take us at our word. We offer to them the same guarantees that we have the right and duty to demand of them. We offer to submit to verification procedures under international control at each step of disarmament.

Let me assure you, Mr. Chairman, that the United States has no interest in controls for the sake of controls. We do not wish to buy control or to trade something for it. We have no stake in playing the host to teams of foreign inspectors within our borders. But there is no other way to dispel mistrust, to exorcise suspicion, to begin to build the mutual confidence upon which peaceful cooperation ultimately depends. So we accept the need for adequate verification procedures. And we recognize the right of others to assure themselves that we, in fact, do what we say we shall do with respect to disarmament.

We must find a basis for a workable agreement. And even as we do, even as we consider the first moves toward disarmament, we can begin right away to strengthen our machinery for keeping the peace. We can do this without hampering our efforts to reach agreement on disarmament. Every step to improve the machinery of peace will make it easier to take the next step in destroying the machinery of war.

We need not even be at a loss as to where to begin or how to proceed. The experience of the United Nations itself gives us a starting point and a guideline.

In its earliest years the United Nations had successful experience with mediation and conciliation.

It defended collective security and the independence of small nations against their assailants in Korea.

Then, at a time of urgent need in the Middle East, the United Nations acquired an effective power to police the lines of an armistice agreement.

At another time of great need in the Congo, it added an effective power to restore order and to prevent a civil war.

Out of such emergencies, the United Nations is becoming a stronger instrument for keeping the peace.

It will have to be much stronger still. And our task now is to strengthen, refine and develop more fully the peace-keeping structure of the United Nations and its capacity to serve as an international police force.

We suggest that all nations make available an inventory of the forces, equipment and logistic support they would be prepared to put at the disposal of the United Nations, and that recent United Nations experience, such as in the Congo, be studied so that manuals can be prepared for the special training of these national units in the special character of United Nations operations.

But a stronger and better organized police force such as this would be needed only when threats to peace have reached dangerous proportions. It must be supplemented, therefore, with improved machinery for settling disputes *before* they reach an explosive stage. And here again our task is to build on the existing resources of the United Nations, including the International Court of Justice, and to avail ourselves more fully of our existing potentials for action.

Moves such as these—and I hope other members will have other suggestions—would permit us to get on with the job of creating the kind of peace-keeping machinery that will be essential for dealing with conflicts in a world free from war. And we can start them at once, even without waiting for agreement on disarmament.

Every such move will help to blunt danger, help to reduce distrust, help to erase fear. The way to start is to start; and a good place to start is at hand. I refer to the proposed treaty, still tabled at Geneva, whose objective it is to outlaw further testing of atomic devices in space, in the atmosphere, on the ground, or under the ground or the sea. We are flexible about first steps; we are adamant only on the point that we begin at once—immediately—to disarm.

I repeat, we *can* begin at once to disarm. To start now in no sense limits or postpones the goal of general and complete disarmament; indeed, this is the way to reach it faster. For some steps can be taken sooner than others, without disadvantage to any nation or groups of nations.

Let no one doubt our seriousness. The President of our nation presented in person to this General Assembly the boldest and most comprehensive plan for disarmament that my nation has ever offered to the world. Since then he has signed into a law an act creating a new Arms Control and Disarmament Agency, directly under his authority and containing an array of expert talent whose counterpart I would be very happy to see in a similar agency in the Soviet Union.

As I said earlier, it is extremely difficult for the mind to grasp a clear vision of a world without arms, for it is a condition totally foreign to the human experience. But, as I also said earlier, it is even more difficult to envision a world turned to a radioactive wasteland, which may well be the alternative. Difficult as it is, then, we must grasp the easier and happier vision.

And I do think we can see, however dimly, the general outlines of such a world. A world disarmed would not be utopia, but one suddenly blessed by freedom from war. It would not usher in world government, but the world community would have the capacity to keep the peace. It would not end national sovereignty, but the sovereign right to commit national suicide would be yielded up forever.

A disarmed world would still be a world of great diversity, in which no one nation could seriously pretend to have the wit and wisdom to manage mankind.

It would be a world in which ideas, for the first time, could compete on their own merits without the possibility of their imposition by force of arms.

It would be a world in which men could turn their talents to an agenda of progress and justice for all mankind in the second half of the twentieth century.

In short, it would not be a perfect world, but a world both safer and more exhilarating for us all to live in.

There is nothing inherently impossible in creating the conditions for a world without war. Our basic problems are not technical, mechanistic or administrative. The basic question is whether every nation will agree to abandon the means to coerce others by force.

If they will not, the arms race will go on. For those who love freedom and have the power to defend it will not be coerced. And uncertain as it is, free people prefer to live on borrowed time than to yield to terror.

Conceivably, the world could survive on this perpetual brink of universal disaster. Conceivably, fortune would spare us from the fatal act of a lunatic, the miscalculation of an uninformed leader, the false step of a nervous young sentry.

But on behalf of my government and my people I propose that this Assembly set the world on the road toward freedom from war.

And I propose that this committee take the first steps by approving a negotiating forum, endorsing the statement of agreed principles already worked out by the United States and the Soviet Union, and recommending that the new forum get on at once with the first business of this dangerous world—general and complete disarmament.

I ask the Soviet delegate whether his country cannot so conduct negotiations now that we and our respective allies may be able to turn to the rest of the members here, and to the hundreds of millions for whom they speak, and say: "We have not failed you."

TO NARROW THE GAP:
THE PEACEFUL USES OF OUTER SPACE

🕊 🕊 *"In outer space we start with a clean slate"—and after urging the United Nations to write boldly, Governor Stevenson presented the broad program which the United States thought should be written on this slate. Even the Soviet Union agreed with the basic premises, and after minor changes, the program was adopted unanimously. Among its key provisions: that outer space and celestial bodies are free for exploration and use by all states in conformity with international law and are not subject to national appropriation; the Secretary General should maintain a public registry of launchings of space vehicles into orbit or beyond; that there should be a worldwide effort in weather research and prediction under the United Nations, and a global system of communications satellites should be instituted.*

This is Year Five in the Age of Space. Already, in four short years, scientific instruments, then animals, then men, have been hurled into space and into orbit around the earth. Within a few more years, satellites will bring vast new developments in weather forecasting and in world-wide telephone, radio and television communications. More than that, rocket booster capacity will become sufficient to launch teams of men on journeys to the moon and to the nearest planets. And after that, one can only speculate what may come next.

Statement to the Political Committee, December 4, 1961.
🕊 53

Unhappily, this astounding progress in space science has not been matched by comparable progress in international cooperation. In the race of history, social invention continues to lag behind scientific invention.

We have already lost valuable time that can never be recovered. Unless we act soon, the space age—like the naval age, like the air age and the atomic age—will see waste and danger beyond description as a result of mankind's inability to exploit his technical advances in a rational social framework.

In short, unless we act soon, we shall be making the old mistakes all over again.

Despite the urgent need for immediate international action, I fear that we come to this subject ill-prepared to think clearly about it. I suspect that we are handicapped by our heritage of thought about the affairs of this single planet.

We are conditioned to think in terms of nations. Our lives and concepts are predicted upon states whose boundaries are fixed by oceans and rivers and mountain ranges, or by the man-made lines drawn sharply across the two-dimensional surface of planet Earth.

We are conditioned to think in terms of nations defined by finite areas expressed in finite measurements, nations with more or less known resources and more or less counted populations.

And especially we are conditioned to think in terms of national sovereignties.

Such concepts have no meaningful application to the unexplored, unbounded and possibly unpopulated reaches of outer space, which surround no nation more than any other nation, and which are innocent of the idea of national sovereignty.

We are further handicapped, many of us, by the impression that the exploration of outer space is a matter of concern only to the great powers because they alone have the capacity to penetrate space. That impression gains force from the belief that outer space is unrelated to the day-to-day problems of nations whose energies are absorbed by such earthly daily questions as growing enough food to feed their peoples.

This impression, I submit, is totally and dangerously wrong. The smallest nation represented here in the United Nations is deeply concerned with this question before us, and so is the poorest of our members. Indeed, they may have far more to gain from the shared benefits of space science—and on just such matters as growing food—than the larger and the richer societies.

Moreover, the small nations have an overriding interest in seeing to it that access to space and the benefits of space science are not pre-empted by a few nations, that space exploration is not carried forward as a competition between big power rivals, that the ideological quarrels which so unhappily afflict this planet are not boosted into space to infect other planets yet unsullied by the quarrels of men.

Finally, all nations can play a part in assuring that mankind derives the maximum advantage from space technology in the here and the now, and not just in the hereafter. Every nation can co-operate in the allocation of radio frequencies for space communications. Every nation can participate in global systems of weather prediction and communications.

In outer space we start with a clean slate, an area yet unmarred by the accumulated conflicts and prejudices of our earthly past. We propose today that the United Nations write on this slate boldly, and in an orderly and a creative way, to narrow the gap between scientific progress and social invention, to offer to all nations, irrespective of the stage of their economy or scientific development, an opportunity to participate in one of the greatest adventures of man's existence.

We cannot afford to delay!

The space programs of the great powers are well advanced. In the months ahead important decisions will have to be made. If the opportunity for United Nations action is missed, it will be increasingly difficult to fit national space programs into a rational pattern of United Nations cooperation.

Our first choice is a program making maximum use of the United Nations for at least three reasons:

—because it could bring new vitality to the United Nations and its family of agencies;

—because it would help to assure that all members of the United

Nations, developed and less developed, could have a share in the adventure of space cooperation;

—because a program of such magnitude should be carried out as far as possible through the organizations of the world community.

As I say, this is our first choice. But the march of science is irreversible. The United States has a responsibility to make the fullest possible use of new developments in space technology—in weather forecasting, in communications and in other areas. These developments are inevitable in the near future. We hope they can take place through cooperative efforts in the United Nations.

I suppose that the great climaxes in the drama of history are seldom evident to those who are on the stage at the time. But there can be little question that man's conquest of outer space is just such a moment, that we—all of us—are on stage, and that how we behave in the immediate future will have a profound impact upon the course of human affairs in the decades ahead.

There is a right and a wrong way to get on with the business of space exploration. In our judgment, the wrong way is to allow the march of science to become a runaway race into the unknown. The right way is to make it an ordered, peaceful, cooperative and constructive forward march under the aegis of the United Nations.

AN INVITATION TO AGGRESSION:

THE "IMPORTANT QUESTION" OF CHINA

❦ ❦ The question of which Chinese government shall represent China in the United Nations has come up in a variety of parliamentary guises at each session since 1950. With the advent of Governor Stevenson as Ambassador to the United Nations, the United States no longer tried to prevent even discussion of the question by keeping it off the agenda—a position that had become progressively unpopular with the membership. Instead the United States agreed to include it in the agenda as "an important question" requiring a two-thirds vote. This is what Governor Stevenson said during the long debate in 1961 as he explained why it was an "important question." The outcome of the vote that followed was that China continued to be represented by the government on Taiwan, the Republic of China, and not by the Communist government on the mainland, the People's Republic of China, as proposed by the Soviet Union. A similar Soviet proposal was rejected—by an even stronger vote—in 1962 after Governor Stevenson pointed out that the Communist Chinese disregard for the principles of the United Nations Charter was again demonstrated in its unprovoked attack on India, an attack carried out even as the debate was underway in the Assembly.

We live in an age when the ever-expanding family of nations is striving anew to realize the vision of the United Nations Charter: a

Statement to the General Assembly, December 1, 1961.
❦ 57

world community, freed from the overhanging menace of war, acting together in equal dignity and mutual tolerance to create a better life for humanity. This very Assembly, in its majestic diversity, is both the physical symbol and the practical embodiment, however imperfect, of that transcendent vision.

, In striving toward that vision, what we decide about the representation of China will have momentous consequences. For more is at stake than the status of certain delegations. More is at stake than the registering or reflecting of existing facts of power. Indeed, the underlying question is how the great people of China, who by a tragedy of history have been forcibly cut off from their own traditions and even led into war against the community of nations, can be enabled to achieve their own desires to live with themselves and with the rest of the world in peace and tolerance.

This question has a long history. For twelve years past, ever since the Communist armies conquered the Chinese mainland and the Republic of China relocated its government in Taipei, the community of nations has been confronted with a whole set of profoundly vexing problems. Most of them have arisen from aggressive military actions by the Chinese Communists—against Korea, against the government of the Republic of China on its island refuge, against Tibet and against South and Southeast Asia.*

The problem before us today, in its simplest terms, is this: The authorities who have carried out those aggressive actions, who have been in continuous and violent defiance of the principles of the United Nations and of the resolutions of the General Assembly, and deaf to the restraining pleas of law-abiding members—these same warlike authorities claim the right to occupy the seat of China here, and demand that we eject from the United Nations the representatives of the Republic of China.

The gravity of this problem is heightened in its world-wide political and moral significance by the fact that the Republic of China's place in the United Nations, since its founding in 1945, has been filled by its representatives with distinction—filled by representatives of a law-abiding government which, under most difficult cir-

* The attack on India was to follow.

cumstances, has done its duty well and faithfully in the United Nations, and against which there is no ground for serious complaint, let alone expulsion.

The United States believes, as we have believed from the beginning, that the United Nations would make a tragic and perhaps irreparable mistake if it yielded to the claim of an aggressive and unregenerate "People's Republic of China" to replace the Republic of China in the United Nations.

I realize that we have sometimes been charged with "unrealism," and even with "ignoring the existence of 600 million people."

That is a strange charge. My country's soldiers fought with other soldiers of the United Nations in Korea for nearly three years against a huge invading army from the mainland of China. And we have done our best at Panmunjom, at Geneva, at Warsaw, to negotiate with the emissaries of Peking.

No country is more aware of their existence. I think it could be said with more justice that it would be dangerously unrealistic if this Assembly were to bow to the demands of Peking to expel and replace the Republic of China in the United Nations; it would be ignoring the warlike character and aggressive behavior of the rulers who dominate 600 million people and who talk of the inevitability of war as an article of faith and refuse to renounce the use of force.

To consider this subject in its proper light, Mr. President, we must see it against the background of the era in which we live. It is an era of revolutionary changes. We cannot clearly see the end.

With dramatic swiftness, the age of empire is drawing to a close. More than one-third of the member states of the United Nations have won their independence since the United Nations itself was founded. Today, together with all other free and aspiring nations, they are working to perfect their independence by developing their economies and training their peoples. Already they play a vital part in the community of nations and in the work of this organization.

Thus, for the first time in history, we have seen an imperial system end, not in violent convulsions and the succession of still another empire, but in the largely peaceful rise of new, independent states, equal members of a world-wide community.

So diverse is that community in traditions and attitudes; so small and closely knit together is our modern world; so much do we have need of one another; and so frightful are the consequences of war that all of us whose representatives gather in this General Assembly hall must more than ever be determined, as the Charter says, "to practice tolerance and live together in peace with one another as good neighbors." For there can be no independence any more except in a community, and there can be no community without tolerance.

Such is one of the great revolutionary changes of our time: a spectacular revolution of emancipation and hope.

But this century has also bred more sinister revolutions born out of reaction to old injustices and out of the chaos of world war. These movements have brought into being a plague of warrior states, the scourge of our age. These regimes have been characterized not by democracy, but by dictatorship; they have been concerned not with people, but with power; not with the consent of the people, but with control of the people; not with tolerance and conciliation, but with hatred, falsehood and permanent struggle. They have varied in their names and their ideologies, but that has been their essential character.

Nowhere have these qualities been carried to a greater extreme, or reached a greater scale, than on the mainland of China under Communist rule. The regime has attempted through intimidation, hunger and ceaseless agitation, and through a so-called "commune" system which even allied Communist states view with distaste, to reduce a brilliant and spirited civilization to a culture of military uniformity and iron discipline. Day and night, by poster and loudspeaker and public harangue, the people are reminded of their duty to hate the foreign enemy.

Into the international sphere the Chinese Communists have carried the same qualities of arrogance, regimentation and aggression. Many people hoped, after their invasion of Korea ended, that they would thereupon give up the idea of foreign conquest. Instead, they sponsored and supplied the communizing of North Vietnam; they resumed their warlike threats against Taiwan; they launched a campaign of armed conquest to end the autonomy of Tibet; and all along their southern borders they have pressed forward into new territory. To this day, in a fashion recalling the early authoritarian emperors of China, they pursue all these policies, and, in addition, seek to use the millions of Chinese residing abroad as agents of their political designs.

In fact, these modern Chinese imperialists have gone further than their imperial ancestors ever dreamed of going. There are at this time in Communist China training centers for guerrilla warfare, with young men from Asia, Africa and Latin America being trained in sabotage and guerrilla tactics for eventual use in their own countries. Thus the strategy of Mao Tse-tung, of "Protracted Revolutionary War in the Rural Areas," has become one of the principal world exports—and no longer an "invisible export"—of Communist China.

We have exact information about some of these activities. For example, we have the testimony of six young men from the Republic of Cameroun who traveled clandestinely from their country to the mainland of China last year. They arrived in China on June 9 and left on August 30. During that period they had a ten-week course from French-speaking instructors in a military academy outside Peking. The curriculum of this educational institution, taken from the syllabus those men brought home, included such items as these:

Correct use of explosives and grenades.

Planning a sabotage operation.

How to use explosives against houses, rails, bridges, tanks, guns, trucks, tractors, etc.

Manufacture of explosives from easily obtained materials.

Manufacture and use of mines and grenades.

Use of semiautomatic rifles and carbines.

Theory and practice of guerrilla warfare; ambushes; attacks on communications.

Political lectures with such titles as "The People's War," "The Party," "The United Front" and—of course—"The Imperialists Are Only Paper Tigers."

This, incidentally, was the fourth in a series of courses to train Camerounians to fight for the overthrow, not of European colonial rulers (for their rule had already ended), but of their own sovereign African government.

Such an affinity for aggressive violence, and for subversive interference in other countries, is against all the rules of the civilized world; but it accords with the outlook and objectives of the Peking rulers.

It was the supreme leader of Chinese Communism, Mao Tse-tung, who summed up his world outlook over twenty years ago in these words: "Everything can be made to grow out of the barrel of a gun." And again: "The central duty and highest form of revolution is armed seizure of political power, the settling of problems by means of war. This Marxist-Leninist principle is universally correct, whether in China or in foreign countries; it is always true."

President Tito of Yugoslavia knows to what extremes this dogma of violence has been carried. In a speech to his people in 1958, he quoted the "Chinese leaders" as saying, with apparent complacency, "that in any possible war . . . there would still be 300 million left: that is to say, 300 million would get killed and 300 million would be left behind."

In an age when reasonable men throughout the world fear and detest the thought of nuclear war, from the Chinese Communist thinkers there comes the singular boast that, after such a war, "on the debris of a dead imperialism the victorious people would create with extreme rapidity a civilization thousands of times higher than the capitalist system and a truly beautiful future for themselves."

In fact, it was these same Chinese Communist leaders who officially acclaimed the resumption of nuclear tests by the Soviet Union as "a powerful inspiration to all peoples striving for world peace." What a shocking idea of world peace they seem to have!

With such a record and such a philosophy of violence and fanaticism, no wonder this regime still has no diplomatic relations with almost two-thirds of the governments of the world. One cannot help wondering what the representatives of such a predatory regime would contribute in our United Nations councils to the solution of the many dangerous questions which confront us.

I believe these facts are enough, Mr. President, to show how markedly Communist China has deviated from the pattern of progress and peace embodied in our Charter and toward which the community of peaceful nations is striving. In its present mood it is a massive and brutal threat to man's struggle to better his lot in his own way, and even, perhaps, to man's very survival. Its gigantic power, its reckless ambition and its unconcern for human values make it the major world problem.

Now—what is to be done about this problem? And what in particular can the United Nations do?

The problem is, in reality, age-old. How can those who prize tolerance and humility, those whose faith commands them to "love those that hate you," how can they make a just reply to the arrogant and the rapacious and the bitterly intolerant? To answer with equal intolerance would be to betray our own humane values. But to answer with meek submission or with a convenient pretense that wrong is not really wrong, this would betray the institutions on which the future of a peaceful world depend.

There are some who acknowledge the illegal and aggressive conduct of the Chinese Communists, but who believe that the United Nations can somehow accommodate this unbridled power and bring it in some measure under the control, or at least the influence, of the community of nations. They maintain that this can be accomplished by bringing Communist China into participation in the United Nations. By this step, so we are told, the interplay of ideas and interests in the United Nations would sooner or later cause these latter-day empire builders to abandon their warlike ways and accommodate themselves to the rule of law and the comity of nations.

This is a serious view and I intend to discuss it seriously. Certainly we must never abandon hope of winning over even the most stubborn antagonist.

But reasons born of sober experience oblige us to restrain our wishful thoughts. There are four principal reasons which I think are of overriding importance, and I most earnestly urge the Assembly to consider them with great care, for the whole future of the United Nations may be at stake.

My first point is that the step advocated, once taken, is irreversible. We cannot try it and then give it up if it fails to work. Given the extraordinary and forbidding difficulty of expulsion under the Charter, we must assume that, once in our midst, the Peking representatives would stay for better or for worse.

Secondly, there are ample grounds to suspect that a power given to such bitter words and ruthless actions as those of the Peking regime, far from being reformed by its experience in the United Nations, would be encouraged by its success in gaining admission to exert, all the more forcefully, by threats and maneuvers, a most disruptive and demoralizing influence on the organization at this critical moment in its history.

Thirdly, its admission, in circumstances in which it continues to violate and defy the principles of the Charter, could seriously shake public confidence in the United Nations—I can assure you it would do so among the people of the United States—and this alone would significantly weaken the organization.

Elementary prudence requires the General Assembly to reflect that there is no sign or record of any intention by the rulers of Communist China to pursue a course of action consistent with the Charter. Indeed, the signs all point the other way. The Peking authorities have shown nothing but contempt for the United Nations. They go out of their way to depreciate it and to insult its members. They refuse to abandon the use of force in the Taiwan Straits. They continue to encroach on the territorial integrity of other states. They apparently don't even get along very well with the U.S.S.R.!

Fourth, Mr. President, and with particular emphasis, let me recall to the attention of my fellow delegates the explicit conditions which the Chinese Communists themselves demand to be fulfilled before they will deign to accept a seat in the United Nations. I quote their Prime Minister, Chou En-lai:

The United Nations must expel the Chiang Kai-shek clique and restore China's legitimate rights, otherwise it would be impossible for China to have anything to do with the United Nations.

In this short sentence are two impossible demands. The first is that we should expel from the United Nations the Republic of China. The second, "to restore China's legitimate rights," in this context and in the light of Peking's persistent demands, can have only one meaning: that the United Nations should acquiesce in Communist China's design to conquer Taiwan and the eleven million people who live there, and thereby to overthrow and abolish the independent government of the Republic of China.

The effrontery of these demands is shocking. The Republic of China, which we are asked to expel and whose conquest and overthrow we are asked to approve, is one of the founding members of the United Nations. Its rights in this organization extend in an unbroken line from 1945, when the Charter was framed and went into effect, to the present.

Mr. President, the Republic of China is a charter member of this organization. The seat of the Republic of China is not empty; it is occupied and should continue to be occupied by the able delegates of the government of the Republic of China.

The fact that control over the Chinese mainland was wrested from the government of the Republic of China by the force of arms, and its area of actual control was thus greatly reduced, does not in the least justify expulsion, nor alter the legitimate rights of the government.

The *de jure* authority of the government of the Republic of China extends throughout the territory of China. Its effective jurisdiction extends over an area of over fourteen thousand square miles, an area greater than the territory of Albania, Belgium, Cyprus, El Salvador, Haiti, Israel, Lebanon or Luxembourg—all of them member states of the United Nations. It extends over eleven million people, that is, over more people than exist in the territory of sixty-five United Nations members. Its effective control, in other words, extends over more people than the legal jurisdiction of two-thirds of the governments represented here.

The economic and social standard of living of the people under its jurisdiction is one of the highest in all Asia, and is incomparably higher than the miserable standard prevailing on the mainland. The progressive agrarian policy of the government of the Republic of China and its progress in political, economic and cultural affairs contrast starkly with the policies of the rulers in Peking, under whom the unhappy lot of the mainland people has been little but oppression, communes, famine and cruelty.

All those who have served with the representatives of the Republic of China in the United Nations know their high standards of conduct, their unfailing dignity and courtesy, their contributions, and their consistent devotion to the principles and the success of our organization.

The notion of expelling the Republic of China is thus absurd and unthinkable. But what are we to say of the other condition sought by Peking—that the United Nations stand aside and let it conquer Taiwan and the eleven million people who live there? In effect, Peking is asking the United Nations to set its seal of approval in advance upon what would be as massive a resort to arms as the world has witnessed since the end of World War II. Of course the United Nations will never stultify itself in such a way.

The issue we face is, among other things, this question—whether it is right for the United Nations to drive the Republic of China from this organization in order to make room for a regime whose appetite seems to be insatiable. It is whether we intend to abandon the Charter requirement that all United Nations members must be peace-loving and to give our implicit blessing to an aggressive and bloody war against those Chinese who are still free in Taiwan.

What an invitation to aggression the Soviet proposal would be— and what a grievous blow to the good name of the United Nations!

In these circumstances the United States earnestly believes that it is impossible to speak seriously today of "bringing Communist China into the United Nations." No basis exists on which such a step could be taken. We believe that we must first do just the opposite: We must instead find a way to bring the United Nations, its law and its spirit, back into the whole territory of China.

The root of the problem lies, as it has from the very beginning, in the hostile, callous and seemingly intractable minds of the Chinese Communist rulers. Let those members who advocate Peking's taking China's seat seek to exert upon its rulers whatever benign influence they can, in the hope of persuading them to accept the standards of the community of nations.

Let those rulers respond to these appeals; let them give up trying to impose their demands on this organization; let them cease their aggression, direct and indirect, and their threats of aggression; let them show respect for the rights of others; let them recognize and accept the independence and diversity of culture and institutions among their neighbors.

Therefore, Mr. President, let the Assembly declare the transcendent importance of this question of the representation of China. Let us reaffirm the position which the General Assembly took ten years ago, that such a question as this "should be considered in the light of the purposes and principles of the Charter."

The issue on which peace and the future of Asia so greatly depend is not simply whether delegates from Peking should take a place in the General Assembly. More profoundly still, it is whether the United Nations, with its universal purposes of peace and tolerance, shall be permitted to take its rightful place in the minds of the people of all of China.

Today the rulers in Peking still repeat the iron maxim of Mao Tse-tung: "All political power grows out of the barrel of a gun." If that maxim had been followed, the United Nations would never have been created, and this world would long since have been covered with radioactive ashes. It is an obsolete maxim, and the sooner it is abandoned, the sooner the people of all of China are allowed to resume their traditionally peaceful policies, the better for the world.

No issue remaining before the United Nations this year has such fateful consequences for the future of this organization. The vital significance which would be attached to any alteration of the current situation needs no explanation. The United States has therefore joined today with the delegations of Australia, Colombia, Italy and Japan in presenting a resolution under which the Assembly would determine that any proposal to change the representation of China would be considered an important question in accordance with the Charter. Indeed, it would be hard to consider such a proposal in any other light, and we trust it will be solidly endorsed by the Assembly.

BY CONSENT OF THE GOVERNED:

A NEW IMPERIALISM

❦ ❦ Colonialism is one of the most emotional of the issues before the United Nations, and the Soviet Union rarely misses a chance to exploit that fact. During the Sixteenth General Assembly it circulated a memorandum accusing the United States of being an "accomplice in all the bloody atrocities" of the other colonial powers. In his reply —also as a memorandum circulated to all United Nations members— Governor Stevenson not only delineated the United States position on colonialism, but he focused attention on the Sino-Soviet record of imperialism and the suppression of freedoms. The following statement, although not delivered in the United Nations, was based on this document, which it summarizes.

On a grander scale than ever before, the world in our generation is being swept by forces which express the fierce determination of men to be free. This liberating force is felt with particular effect in the colonial empires which Western nations have created in Africa and Asia in the centuries since the age of discovery began.

Some forty new nations,* embracing about a billion people, have joined into the Family of Nations since 1945. The colonial empires

Remarks on Armstrong Circle Theatre, CBS-TV, January 3, 1962.

* As of May 15, 1963, the number was 47.

of the West have shrunk to a fraction of their former size. The age of imperialism and colonialism is in its twilight.

The colonial age was neither all good nor all bad. It developed material resources previously unknown. It kept peace and order and taught warring groups and tribes to live in peace. It educated leaders and technicians. At its best, it implanted liberal political and social institutions.

But by its very nature this colonial system, if carried on at all humanely, was destined to work itself out of a job. It was dominated by aliens from abroad, and this basic fact was found to clash with the growing education and political awareness which colonialism itself made possible among the subject peoples. Inevitably these people demanded the right to the same free institutions of which they learned from their conquerors.

The American colonies walked this same path in the eighteenth century. Our turn came first, perhaps, because the American colonists were of the same race and culture as the ministers in London who oppressed them. But in *our* time it has turned out that the thirst for freedom is universal and has nothing to do with racial similarities or differences. Government by consent of the governed—that is the root principle. And we are living today in the era in which that principle is marching in triumph across the old colonial world.

Now, in this same era we see a tragically contrasting fact—the huge fact of the Communist empires of Soviet Russia and Communist China, which together operate the largest and most populous colonial empires in the history of the world.

According to their own rulers, the peoples of the Soviet Union enjoy the right of self-determination. The Soviet regime, at its founding over forty years ago, proclaimed "The Right of the Nations of Russia to Free Self-Determination, including the Right to Secede and Form Independent States."

Unfortunately, this turned out to be more double-talk.

During and after the Second World War, as we all know, whole nations and peoples were swallowed up behind the Iron Curtain in violation of agreements and without a free vote of the peoples concerned. These included Latvia, Lithuania, Estonia, Poland,

Hungary, Rumania, Bulgaria, Albania and Czechoslovakia. East Germany was made a satellite. In Asia a similar fate overtook North Korea, North Vietnam and, most recently, Tibet.

Chairman Khrushchev has called Western colonialism "disgraceful, barbarous and savage." But Soviet imperial rule has not been sweet, gentle and kind. One proof of this is the fact that more than twelve million persons have escaped since the Second World War from the Soviet Union, Communist China and the areas they control. Since the end of the Second World War, more than three million Germans have fled from the Soviet-controlled Eastern Zone and East Berlin. Even the famous wall has not stopped them altogether. Nor can we forget, five years later, that nearly 200,000 Hungarians fled after the revolt of October, 1956, was crushed by Soviet troops.

The urge to express one's national identity is a potent force indeed. Even the Soviet Communist party program, newly adopted this fall, admits what a tough task is "the obliteration of national features, particularly of the language differences." And Mr. Khrushchev felt constrained to warn only two months ago that "even the slightest vestiges of nationalism should be eradicated with uncompromising Bolshevik determination."

Thus, although the Soviet state has possessed nearly total control of mass propaganda and education for two generations, it is *still* struggling to wipe out the national characteristics that differentiate the Uzbek from the Ukrainian, the Kazakh from the Armenian, the non-Russian from the Russian.

Now there are perfectly clear historical reasons for this contrast. The nations of the West which established colonial empires between the age of Columbus and the age of Cecil Rhodes were most of them children of the renaissance, of the "enlightenment" and of the doctrines of human freedom on which the United States itself was founded. But these liberating winds did not blow very much across the Russian steppes, except very briefly and feebly in the eighteenth and nineteenth centuries—and even then they were followed by periods of bloody reaction under the Czars.

And today, although we may have some reason to hope that the evolution of the Soviet Union is moving in liberal directions, we know that there is a very long road ahead.

So there are historical reasons for this contrast. But there is hardly any excuse for the Soviet Union—let alone the despots of Communist China—to set themselves up as sponsors or leaders of the liberation movement in Africa and Asia. On their own records they are just about the last whom history would nominate for such an honor.

Yet that is the pretension which Moscow, in particular, makes today. And it may be well for us to think for a minute about the Soviet doctrine of political strategy that underlies this effort.

It is Soviet doctrine that the political development of newly independent states is to proceed in two distinct phases—and now I am quoting Academician Y. E. Zhukov in *Pravda* on August 26, 1960—"The majority of the new Asian and African *National* states are headed by *bourgeois* politicians under the banner of *Nationalism.*" In other words, they are not under control either of Moscow or of local Communist parties.

But at the same time, local Communists are instructed to prepare for the future day of direct action. In this initial period, Communists are to concentrate on obtaining key positions in trade-union and student movements, and front organizations of all types.

As Moscow sees it, most of the African and Asian countries are now in that first phase. As Academician Zhukov phrases it: "One cannot, therefore, term *Socialist* [which is the jargon for Communist] those general democratic measures which to some degree are implemented in India, Indonesia, the United Arab Republic, Iraq and other independent countries of Asia and Africa." At the appropriate stage, therefore, the Communist parties must come forth frankly and openly with their bid for power. And that is the "second phase."

The national independence for which patriots under colonial domination have yearned so long, and which most of them have now achieved in very great measure, is for them a tremendous victory, to be celebrated with rejoicing and bonfires and dancing in the streets. And that is what we have seen all the way across Africa and Asia.

But this same thing called "independence," or "freedom," is in the eyes of Soviet strategy nothing better than a way station on the road to the world Communist system of the future, in which all peoples will take their orders from Moscow. Or will it be Peking?

Some of the African and Asian patriots have perhaps been slow to learn these bitter truths. Many of them are understandably impatient, and are tempted from time to time, in their quarrels with the European ruler, to fall for that ancient fallacy, "The enemy of my enemy is my friend."

Any who still think that way, however, would do well to study Soviet strategy as it applies to them, and also to study the Soviet and Chinese Communist empires as they really are.

The Communist empires are the only imperial systems which are not liquidating themselves, as other empires have done, but are still trying energetically to expand in all directions.

By the ruthless use of police control, by systematic falsehood, and by the erection of artificial barriers to communication, these regimes have suppressed all movements in the direction of freedom. They have labored to eradicate all national identity in the people, as well as all religious loyalties, and have held their peoples in virtual isolation from the outside world.

Finally, the Soviet colonial empire is the only modern empire in which no subject peoples have ever been offered any choice concerning their future and their destiny. That destiny was "decided" once and for all—at gunpoint. Until Moscow and Peking change their basic outlook, no chance will be given to any of their subject peoples to reconsider this so-called "choice."

The United States is against colonialism, wherever and whenever it occurs. We believe that the promise of our Declaration of Independence, that "all men are created equal," literally means what it says—not Americans only, or Westerners only, but "all men."

We shall never join with any nation for the purpose of planning, financing or waging colonial wars. The military alliances we have formed with others have no such aims; they are defensive alliances created as a shield for free men and free nations. But the key to our policy is not arms; it is freedom.

As a nation we believe that man—a physical, intellectual and spiritual being, not an economic animal—has individual rights, divinely bestowed, limited only by the obligation to avoid infringement upon the equal rights of others.

We do not claim perfection in our own society and in our own lives. But we do maintain that the direction we take is always that of greater liberty.

We believe that justice, decency and liberty, in an orderly society, are concepts which have raised man above the beasts of the field. To deny any person the opportunity to live under their shelter is an offense against all humanity.

Our Republic is the product of the first successful revolution against colonialism in modern times. Our people, drawn from all the nations of the world, have come to these shores in the search for freedom and opportunity in a progressive society. We have never forgotten either our origins or the nature of the world we live in.

And that is why we Americans do not fear the winds of change and the winds of freedom which are blowing across so much of the world. To us they make a wonderful sound; and as the seeds they carry take root and grow, we will feel that America's great purpose in this world is being fulfilled.

A PRIVILEGE ABUSED:
100 SOVIET VETOES

✌ ✌ *On June 22, 1962, the Soviet Union cast its one hundredth veto in the Security Council. Under the terms of the Charter, a negative vote by any one of the five permanent members—the United States, the U.S.S.R., the United Kingdom, France, the Republic of China— is sufficient to kill a proposal. The issue before the Security Council on this occasion involved the India-Pakistan dispute over Kashmir, and the veto prevented the Security Council from urging the governments of India and Pakistan to enter into negotiations and to refrain from actions or statements that would aggravate the situation. In his statement after the vote, Governor Stevenson gave a history of the veto—never resorted to by the United States— and how the Soviet Union has used it.*

I hope the members of the Security Council will not object and will indulge me while I make a few remarks on this historic day in the Security Council. It is a day that should not pass without notice. A permanent member of the Security Council has just cast its one hundredth veto.

From the beginning of the United Nations, one of its special characteristics has been the voting procedure in the Security Council. We all recall the serious deliberations which took place at San Francisco concerning the nature and the import for the future of

Statement to the Security Council, June 22, 1962.

the veto right for the permanent members of the Security Council. That right was given to them primarily because it would be their military and economic power which would have to be used to sustain and enforce Security Council decisions directly affecting vital world interests.

Representatives of small and middle-sized states emphasized their anxiety that the veto might be used to paralyze the Security Council. In order to meet such fears, the four sponsoring members of the conference set forth their conception at that time of the unanimity rule, with which the delegation of France also associated itself.

The big powers, including the Soviet Union, specifically stated, "It is not to be assumed . . . that the permanent members, any more than the non-permanent members, would use their veto willfully to obstruct the operation of the Council."

That was the way we started, Mr. President, at San Francisco seventeen years ago, this very week, I believe. What has happened since? Before the first year was out the Soviet Union had cast nine vetoes. The Soviet member of the Council has today cast its one hundredth veto. For seventeen years the U.S.S.R. on occasion after occasion has sought to obstruct the operations of the Council, sometimes where Soviet plans and prestige were directly and clearly involved and at other times when the continuation of friction might contribute to Soviet objectives.

The Soviet Union has used the veto lavishly to prevent states from assuming their rightful place in the United Nations. In fact, fifty-one of these vetoes were cast on applications for membership in the United Nations.

Ireland, a member of this Council, was denied membership for nine years. So were Jordan and Portugal. Austria, Finland and Italy were kept out for eight years. Ceylon was kept out for seven years, Nepal for six years. Mauritania was vetoed in 1960, and Kuwait in 1961. Korea is still not a member.

The veto has been used to tie the admission of clearly qualified states for which there was widespread support to the admission of states and regimes about whose qualifications for membership there were grave doubts. This, despite the fact that the tying of the admission of one applicant to that of another has been specifically held by the International Court of Justice to be contrary to the Charter.

The Soviet delegate used the veto thirteen times to assist Soviet bloc activities against the territorial integrity and political independence of other states. When the Soviet subverted Czechoslovakia in 1948, the Soviet delegate vetoed Security Council moves to investigate the case. When Communist-supported guerrillas tried to overturn the independence of Greece in 1946 and 1947, the Soviet again vetoed a Security Council resolution. And when Thailand asked the Security Council to act against attempted infiltration from Indochina in 1954, the Soviet again vetoed.

After realizing its mistake in boycotting the Council during the North Korean aggression against the Republic of Korea in 1950, I remind the members of the Council that the Soviet Union finally returned in August and immediately began to veto Security Council decisions designed to uphold the independence of that country. Fortunately for the Korean people and for this organization, that effort failed because we were able to proceed through the General Assembly.

Similarly, in 1956, the United Nations was forced to move in the General Assembly to condemn Soviet intervention in Hungary after the Soviet Union supported its aggression against the Hungarian people by invocation of the veto.

And, most recently, in 1960, the Soviet Union vetoed a resolution on the Congo sponsored by Ceylon and Tunisia because the resolution was designed in part to resist Soviet efforts to intervene in the Congo despite the fact that the United Nations peace-keeping operation was already in action. Again an emergency session of the General Assembly was required before the United Nations could do what was necessary.

There are still more areas in which the veto has been used to obstruct the operation of the Council. On at least four occasions, with the use of six vetoes, the Soviet Union refused, after using the Security Council to air its charges, to let its own assertions be examined.

I invite your attention to 1950; when the Soviet Union charged the United States Air Force with the bombing of Communist-held areas of China it vetoed a commission of investigation.

In 1952, the Soviet representative climaxed one of the most shameless falsehoods in history—the long crescendo of accusations that the United States and the United Nations troops were employing germ warfare in Korea—by bringing the issue before the Security Council, and then promptly vetoing a proposal for an impartial investigation.

In 1958, when the Soviet Union purported to be concerned about United States flights over the Arctic Circle, the United States proposed an Arctic Inspection Zone. That, too, was vetoed. In 1960, when Soviet fighter planes destroyed a United States RB-47 airplane over international waters, the Soviet Union vetoed two separate proposals for investigations, one of them asking only that the International Red Cross be permitted to assist any surviving member of the plane.

In each of these cases the Security Council tried to exercise its proper peace-keeping function through systematic investigations. In each case, after having brought the charge, the Soviets vetoed the attempt at a remedy.

One of the most disturbing facts also revealed in the history of a hundred vetoes is the consistent effort to prevent the Security Council from developing processes of peaceful settlement. Not only do many of the vetoes I have referred to fall into this category, but most of the remaining ones were also cast against efforts to promote peaceful settlements: four times with respect to Spain in 1946; once against a resolution on troop withdrawals from Syria and Lebanon in 1946, not because the resolution was wrong, but because it was not extreme enough; twice in connection with problems arising at the time of Indonesian independence; once against the Security Council recommendations for a solution of the Berlin blockade in 1948; once on Goa; twice to prevent extension of United Nations peace-keeping functions in Lebanon in 1958, and five times since 1960 in the Security Council's consideration of the Congo. The U.S.S.R. also vetoed four resolutions in the field of disarmament.

Distortion of the veto power has been a fact of life in this Council.

It is the fact that led to the Uniting for Peace procedure, which added to the United Nations peace-keeping machinery a flexible means whereby members can make sure that the United Nations' primary function of preserving the peace will be carried out.

The veto does exist, within its proper context, as a recognition of political reality, but it is a privilege to be used not abused. And abused it has been, for the Soviet Union has willfully obstructed the operation of this Council over and over. It has violated that part of the Four Power Declaration at San Francisco, in which the powers agreed not to use their veto willfully to obstruct the operation of this Council.

Now, so much for yesterday and for today. What of the future? The Council is a vital and purposeful organ of the United Nations in spite of the veto. It provides vital and purposeful direction and leadership. And in areas of its work where the veto does not apply, we believe the Council might well widen its activities and increasingly provide that direction and that leadership to our affairs.

As for the veto itself, we hope that long before the Soviet Union approaches its two hundredth veto, it will realize that its own interests lie not in national obstruction, but in international cooperation, not in willful vetoes for narrow ends, but in willing assents for the broad and common good for which the United Nations stands.

A THREAT TO THE WORLD:
SOVIET MISSILES IN CUBA

❦ ❦ *Tuesday, October 23, 1962 is an historic date in the United Nations. At an emergency meeting of the Security Council, Governor Stevenson described the threat confronting the Americas and the world as a result of the secret Soviet nuclear missile build-up in Cuba. The issue of Cuba had come up many times before, both in the Security Council and in the General Assembly, but not once were Cuban or Soviet charges against the United States substantiated or upheld by votes of the other members. Only a few days earlier, in an immediate reply to President Dorticos of Cuba—who had utilized a ceremonial occasion to launch new and old charges against the United States—Governor Stevenson declared that if the Cuban regime wished to renounce Communism and establish normal relations in this hemisphere, "the way is clear, and the choice is Cuba's." Then, the night before the emergency meeting of the Council, President Kennedy announced the discovery of the missile sites, and now it no longer was the danger of Communism in Cuba, it was one of nuclear war. Speaking solemnly, grimly, Adlai Stevenson told a crowded, tense Security Council chamber the details of the Soviet Union's "ominous adventure." It was a speech that none who heard it will forget.*

I have asked for an emergency meeting of the Security Council to bring to your attention a grave threat to the Western Hemisphere and to the peace of the world.

Statement to the Security Council, October 23, 1962.

❦ 79

Last night, the President of the United States reported the recent alarming developments in Cuba. Permit me to remind you of the President's sobering words:

Within the past week, unmistakable evidence has established the fact that a series of offensive missile sites is now in preparation on that imprisoned island. The purpose of these bases can be none other than to provide a nuclear strike capability against the Western Hemisphere. Upon receiving the first preliminary hard information of this nature last Tuesday morning at 9 A.M., I directed that our surveillance be stepped up. And having now confirmed and completed our evaluation of the evidence and our decision on a course of action, this Government feels obliged to report this new crisis to you in full detail.

The characteristics of these new missile sites indicate two distinct types of installations. Several of them include medium range ballistic missiles, capable of carrying a nuclear warhead for a distance of more than 1,000 nautical miles. Each of these missiles, in short, is capable of striking Washington, D.C., the Panama Canal, Cape Canaveral, Mexico City, or any other city in the Southeastern part of the United States, in Central America or in the Caribbean area.

Additional sites not yet completed appear to be designed for intermediate range ballistic missiles—capable of traveling more than twice as far—and thus capable of striking most of the major cities in the Western Hemisphere, ranging as far north as Hudson's Bay, Canada, and as far south as Lima, Peru. In addition, jet bombers, capable of carrying nuclear weapons, are now being uncrated and assembled in Cuba, while the necessary air bases are being prepared.

In view of this transformation of Cuba into a base for offensive weapons of sudden mass destruction, the President announced the initiation of a strict quarantine on all offensive military weapons under shipment to Cuba. He did so because, in the view of my government, the recent developments in Cuba—the importation of the cold war into the heart of the Americas—constitute a threat to the peace of this hemisphere, and, indeed, to the peace of the world.

Mr. President, seventeen years ago the representatives of fifty-one nations gathered in San Francisco to adopt the Charter of the United Nations. These nations stated with clarity and eloquence the high purpose which brought them together.

They announced their common determination "to save succeeding generations from the scourge of war . . . to reaffirm faith in fundamental human rights . . . to establish conditions under which justice and respect for the obligations arising from treaties and other sources of international law can be maintained, and to promote social progress and better standards of life in larger freedom." And in one sentence, paragraph 4, Article 2, they defined the necessary condition of a community of independent peoples:

All members shall refrain in their international relations from the threat or use of force against the territorial integrity or political independence of any state, or in any other manner inconsistent with the Purposes of the United Nations.

In this spirit, these fifty-one nations solemnly resolved to band together in a great cooperative quest for world peace and world progress. The adventure of the United Nations held out to humanity the bright hope of a new world—a world securely founded in international peace, in national independence, in personal freedom, in respect for law, for social justice and betterment, and, in the words of the Charter, for "equal rights and self-determination of peoples."

The vision of San Francisco was the vision of a world community of independent nations, each freely developing according to its own traditions and its own genius, bound together by a common respect for the rights of other nations and by a common loyalty to the larger international order. This vision assumes that this earth is quite large enough to shelter a great variety of economic systems, political creeds, philosophical beliefs and religious convictions. The faith of the Charter is in a pluralistic world, a world of free choice, respecting the infinite diversity of mankind and dedicated to nations living together as good neighbors, in peace.

Like many peoples, we welcomed the world of the Charter, for our society is based on principles of choice and consent.

We believe the principles of an open society in the world order survive and flourish in the competitions of peace. We believe that freedom and diversity are the best climate for human creativity and social progress. We reject all fatalistic philosophies of history and all theories of political and social predestination. We doubt whether any nation has so absolute a grip on absolute truth that it is entitled to impose its idea of what is right on others. And we know that a world community of independent nations accepting a common frame of international order offers the best safeguard for the safety of our shores and the security of our people. Our commitment to the world of the Charter expresses both our deepest philosophical traditions and the most realistic interpretation of our national interest.

Had we any other vision of the world, had we sought the path of empire, our opportunities for self-aggrandizement immediately after the war were almost unparalleled. In 1945, the United States was incomparably the greatest military power in the world. Our troops and planes were dispersed at strategic points around the globe. We had exclusive possession of the terror and promise of atomic energy. Our economic strength was unmatched. If the American purpose had been world dominion, there could have been no more propitious moment to set out on such a course.

Instead, our commitment, then as now, was to the world of the Charter—the creation of a community of freely cooperating, inde-dependent states bound together by the United Nations. In the service of this commitment and without waiting for the peace treaties, we dismantled the mightiest military force we had ever assembled. Armies were disbanded wholesale. Vast supplies of war equipment were liquidated or junked. Within two years after the end of the war, our defense spending had fallen by nearly $70 billion. Our armed forces were slashed from more than twelve million to one and a half million men. We did not retain a single division in a state of combat readiness. We did not have a single military alliance anywhere in the world. History has not seen, I believe, a more complete and comprehensive demonstration of a great nation's hope for peace and amity.

Instead of using our monopoly of atomic energy to extend our national power, we offered in 1946 to transfer the control of atomic energy to the United Nations.

Instead of using our overwhelming economic strength to extend our national power, we contributed more than $2.6 billion to the United Nations Relief and Rehabilitation Administration, much of which went to the relief of suffering in the Communist countries.

And after 1948, we contributed many more billions to the economic restoration of Europe—and invited the Communist countries to participate as recipients of our assistance.

Instead of using our substance and strength to extend our national power, we supported the movement for independence which began to sweep through Asia and Africa, the movement which has added so many new members to the United Nations in the years since 1945. Since the war, we have contributed $97 billion of economic and military assistance to other nations—and, of this sum, $53 billion has gone to the nations of Asia, Africa and Latin America.

I have often wondered what the world would be like today if the situation at the end of the war had been reversed—if the United States had been ravaged and shattered by war, and if the Soviet Union had emerged intact in exclusive possession of the atomic bomb and overwhelming military and economic might. Would it have followed the same path and devoted itself to realizing the world of the Charter?

To ask this question suggests the central paradox of the United Nations. For among the states which pledged their fidelity to the idea of a pluralistic world in San Francisco were some who had an incompatible vision of the future world order.

Has the Soviet Union ever really joined the United Nations? Or does its philosophy of history and its conception of the future run counter to the pluralistic concept of the Charter?

Against the idea of diversity, Communism asserts the idea of uniformity; against freedom, inevitability; against choice, compulsion; against democracy, dogma; against independence, ideolgy; against tolerance, conformity. Its faith is that the iron laws of history will require every nation to traverse the same predestined path to the same predestined conclusion. Given this faith in a monolithic world, the very existence of diversity is a threat to the Communist future.

I do not assert that Communism must always remain a messianic faith. Like other fanaticisms of the past, it may in time lose its sense of infallibility and accept the diversity of human destiny. Already in some countries we see Communism subsiding into a local and limited ideology. There are those who have discerned the same evolution in the Soviet Union itself; and we may all earnestly hope that Chairman Khrushchev and his associates will renounce the dream of making the world over in the image of the Soviet Union. It must be the purpose of other nations to do what they can to hasten that day.

But that day has not yet arrived. The conflict between absolutist and pluralistic conceptions of the destiny of mankind remains the basic source of discord within the United Nations. It has given rise to what is known as the cold war. Were it not for this conflict, this organization would have made steady progress toward the world of choice and justice envisaged at San Francisco.

But because of the Soviet rejection of an open world, the hope for progress and for peace has been systematically frustrated. And in these halls we spend much of our time and energy either engaged in or avoiding this incessant conflict.

It began even before the nations gathered at San Francisco. As soon as the defeat of the Nazis appeared certain, the Soviet Union began to abandon the policy of wartime cooperation to which it had turned for self-protection. In early 1945, Moscow instructed the Communist parties of the West to purge themselves of the sin of cooperation, and to return to their prewar view that democratic governments were by definition imperialistic and wicked. Within a few weeks after the meeting at Yalta, the Soviet Union took swift action in Rumania and Poland in brutal violation of the Yalta pledges of political freedom.

At the same time, it began a political offensive against the United States, charging that the American Government—the government of Franklin Roosevelt—was engaged in secret peace negotiations with Hitler. Roosevelt replied to Stalin that he deeply resented these "vile misrepresentations." At the end of March, 1945, Roosevelt cabled Winston Churchill that he was "watching with anxiety and concern the development of the Soviet attitude" and that he was "acutely aware of the dangers inherent in the present course of events, not only for the immediate issue, but also the San Francisco Conference and future world cooperation."

It is important to recall these facts, because the Soviet Union has tried in the years since to pretend that its policy of aggression was a defensive response to the change of Administration in the United States, or to Churchill's 1946 speech at Fulton, Missouri, or to some other event after the death of Roosevelt. But the historical record is clear. As soon as the Soviet Government saw no further military need for the wartime coalition, it set out on its expansionist adventures.

The ink was hardly dry on the Charter before Moscow began its war against the world of the United Nations. The very first meeting of the Security Council—and I was there—was called to hear a complaint by Iran that Soviet troops had failed to withdraw from the northern part of that country on the date on which they had agreed to leave. Not only had they declined to go; they had installed a puppet regime on Iranian soil and had blocked Iranian troops from entering part of Iran's territory. The Soviet Union, in short, was violating the territorial integrity and denying the political independence of Iran—and doing so by armed force. Eventually the United Nations forced a reluctant agreement from the Soviet Union to live up to its pledge.

This was only the beginning. At the time of the German surrender, the Red Army was in occupation of Rumania, Bulgaria, Hungary, Poland, Eastern Germany and most of Czechoslovakia. And there the Red Army stayed. It stayed in violation of the agreement reached at Yalta by the heads of the Allied powers—the agreement which pledged independence of and free elections to these nations. By 1948, five nations and half of a sixth, with a combined population of more than ninety million people, had been absorbed into the Communist empire. To this day the peoples of Eastern Europe have never been permitted to exercise the Charter right of self-determination.

Before the suppression of Eastern Europe was complete, the Soviet Union was fomenting guerrilla warfare and sabotaging economic recovery in Greece and Turkey, and assailing neighboring regimes through all the instrumentalities of propaganda and subversion.

Nor were such activities confined to Europe. In Malaya, in the

Philippines, in Burma, in Indochina the Communists encouraged and supported guerrilla uprisings against constituted governments.

In one event after another, on one stage after another—the rejection in the United Nations of the American plan for the internationalization of atomic energy, the rejection of the Marshall Plan, the blockade of Berlin and, finally, the invasion of South Korea—the Soviet Union assailed political independence, repudiated the concepts of the Charter and tried to impose its design of a Communist future.

Let me recall the record with regard to international agreements.

The Soviet Government has signed treaties of non aggression—as it did with the Baltic states and Finland—and then systematically invaded the countries whose integrity it had solemnly promised to respect.

At Yalta and in a succession of peace treaties, it pledged to the liberated countries of Eastern Europe "the right of all peoples to choose the form of government under which they will live—the restoration of sovereign rights and self-government to those peoples who have been forcibly deprived of them"—and then systematically denied those rights and consolidated that deprivation.

In 1945 it signed a thirty-year pact of mutual assistance and non-aggression with China, pledging that its military aid and economic support would be "given entirely to the National Government as the Central Government of China"—and violated that treaty almost before the Chinese negotiators had left Moscow.

At Potsdam it promised that "all democratic political parties with rights of assembly and of public discussion shall be allowed and encouraged throughout Germany"—and within its own zone promptly repudiated that promise. At Geneva in 1954 it agreed not to introduce arms into Vietnam—and sent guns and ammunition to the Viet Minh.

It denounced nuclear testing—and then violated the moratorium which for three years had spared the world the danger of nuclear tests.

Within this Council, it has thwarted the majority will one hundred times by the use of the veto.

The record is clear: treaties, agreements, pledges and the morals of international relations were never an obstacle to the Soviet Union under Stalin. And no one has said so more eloquently than Chairman Khrushchev.

With the death of Stalin in 1953, the world had a resurgence of hope. No one can question that Chairman Khrushchev has altered many things in the Soviet Union. He has introduced welcome measures of normalization in many sectors of Soviet life. He has abandoned the classic Communist concept of the inevitability of war. He has recognized, intermittently, at least, the appalling dangers of nuclear weapons.

But there is one thing he has not altered, and that is the basic drive to abolish the world of the Charter, to destroy the hope of a pluralistic world order. He has not altered the basic drive to fulfill the prophecies of Marx and Lenin and make all the world Communist. And he has demonstrated his singleness of purpose in a succession of aggressive acts—the suppression of the East German uprisings in 1953 and the Hungarian Revolution in 1956, in the series of manufactured crises and truculent demands that the Allies get out of West Berlin, in the resumption of nuclear testing, in the explosion—defying a resolution of the General Assembly—of a 50-megaton bomb, in the continued stimulation of guerrilla and subversive warfare all over the globe, in the compulsive intervention in the internal affairs of other nations, whether by diplomatic assault, by economic pressure, by mobs and riots, by propaganda or espionage.

The world welcomed the process known as "de-Stalinization" and the move toward a more normal life within the Soviet Union. But the world has not yet seen comparable changes in Soviet foreign policy.

It is this which has shadowed the world since the end of the Second World War, which has dimmed our hopes of peace and progress, which has forced those nations determined to defend their freedom to take measures in their own self-defense.

In this effort, the leadership has inevitably fallen in large degree on the United States. I do not believe that every action we have taken in the effort to strengthen the independence of nations has necessarily been correct; we do not subscribe to the thesis of national infallibility for any nation. But we do take great pride in the role we have performed.

Our response to the remorseless Soviet expansionism has taken many forms.

We have sought loyally to support the United Nations, to be faithful to the world of the Charter, and to build an operating system that acts, and does not talk, for peace.

We have never refused to negotiate. We have sat at conference after conference seeking peaceful solutions to menacing conflicts.

We have worked for general and complete disarmament under international supervision. We have tried earnestly—and we won't stop trying—to reach an agreement to end all nuclear testing.

We have declined to be provoked into actions which might lead to war, in face of such challenges as the Berlin blockade, such affronts to humanity as the repression of the Hungarian revolt, such atrocities as the erection of that shameful wall to fence in the East Germans who had fled to the West in such vast multitudes.

We have assisted nations, both allied and unaligned, who have shown a will to maintain their national independence. To shield them and ourselves, we have rebuilt our armed forces, established defensive alliances and, year after year, reluctantly devoted a large share of our resources to national defense.

Together with our allies, we have installed certain bases overseas as a prudent precaution in response to the clear and persistent Soviet threats. In 1959, eighteen months after the boasts of Chairman Khrushchev had called the world's attention to the threat of Soviet long-range missiles, the North Atlantic Treaty Organization, without concealment or deceit, as a consequence of agreements freely negotiated and publicly declared, placed intermediate-range ballistic missiles in the NATO area. The warheads of these missiles remain in the custody of the United States, and the decision for their use rests in the hands of the President of the United States of America in association with the governments involved.

I regret that people here at the United Nations seem to believe

that the cold war is a private struggle between two great super-
powers. It isn't a private struggle; it is a world civil war, a contest
between the pluralistic world and the monolithic world, a contest
between the world of the Charter and the world of Communist
conformity. Every nation that is now independent and wants to remain independent is involved, whether it knows it or not. Every
nation is involved in this grim, costly, distasteful division in the
world, no matter how remote and how uninterested.

We all recognized this in 1950, when the Communists decided to
test how far they could go by direct military action and unleashed
the invasion of South Korea. The response of the United Nations
taught them that overt aggression would produce not appeasement,
but resistance. This remains the essential lesson. The United Nations
stood firm in Korea because we knew the consequences of appeasement.

The policy of appeasement is always intended to strengthen the
moderates in the country appeased; but its effect is always to strengthen
the extremists. We are prepared to meet and reconcile every legitimate Soviet concern; but we have only contempt for blackmail. We
know that every retreat before intimidation strengthens those who say
that the threat of force can always achieve Communist objectives,
and undermines those in the Soviet Union who are urging caution
and restraint, even cooperation.

Reluctantly and repeatedly, we have to face the sad fact that the
only way to reinforce those on the other side who are for moderation and peaceful competition is to make it absolutely clear that
aggression will be met with resistance, and force with force.

The time has come for this Council to decide whether to make
a serious attempt to bring peace to the world or to let the United
Nations stand idly by while the vast plan of piecemeal aggression
unfolds, conducted in the hope that no single issue will seem con-
sequential enough to mobilize the resistance of the free peoples.
For my own government, this question is not in doubt. We remain
committed to the principles of the United Nations Charter, and we
intend to defend them.

We are engaged today in a crucial test of those principles. Nearly four years ago revolution took place on the island of Cuba. This revolution overthrew a hated dictatorship in the name of democratic freedom and social progress. Dr. Castro made explicit promises to the people of Cuba. He promised them the restoration of the 1940 constitution abandoned by the Batista dictatorship; a "provisional government of entirely civilian character that will return the country to normality and hold general elections within a period of no more than one year"; "truly honest" elections along with "full and untrammeled" freedom of information and political activity.

That is what Dr. Castro offered the people of Cuba. This is what the people of Cuba accepted. Many in my own country and throughout the Americas sympathized with Dr. Castro's stated objectives. The United States Government offered immediate diplomatic recognition and stood ready to provide the revolutionary regime with economic assistance.

But a grim struggle took place within the revolutionary regime, between its democratic and its predominant Communist wings, between those who overthrew Batista to bring freedom to Cuba and those who overthrew Batista to bring Cuba to Communism. In a few months the struggle was over. Brave men who had fought with Castro in the Sierra Maestra and who had organized the underground against Batista in the cities were assailed, arrested and driven from office into prisons or exile, all for the single offense of anti-Communism, all for the single offense of believing in the principles of the revolution they fought for. By the end of 1959, the Communist party was the only party in Cuba permitted freedom of political action. By early 1960, the Castro regime was entering into intimate economic and political relations with the Soviet Union.

It is well to remember that all these events took place months before the United States stopped buying Cuban sugar in the summer of 1960—and many more months before exactions upon our embassy in Havana forced the suspension of diplomatic relations in December, 1960.

As the communization of Cuba proceeded, more and more democratic Cubans, men who had fought for freedom in the front ranks, were forced into exile. They were eager to return to their homeland

and to save their revolution from betrayal. In the spring of 1961, they tried to liberate their country, under the political leadership of Dr. Castro's first Prime Minister and of a Revolutionary Council composed without exception of men who had opposed Batista and backed the revolution.

The people and government of the United States sympathized with these men, as throughout our history Americans have always sympathized with those who sought to liberate their native lands from despotism. But I would point out that my government refrained from direct intervention. It sent no American troops to Cuba.

In the year and a half since, Dr. Castro has continued the communization of his unfortunate country. The 1940 constitution was never restored. Elections were never held and their promise withdrawn, though Dr. Castro's twelve months have stretched to forty-two. The Castro regime fastened on Cuba an iron system of repression. It eradicated human and civil rights. It openly transformed Cuba into a Communist satellite and a police state. Whatever benefit this regime might have brought to Cuba has long since been canceled out by the firing squads, the drumhead executions, the hunger and misery, the suppression of civil and political and cultural freedom.

Yet even these violations of human rights, repellent as they are —even this dictatorship, cruel as it may be—would not, if kept within the confines of one country, constitute a direct threat to the peace and independence of other states. The threat lies in the submission of the Castro regime to the will of an aggressive foreign power. It lies in its readiness to break up the relations of confidence and cooperation among the good neighbors of this hemisphere, at a time when the Alliance for Progress, that vast effort to raise living standards of all peoples of the Americas, has given new vitality and hope to the inter-American system.

Let me make it absolutely clear what the issue of Cuba is. It is not an issue of revolution. This hemisphere has seen many revolutions, including the one which gave my own nation its independence.

It is not an issue of reform. My nation has lived happily with other countries which have had thoroughgoing and fundamental social transformations, like Mexico and Bolivia. The whole point of the

Alliance for Progress is to bring about an economic and social revolution in the Americas.

It is not an issue of socialism. As Secretary of State Rusk said at Punta del Este: "Our hemisphere has room for a diversity of economic systems."

It is not an issue of dictatorship. The American republics have lived with dictators before. If this were his only fault, they could even live with Dr. Castro.

The foremost objection of the states of the Americas to the Castro regime is not because it is revolutionary, not because it is socialistic, not because it is dictatorial, not even because Dr. Castro perverted a noble revolution in the interests of a squalid totalitarianism. It is because he has aided and abetted an invasion of this hemisphere, and an invasion at just the time when the hemisphere is making a new and unprecedented effort for economic progress and social reform.

The crucial fact is that Cuba has given the Soviet Union a bridgehead and staging area in this hemisphere; that it has invited an extra-continental, antidemocratic and expansionist power into the bosom of the American family; that it has made itself an accomplice in the Communist enterprise of world dominion.

There are those who seek to equate the presence of Soviet bases in Cuba with the presence of NATO bases in parts of the world near the Soviet Union.

Let us subject this facile argument to critical consideration.

It is not only that the Soviet action in Cuba has created a new and dangerous situation by sudden and drastic steps which imperil the security of all mankind. It is necessary further to examine the purposes for which missiles are introduced and bases established.

Missiles which help a country defend its independence, which leave the political institutions of the recipient countries intact, which are not designed to subvert the territorial integrity or political independence of other states, which are installed without concealment or deceit—assistance in this form and with these purposes is consistent with the principles of the United Nations. But missiles which introduce a nuclear threat into an area now free of it, which threaten the security and independence of defenseless neighboring states, which are installed by clandestine means, which result in the most formidable nuclear base in the world outside existing treaty systems— assistance in this form and with these purposes is radically different.

Let me state this point very clearly. The missile sites in NATO countries are established in response to missile sites in the Soviet Union directed at the NATO countries. The NATO states had every right and necessity to respond to the installation of these Soviet missiles by installing missiles of their own. These missiles were designed to deter a process of expansion already in progress. Fortunately, they have helped to do so.

The United States and its allies established their missile sites after free negotiation, without concealment and without false statements to other governments.

There is, in short, a vast difference between the long-range missile sites established years ago in Europe and the long-range missile sites established by the Soviet Union in Cuba during the last three months.

There is a final significant difference. For one hundred and fifty years the nations of the Americas have painfully labored to construct a hemisphere of independent and cooperating nations, free from foreign threats. An international system far older than this one, the inter-American system, has been erected on this principle. The principle of the territorial integrity of the Western Hemisphere has been woven into the history, the life and the thought of all the people of the Americas. In striking at that principle the Soviet Union is striking at the strongest and most enduring strain in the policy of this hemisphere. It is disrupting the convictions and aspirations of a century and a half. It is intruding on the firm policies of twenty nations. To allow this challenge to go unanswered would be to undermine a basic and historic pillar of the security of this hemisphere.

Twenty years ago the nations of the Americas were understandably disturbed by the threat of Nazism. Just as they would have reacted with vigor had any American republic given itself over to the doctrines and agents of Nazism, so today they look with equal concern on the conquest of Cuba by a foreign power and an alien ideology.

They do not intend to applaud and assist while Dr. Castro and his new friends try to halt the march of free and progressive democracy in Latin America.

Yet, despite the ominous movement of affairs in Cuba, the reaction of the hemisphere, and of my own government, continued to be marked by forbearance. Despite Dr. Castro's verbal assaults on other nations in the hemisphere, despite his campaign of subversion against their governments, despite the insurrectionary expeditions launched from Cuba, the nations of the Americas retained their hope that the Cuban Revolution would free itself. But Dr. Castro's persistence in his campaigns against the governments of this hemisphere—his decision to become the junior partner of Moscow—finally destroyed that hope.

If Cuba has withdrawn from the American family of nations, it has been Dr. Castro's own act. If Cuba is today isolated from its brethren of the Americas, it is self-inflicted isolation. If the present Cuban Government has turned its back on its own history, tradition, religion and culture, if it has chosen to cast its lot with the Communist empire, it must accept the consequences of its decision. The hemisphere has no alternative but to accept the tragic choice Dr. Castro has imposed on his people—that is, to accept Cuba's self-exclusion from the hemisphere.

One after another, the other governments of this hemisphere have withdrawn their diplomatic representatives from Cuba. Today only three still have their ambassadors in Havana. Last February the American states unanimously declared that the Castro regime was incompatible with the principles on which the Organization of American States had been founded and, by a two-thirds vote, excluded that regime from participation in the inter-American system.

All this took place before Soviet arms and technicians began to move into Cuba in a massive, continuous stream. But, even then, the governments of the hemisphere were willing to withhold final judgment so long as the Soviet weapons were defensive. And my government—and the United Nations—were solemnly assured by the representatives of both Soviet Russia and Cuba that the Soviet arms pouring into the island were, in fact, purely defensive weapons.

On September 22, the Soviet Government said in an official statement: "The armaments and military equipment sent to Cuba are designed exclusively for defensive purposes." The Soviet Government added that Soviet rockets were so powerful that "there is no need to search for sites for them beyond the boundaries of the Soviet Union." And last week, on October 18, Mr. Gromyko, the Soviet Foreign Minister, told the President of the United States at the White House that Soviet assistance to Cuba "pursued solely the purpose of contributing to the defense capabilities of Cuba," that "training by Soviet specialists of Cuban nationals in handling defensive armaments was by no means offensive," and that "if it were otherwise, the Soviet Government would have never become involved in rendering such assistance."

Yet this once peaceable island is being transformed into a formidable missile and strategic air base armed with the deadliest, far-reaching modern nuclear weapons.

The statement issued by the Soviet Government this morning does not deny these facts—which is in refreshing contrast to the categoric assurances on this subject which it had previously given.

However, this same statement repeats the extraordinary claim that Soviet arms in Cuba are of a "defensive character." I should like to know what the Soviets consider "offensive" weapons. In the Soviet lexicon evidently all weapons are purely defensive, even weapons that can strike from one to two thousand miles away. Words can be stretched only so far without losing their meaning altogether. But semantic disputes are fruitless, and the fact remains that the Soviet has upset the precarious balance and created a new and dangerous situation in a new area.

This is precisely the sort of action which the Soviet Government is so fond of denouncing as "a policy of positions of strength." Consequently, I invite the attention of the Council to another remark in the Soviet Government's statement of this morning: "Only madmen bank on a policy of positions of strength and believe that this policy will bring any success; will help make it possible to impose their orders on other States."

I need only mention one other curious remark in the Soviet Government's statement of today, and I quote once more: "Who gave the United States the right to assume the role of the master of destinies of other countries and peoples? . . . Cuba belongs to the Cuban people and only they can be masters of their destiny." This latter sentence is, of course, a succinct statement of United States policy toward Cuba. It is, however, very far from being Soviet policy toward Cuba.

When the Soviet Union sends thousands of military technicians to its satellite in the Western Hemisphere; when it sends jet bombers capable of delivering nuclear weapons; when it installs in Cuba missiles capable of carrying atomic warheads and of obliterating the Panama Canal, Mexico City and Washington; when it prepares sites for additional missiles with a range of 2,200 miles and a capacity to strike at targets from Peru to Hudson's Bay; when it does these things under the cloak of secrecy and to the accompaniment of premeditated deception; when its actions are in flagrant violation of the policies of the Organization of American States and of the Charter of the United Nations—this clearly is a threat to this hemisphere. And when it thus upsets the precarious balance in the world, it is a threat to the whole world.

We now know that the Soviet Union, not content with Dr. Castro's oath of fealty, not content with the destruction of Cuban independence, not content with the extension of Soviet power into the Western Hemisphere, not content with a challenge to the inter-American system and the United Nations Charter, has decided to transform Cuba into a base for Communist aggression, into a base for putting all of the Americas under the nuclear gun and thereby intensify the Soviet diplomacy of blackmail in every part of the world.

In our passion for peace, we have forborne greatly. But there must be limits to forbearance, if forbearance is not to become the diagram for the destruction of this organization. Dr. Castro transformed Cuba into a totalitarian dictatorship with impunity; he extinguished the rights of political freedom with impunity; he aligned himself with the Soviet bloc with impunity; he accepted defensive weapons from the Soviet Union with impunity; he welcomed thousands of Communists into Cuba with impunity; but when, with cold deliberation, he turns

his country over to the Soviet Union for a long-range missile launching base, and thus carries the Soviet program for aggression in the
heart of the Americas, the day of forbearance is past.

If the United States and the other nations of the Western Hemisphere should accept this new phase of aggression, we would be
delinquent in our obligations to world peace. If the United States
and the other nations of the Western Hemisphere should accept this
basic disturbance of the world's structure of power, we would invite
a new surge of Communist aggression at every point along the frontier
which divides the Communist world from the democratic world. If
we do not stand firm here, our adversaries may think that we will
stand firm nowhere, and we guarantee a heightening of the world
civil war to new levels of intensity and danger.

We hope that Chairman Khrushchev has not made a miscalculation, that he has not mistaken forbearance for weakness. We cannot
believe that he has deluded himself into supposing that though we
have power, we lack nerve; that, though we have weapons, we are
without the will to use them.

We still hope, we still *pray,* that the worst may be avoided, that
the Soviet leadership will call an end to this ominous adventure.
Accordingly, the President has initiated steps to quarantine Cuba
against further imports of offensive military equipment. Because the
entire inter-American system is challenged, the President last night
called for an immediate meeting of the Organ of Consultation of the
Organization of the American States, to consider this threat to hemispheric security and to invoke Articles 6 and 8 of the Rio Treaty in
support of all necessary action. It is meeting now, and, Mr. President, I have just been informed that it has adopted a resolution—
by nineteen affirmative votes—containing the following operative
paragraphs:

The Council of the Organization of Inter-American States, meeting as
the Provisional Organ of Consultation, resolved:
1. To call for the immediate dismantling and withdrawal from Cuba of
all missiles and other weapons with any offensive capability;
2. To recommend that the Member States in accordance with Articles
6 and 8 of the Inter-American Treaty of Reciprocal Assistance take all

measures individually and collectively, including the use of armed force which they may deem necessary, to insure that the government of Cuba cannot continue to receive from the Sino-Soviet power military material and related supplies which may threaten the peace and the security of the continent and to prevent the missiles in Cuba with offensive capability from ever becoming an active threat to the peace and the security of the continent;

3. Decides to inform the Security Council of the United Nations of this resolution in accordance with Article 54 of the Charter of the United Nations, and expresses the hope that the Security Council will, in accordance with the resolution introduced by the United States, dispatch United Nations observers to Cuba at the earliest moment.

Mr. President, I am submitting today a resolution to the Security Council designed to find a way out of this calamitous situation.

This resolution calls, as an interim measure under Article 40 of the Charter, for the immediate dismantling and withdrawal from Cuba of all missiles and other offensive weapons.

It further authorizes and requests the Acting Secretary General to dispatch to Cuba a United Nations observer corps to assure and report on compliance with this resolution.

Upon United Nations certification of compliance, it calls for the termination of the measures of quarantine against military shipments to Cuba.

And, in conclusion, it urgently recommends that the United States of America and the Soviet Union confer promptly on measures to remove the existing threat to the security of the Western Hemisphere and the peace of the world, and to report thereon to the Security Council.

Mr. President, the issue which confronts the Security Council today is grave. Since the end of the Second World War, there has been no threat to the vision of peace so profound, no challenge to the world of the Charter so fateful. The hopes of mankind are concentrated in this room. The action we take may determine the future of civilization. I know that this Council will approach the issue with a full sense of our responsibility and a solemn understanding of the import of our deliberations.

There is a road to peace. The beginning of that road is marked out in the resolution I have submitted for your consideration. If we act promptly, we will have another chance to take up again the dreadful questions of nuclear arms and military bases and the means and causes of aggression and war—to take them up and do something about them.

This is a solemn and significant day for the life of the United Nations and the hope of world community. Let it be remembered, not as the day when the world came to the edge of nuclear war, but as the day when men resolved to let nothing thereafter stop them in their quest for peace.

A PREMEDITATED ATTEMPT:
THE DREAD REALITIES

❦ ❦ Perhaps the single most dramatic moment of any UN meeting occurred in the Security Council on October 25, 1962. For two days the world had stood at the abyss following President Kennedy's announcement that Soviet missiles had been installed in Cuba and that the U.S. Navy would quarantine the island against further arms shipments. The Organization of American States acted immediately. Secretary General U Thant of the United Nations made mediation proposals, and Soviet ships bound for Cuba changed course. In the hushed Security Council chamber the discussion of the United States complaint ended abruptly after a memorable exchange between Governor Stevenson and Ambassador Zorin. Asked if there were any Soviet missiles in Cuba, the Soviet delegate evaded a "yes" or "no" answer; and then Governor Stevenson presented the photographic evidence. After President Kennedy and Chairman Khrushchev reached agreement on the removal of the weapons, the high drama of those days was replaced by prolonged negotiations between Soviet representatives and Governor Stevenson and John J. McCloy, special U.S. negotiator on the Cuban matter. The Security Council was finally "deseized" of the issue on January 7, 1963.

Today we must address our attention to the realities of the situation posed by the build-up of nuclear striking power in Cuba.

    I want to say at the outset that the course adopted by the Soviet

Statements to the Security Council, October 25, 1962.

Union yesterday to avoid direct confrontations in the zone of quarantine is welcome to my government. We also welcome the assurance by Chairman Khrushchev in his letter to Earl Russell that the Soviet Union will "take no reckless decisions" with regard to this crisis. And we welcome most of all the report that Mr. Khrushchev has agreed to the proposals advanced by the Secretary General.

My government is most anxious to effect a peaceful resolution of this affair. We continue to hope that the Soviet Union will work with us to diminish not only the new danger which has suddenly shadowed the peace, but all of the conflicts that divide the world.

I shall not detain you with any detailed discussion of the Soviet and the Cuban responses to our complaint. The speeches of the Communist delegates were entirely predictable. I shall make brief comment on some points suggested by these speeches and some other points which may have arisen in the minds of members of the United Nations.

Both Chairman Khrushchev in his letter to Earl Russell and Ambassador Zorin in his remarks to this Council argued that this threat to the peace had been caused, not by the Soviet Union and Cuba, but by the United States.

We are here today and have been this week for one single reason— because the Soviet Union secretly introduced this menacing, offensive, military build-up into the island of Cuba while assuring the world that nothing was further from their thoughts.

The Soviet argument, in its essence, is that it was not the Soviet Union which created the threat to peace by secretly installing these weapons in Cuba, but that it was the United States which created the crisis by discovering and reporting the facts.

This is the first time that I have ever heard it said that the crime is not the burglary, but the discovery of the burglar—and that the threat is not the clandestine missiles in Cuba, but their discovery and the measures taken to quarantine further infection.

The peril arises not because the nations of the Western Hemisphere have joined together to take necessary action in their self-defense, but because the Soviet Union has extended its nuclear threat into the Western Hemisphere.

I noted that there are still some delegates in the Council—I suspect, very few—who say that they do not know whether the Soviet Union has, in fact, built in Cuba installations capable of firing nuclear missiles over ranges from one to two thousand miles.

Chairman Khrushchev did not deny these facts in his letter to Earl Russell, nor did Ambassador Zorin on Tuesday evening. And if further doubt remains on this score, we shall gladly exhibit the photographic evidence to the doubtful.

One other point. I would like to invite attention to the casual remark of the Soviet representative claiming that we have thirty-five bases in foreign countries. The facts are that missiles comparable to those placed in Cuba are with the forces of only three of our allies, and were only established there by a decision of the heads of these governments, meeting in December, 1957, who were compelled to authorize such arrangements by virtue of a prior Soviet decision to display missiles capable of destroying the countries of Western Europe.

In the next place, there are some troublesome questions in the minds of members that are entitled to serious answers. There are those who say that, conceding the fact that the Soviet Union has installed offensive weapons in Cuba, conceding the fact that this creates a grave threat to the peace of the world, why was it necessary for the nations of the Western Hemisphere to act with such speed? Why could not the quarantine against the shipment of offensive weapons have been delayed until the Security Council and the General Assembly had a full opportunity to consider the situation and make recommendations?

Let me remind the members that the United States was not looking for some pretext to raise the issue of the transformation of Cuba into a military base. On the contrary, the United States made no objection whatever to the shipment of *defensive* arms by the Soviet Union to Cuba, even though such shipments offended the traditions of this hemisphere.

Even after the first hard intelligence reached Washington concerning the change in the character of Soviet military assistance to

Cuba, the President of the United States responded by directing an intensification of surveillance. And only after the facts and the magnitude of the build-up had been established beyond all doubt did we begin to take this limited action of barring only these nuclear weapons equipment and aircraft.

To understand the reasons for this prompt action, it is necessary to understand the nature and the purpose of this operation. It has been marked, above all, by two characteristics—speed and stealth. As the photographic evidence makes clear, the installation of these missiles—the erection of these missile sites—has taken place with extraordinary speed. One entire complex was put up in twenty-four hours. This speed not only demonstrates the methodical organization and careful planning involved; but it also demonstrates a premeditated attempt to confront this hemisphere with a *fait accompli*. By quickly completing the whole process of nuclearization of Cuba, the Soviet Union would be in a position to demand that the *status quo* be maintained and left undisturbed.

If we were to have delayed our counteraction, the nuclearization of Cuba would have been quickly completed. This is not a risk which this hemisphere is prepared to take.

When we first detected the secret offensive installations, could we reasonably be expected to have notified the Soviet Union in advance, through the process of calling the Security Council, that we had discovered its perfidy, and then to have done nothing but wait while we debated, and then have waited further while the Soviet representative in the Security Council vetoed a resolution, as he has already announced that he will do? In different circumstances, we would have. But today we are dealing with dread realities and not with wishes.

One of the sites, as I have said, was constructed in twenty-four hours. One of these missiles can be armed with its nuclear warhead in the middle of the night, pointed at New York, and landed above this room five minutes after firing. No debate in this room could affect in the slightest the urgency of these terrible facts or the immediacy of the threat to the peace.

There was only one way to deal with that urgency and with that immediacy, and that was to act, and to act at once—but with the utmost restraint consistent with the magnitude of this threat to the peace.

And we came to the Security Council, I remind you, immediately and concurrently with the meeting of the Organization of American States. We did not even wait for the OAS to meet and to act. We came here at the same time. We immediately put into process the political machinery that, we pray, will achieve a solution of this grave crisis. And we did not act until the American republics had acted to make the quarantine effective.

We did not shirk our duties to ourselves, to the hemisphere, to the United Nations or to the world. We are now in the Security Council on the initiative of the United States precisely because, having taken the hemispheric action which has been taken, we wish the political machinery of the United Nations to take over, to reduce these tensions, to interpose itself to eliminate this aggressive threat to the peace, and to assure the removal from this hemisphere of offensive nuclear weapons with the corresponding lifting of the quarantine.

There are those who say that the quarantine is an inappropriate and extreme remedy, that the punishment does not fit the crime. But I ask those who take this position to put themselves in the position of the Organization of American States, to consider what you would have done in the face of the nuclearization of Cuba. Were we to do nothing until the knife was sharpened? Were we to stand idly by until it was at our throats? What were the alternatives available?

On the one hand, the Organization of American States might have sponsored an invasion, or destroyed the bases by an air strike, or imposed a total blockade on all imports to Cuba, including medicine and food. On the other hand, the OAS and the United States might have done nothing. Such a course would have confirmed the greatest threat to the peace of the Americas known to history and would have encouraged the Soviet Union in similar adventures in other parts of the world. And it would have discredited our will, our determination, to live in freedom and to reduce, not increase, the perils of this nuclear age.

The course we have chosen seems to me perfectly graduated to meet the character of the threat. To have done less would have been to fail in our obligation to peace.

To those who say that a limited quarantine was too much in spite of the provocation and the danger, let me tell you a story—attributed like so many of our American stories to Abraham Lincoln —about the passerby out in my part of the country who was charged by a farmer's ferocious boar. He picked up a pitchfork and met the boar head on. It died. The irate farmer denounced him and asked him why he didn't use the blunt end of the pitchfork. And the man replied, "Why didn't the boar attack me with his blunt end?"

Some here have attempted to question the legal basis of the defensive measures taken by the American republics to protect the Western Hemisphere against Soviet long-range nuclear missiles.

I would gladly expand on our position on this, but in view of the proposal now before us presented last night by the Secretary General, perhaps that is a matter and a discussion, in view of its complexity and length, which could be more fruitfully delayed to a later time.

Finally, let me say that no twisting of logic, no distortion of words can disguise the plain, the obvious, the compelling, common-sense conclusion that the installation in Cuba of nuclear weapons by stealth, weapons of mass destruction, poses a dangerous threat to the peace, a threat which contravenes Article 2, paragraph 4 of the Charter, and a threat which the American republics are entitled to meet, as they have done, with appropriate regional defensive measures.

Nothing has been said by the representatives of the Communist states here which alters the basic situation. There is one fundamental question to which I solicit your attention. The question is this: What action serves to strengthen the world's hope for peace?

Can anyone claim that the introduction of long-range nuclear missiles into Cuba strengthens the peace?

Can anyone claim that the speed and stealth of this operation strengthen the peace?

Can anyone suppose that this whole undertaking is anything more than an audacious effort to increase the nuclear striking powers of the Soviet Union against the United States? When we are about to debate how to stop the dissemination of nuclear weapons, does their introduction in a new hemisphere by an outside state advance sanity and peace? Does anyone suppose that, if this Soviet adventure should go unchecked, the Soviet Union would refrain from similar adventures in other parts of the world?

The one action in the last few days which has strengthened the peace is the determination to stop this further spread of weapons in this hemisphere.

In view of the situation that now confronts us and the proposals made here yesterday by the Acting Secretary General, I will not extend my remarks this afternoon, I will conclude by reading to the members of the Council a letter from the President of the United States which was delivered to the Acting Secretary General just a few minutes ago in reply to his appeal of last night. The letter says:

> I deeply appreciate the spirit which prompted your message of yesterday.
>
> As we made clear in the Security Council, the existing threat was created by the secret introduction of offensive weapons into Cuba, and the answer lies in the removal of such weapons.
>
> In your message and your statement to the Security Council last night, you have made certain suggestions and have invited preliminary talks to determine whether satisfactory arrangements can be assured.
>
> Ambassador Stevenson is ready to discuss these arrangements with you promptly.
>
> I can assure you of our desire to reach a satisfactory and peaceful solution of this matter.

I have nothing further to say at this time, Mr. President.

A PREMEDITATED ATTEMPT:
THE BUILDING OF THE SITES

I want to say to you, Mr. Zorin, that I do not have your talent for obfuscation, for distortion, for confusing language and for double-talk. And I must confess to you that I am glad that I do not!

But if I understood what you said, it was that my position had changed, that today I was defensive because we did not have the evidence to prove our assertions that your government had installed long-range missiles in Cuba.

Well, let me say something to you, Mr. Ambassador—we do have the evidence. We have it, and it is clear and it is incontrovertible. And let me say something else—those weapons must be taken out of Cuba!

Next, if I understood you, you said—with a trespass on credibility that excels your best—that our position had changed since I spoke here the other day because of the pressures of world opinion and the majority of the United Nations. Well, let me say to you, sir—you are wrong again. We have had no pressure from anyone whatsoever. We came here today to indicate our willingness to discuss U Thant's proposals, and that is the only change that has taken place.

But let me also say to you, sir, that there *has* been a change. You—the Soviet Union *has* sent these weapons to Cuba. You—the Soviet Union *has* upset the balance of power in the world. You—the Soviet Union *has* created this new danger, not the United States.

And you ask with a fine show of indignation why the President did not tell Mr. Gromyko on last Thursday about our evidence, at

Further statement to the Security Council, October 25, 1962

the very time that Mr. Gromyko was blandly denying to the President that the U.S.S.R. was placing such weapons on sites in the new world.

Well, I will tell you why—because we were assembling the evidence, and perhaps it would be instructive to the world to see how far a Soviet official would go in perfidy. Perhaps we wanted to know if this country faced another example of nuclear deceit like that one a year ago when, in stealth, the Soviet Union broke the nuclear test moratorium.

And while we are asking questions, let me ask you why your government, your Foreign Minister deliberately, cynically deceived us about the nuclear build-up in Cuba?

And, finally, the other day, Mr. Zorin, I remind you that you did not deny the existence of these weapons. Instead, we heard that they had suddenly become *defensive* weapons. But today, again, if I heard you correctly, you now say, with another fine flood of rhetorical scorn, they do not exist, or that we haven't proved they exist.

All right, sir, let me ask you one simple question: Do you, Ambassador Zorin, deny that the U.S.S.R. has placed and is placing medium and intermediate-range missiles and sites in Cuba? Yes or no? Don't wait for the translation. Yes or no?

[Ambassador Zorin refused to answer, maintaining he was "not in an American courtroom."]

You are in the courtroom of world opinion. You have denied they exist, and I want to know if I understood you correctly.

I am prepared to wait for my answer until hell freezes over, if that's your decision. And I am also prepared to present the evidence in this room—now!

[Instead of answering, Ambassador Zorin, as President of the Security Council, called on the representative of Chile to speak; however, the United States retained the floor.]

I have not finished my statement. I asked you a question. I have had no reply to the question, and I will now proceed, if I may, to finish my statement.

I doubt if anyone in this room, except possibly the representative of the Soviet Union, has any doubt about the facts. But in view of his statements and the statements of the Soviet Government up until last Thursday, when Mr. Gromyko denied the existence or any intention of installing such weapons in Cuba, I am going to make a portion of the evidence available right now. If you will indulge me for a moment, we will set up an easel here in the back of the room where I hope it will be visible to everyone.

[Enlargements of aerial photographs were then placed on display, one by one, in the Security Council chamber.]

The first of these exhibits shows an area north of the village of Candelaria, near San Cristóbal, southwest of Havana. A map, together with a small photograph, shows precisely where the area is in Cuba.

The first photograph shows the area in late August, 1962; it was then, if you can see from where you are sitting, only a peaceful countryside.

The second photograph shows the same area one day last week. A few tents and vehicles had come into the area, new spur roads had appeared, and the main road had been improved.

The third photograph, taken only twenty-four hours later, shows facilities for a medium-range missile battalion installed. There are tents for four or five hundred men. At the end of the new spur road there are seven one-thousand-mile missile trailers. There are four launcher-erector mechanisms for placing these missiles in erect firing position. This missile is a mobile weapon, which can be moved rapidly from one place to another. It is identical with the thousand-mile missiles which have been displayed in Moscow parades.

All of this, I remind you, took place in twenty-four hours.

The second exhibit, which you can all examine at your leisure, shows three successive photographic enlargements of another missile base of the same type in the area of San Cristóbal. These enlarged photographs clearly show six of these missiles on trailers and three erectors.

And that is only one example of the first type of ballistic missile installation in Cuba.

A second type of installation is designed for a missile of intermediate range—a range of about 2,200 miles. Each site of this type has four launching pads.

The exhibit on this type of missile shows a launching area being constructed near Guanajay, southwest of the city of Havana. As in the first exhibit, a map and small photograph show this area as it appeared in late August, 1962; when no military activities were apparent.

A second large photograph shows the same area about six weeks later. Here you will see a very heavy construction effort to push the launching area to rapid completion. The pictures show two large concrete bunkers or control centers in process of construction, one between each pair of launching pads. They show heavy concrete retaining walls being erected to shelter vehicles and equipment from rocket blast-off. They show cable scars leading from the launch pads to the bunkers. They show large reinforced concrete buildings under construction. A building with a heavy arch may well be intended as the storage area for the nuclear warheads. The installation is not yet complete and no warheads are yet visible.

The next photograph shows a closer view of the same intermediate-range launch site. You can clearly see one of the pairs of large concrete launch pads with a concrete building from which launching operations for three pads are controlled. Other details are visible, such as fuel tanks.

And that is only one example, one illustration of the work being furnished in Cuba on intermediate-range missile bases.

Now, in addition to missiles, the Soviet Union is installing other offensive weapons in Cuba. The next photograph is of an airfield at San Julian in western Cuba. On this field you will see twenty-two crates designed to transport the fuselages of Soviet Ilyushin-28 bombers. Four of the aircraft are uncrated and one is partially assembled. These bombers, sometimes known as Beagles, have an operating radius of about 750 miles and are capable of carrying nuclear weapons. At the same field you can see one of the surface-to-air antiaircraft guided missile bases, with six missiles per base, which now ring the entire coastline of Cuba.

Another set of two photographs covers still another area of deployment of medium-range missiles in Cuba. These photographs are on a larger scale than the others and reveal many details of an improved field-type launch site. One photograph provides an over-all view of most of the site; you can see clearly three of the four launching pads. The second photograph displays details of two of these pads. Even an eye untrained in photographic interpretation can clearly see the buildings in which the missiles are checked out and maintained ready to fire, a missile trailer, trucks to move missiles out to the launching pad, erectors to raise the missiles to launching position, tank trucks to provide fuel, vans from which the missile firing is controlled—in short, all of the requirements to maintain, load and fire these terrible weapons.

These weapons, gentlemen, these launching pads, these planes—of which we have illustrated only a fragment—are a part of a much larger weapons complex, what is called a weapons system.

To support this build-up, to operate these advanced weapons systems, the Soviet Union has sent a large number of military personnel to Cuba, a force now amounting to several thousand men.

I have nothing further to say at this time.

[Ambassador Zorin, still offering no answer, questioned the authenticity of the photographs.]

Mr. President and gentlemen, I shall detain the Council only a moment.

I have not had a direct answer to my question. The representative of the Soviet Union says that the official answer of the U.S.S.R. was a statement carried by Tass that it does not need to locate missiles in Cuba. I agree—the U.S.S.R does not need to. But the question is not whether the U.S.S.R. *needs* missiles in Cuba; the question is: *Has* the U.S.S.R. missiles in Cuba? And that question remains unanswered. I knew it would remain unanswered.

As to the authenticity of the photographs which Mr. Zorin has spoken about with such scorn, I wonder if the Soviet Union would ask its Cuban colleague to permit a United Nations team to go to these sites. If so, Mr. Zorin, I can assure you that we can direct them to the proper places very quickly.

And now I hope that we can get down to business, that we can stop this sparring. We know the facts and so do you, sir, and we are ready to talk about them. Our job here is not to score debating points. Our job, Mr. Zorin, is to save the peace. And if you are ready to try, we are.

SHE WOULD RATHER LIGHT CANDLES:

THE DEATH OF ELEANOR ROOSEVELT

❦ ❦ *Cuba and other crises of the Seventeenth General Assembly were put aside one morning, and delegate after delegate mounted the rostrum of the General Assembly to express grief at the death of Mrs. Eleanor Roosevelt. The tribute was unusual in that, when she died, she held no official office or had any connection with the United Nations. It marked the first time any private citizen was so honored. Governor Stevenson, who earlier that year had gone to the same rostrum to eulogize Dag Hammarskjöld, spoke officially for the United States and personally for himself. Some days after the United Nations tribute, Governor Stevenson delivered a public eulogy for Mrs. Roosevelt (page 290). Both eulogies, he later said, were the most difficult, and certainly the saddest, of any tasks he had ever been called upon to perform.*

I stand here for the second time in little more than a year sad in heart and in spirit. The United States, the United Nations, the world, has lost one of its great citizens. Mrs. Eleanor Roosevelt is dead; a cherished friend of all mankind is gone.

Yesterday I said I had lost more than a friend; I had lost an inspiration. She would rather light candles than curse the darkness, and her glow had warmed the world.

Statement to the General Assembly, November 9, 1962.
❦ 113

My country mourns her, and I know that all in this Assembly mourn with us. But even as we do, the sadness we share is enlivened by the faith in her fellowman and his future which filled the heart of this strong and gentle woman.

She imparted this faith, not only to those who shared the privilege of knowing her and of working by her side, but to countless men, women and children in every part of the world who loved her even as she loved them. For she embodied the vision and the will to achieve a world in which all men can walk in peace and dignity. And to this goal, a better life, she dedicated her tireless energy, the strange strength of her extraordinary personality.

I do not think it amiss to suggest that the United Nations is, in no small way, a memorial to her and to her aspirations. To it she gave the last fifteen years of her restless life. She breathed life into this organization. The United Nations has meaning and hope for millions, thanks to her labors, her love, no less than to her ideals—ideals that made her, only weeks after Franklin Roosevelt's death, put aside all thoughts of peace and quiet after the tumult of their lives, to serve as one of this nation's delegates to the first regular session of the General Assembly. Her duty then, as always, was to the living, to the world, to peace.

Some of you in this hall were present at that first historic Assembly in London seventeen years ago. More of you were witnesses to her work in subsequent Assemblies in the years that followed. The members of the Third Committee—the Committee on Social, Humanitarian and Cultural Questions—and the Commission on Human Rights, which she served so long as chairman—you in particular will remember the warmth, the intelligence and infectious buoyancy which she brought to her tasks. You know, better than any of us, the unceasing crusade that helped give the world, after years of painstaking, patient travail, one of the noblest documents of mankind: The Declaration of Human Rights.

This is not the time to recount the infinite services of this glorious, gracious lady; the list is as inexhaustible as her energies! But devotion to the world of the Charter, to the principles of the United Nations, to a world without war, to the brotherhood of man, underscored them all. And, happily for us all, she could communicate her devotion, her enthusiasm to others. She saw clearly; she spoke simply. The power of her words came from the depth of her conviction.

"We must be willing," she said, "to learn the lesson that cooperation may imply compromise, but if it brings a world advance it is a gain for each individual nation. There will be those who doubt their ability to rise to those new heights, but the alternative is not possible to contemplate.

"We must build faith in the hearts of those who doubt, we must rekindle faith in ourselves when it grows dim, and find some kind of divine courage within us to keep on till on Earth we have Peace and Good Will among Men."

While she lived, Mrs. Roosevelt rekindled that faith in ourselves. Now that she is gone, the legacy of her lifetime will do no less. Albert Schweitzer wrote:

> No ray of sunlight is ever lost,
> but the green which it wakes . . .
> needs time to sprout, and it is not
> always granted to the sower to live
> to see the harvest. All work that
> is worth anything is done in faith.

Mr. President, I trust you will forgive me for having taken the time of this Assembly with these very personal thoughts. The issues we debate in this hall are many and grave. But I do not think we are divided in our grief at the passing of the great and gallant human being who was called the First Lady of the World.

PART III

OUR STAKE
IN THE UN

WHAT'S IN IT FOR US?
OUR MEMBERSHIP

❦ ❦ *Of what value is America's membership in the UN? Governor Stevenson gave his first answer to this oft-repeated question to the Senate Committee on Foreign Relations on January 18, 1961, when he said it was "our best hope for fashioning a peace marked with freedom and justice." Then, in testimony before the same committee on February 8, 1962, on the matter of the purchase of United Nations Bonds to help finance the UN's peacekeeping operations, he explained that Americans had spent "only $1.06 per capita on the United Nations in 1961. . . ," a cost, as he later told the House Committee on Foreign Relations on June 27, 1962, that was "very modest indeed compared to the cost . . . both in dollars and in lives, if our own armed forces were engaged in keeping the peace." This statement—also given in testimony before Congress—sums up his thinking on the issue of America's membership, and he does so in answer to a question—a crude one, as he describes it, but one he asks with no apologies: "What's in it for us?"*

The United Nations is a big subject, one which can be approached from many points of view. From one point of view it is a symbol of the aspirations of most of humanity for peace, for decency and human dignity. From another point of view it is an institution of 110 members pioneering the arts of parliamentary diplomacy on a

Statement to the United States Senate Subcommittee on Foreign Relations, March 13, 1963.

❦ 119

near-universal level. From still another, it is a very large operating mechanism performing such varied activities as stopping a war, spraying tropical villages to combat malaria, and drafting a convention on some aspect of human rights. There is even a point of view, albeit a narrow one, from which the United Nations appears to be the symbol of wicked one-worldliness, a sinister threat to the national sovereignty, and a joint convention of international do-gooders and bobby-soxers.

So, like a novelist approaching some universal theme, anyone preparing to say or write something about the United Nations must somehow come to grips with his material, determine his point of view, decide where to focus, what to put in and what to leave out. In the process, many arbitrary choices must be made.

My arbitrary choice is to focus briefly but sharply on this question: How and to what extent does our membership in the United Nations serve the foreign policy interests of the United States of America? Or, more crudely, what's in it for us?

I make no apology to the most sensitive supporter of the United Nations for phrasing it that way. After all, if the very considerable effort and time and money which we have invested in the United Nations have not been a good investment from the United States point of view, then we should say so and behave accordingly—as, I feel sure, every other member does.

I shall try to test this question of what's in it for us against two criteria: first, against the record of the Seventeenth General Assembly, which had just over one hundred items on its agenda; and second, against the roles of the United Nations in two of the greatest crises of recent history—the collapse of the Congo and the discovery of Soviet missile bases in Cuba. These are tough tests: one covers a virtual compendium of the ongoing problems which beset the modern world; the other raises specific issues of peace and war in specific areas at specific times.

But before coming to these two tests of how well or how badly our membership in the United Nations serves the national interest, it is worthwhile to pose a prior test: Is the United Nations relevant to the real world of the second half of the twentieth century? For if the United Nations does not reflect the real world, it is unlikely to be able to do anything useful about it.

What then are the dominant factors that make the real world what it is in our tumultuous times?

First is the great confrontation which goes under the name of the East-West conflict or the cold war, and the nuclear arms race which is its most dangerous manifestation. This has brought into conflict two sets of ideas about the value of human dignity which cannot be bridged philosophically. It also has brought into conflict two great and powerful nations whose national differences must be bridged politically if either is to survive. The proceedings of the United Nations consistently reflect both aspects of this so-called East-West confrontation.

The second factor dominating contemporary history is the revolutionary wave of national independence which, in an incredibly short period, has brought political independence to nearly one billion people, leaving less than 2 per cent of the former colonial peoples in dependent status—an historic convulsion which perhaps offered Communism its greatest opportunity to absorb vast areas of the world. The United Nations has itself administered a number of these changes from dependent to independent status and is deeply involved with the difficult and emotional final stages of liquidating the old colonial system and the race problems embedded in it.

The third factor is the so-called Revolution of Rising Expectations, which has put a spotlight on the glaring gap between the material conditions of the rich minority and the poor majority among the world's peoples. Some 85 per cent of the entire staffs of the United Nations system is occupied with the first systematic effort at international cooperation in the field of economic and social affairs— certainly one of the great phenomena of contemporary times.

Fourth is the fantastic pace of discovery and invention, which romps ahead oblivious to the political and social consequences and which makes the demands for a decent life for all a practical proposition for the first time in history. The United Nations is concerned increasingly with the complex and little- understood problems of how to transfer effectively science and technology from one cultural setting to another.

Fifth is the fitful emergence of a restless, teeming, volatile, frequently quarrelsome open society of nation-states—a society of enormous diversity of cultures, races, and political, economical and social systems. The United Nations is, of course, the institutional center of this open international society, partly the cause and partly the result of the forces which impel an interdependent world into more intimate association on an expanding agenda of political and human problems.

If these are the principal factors which mold our times—the cold war, the liquidation of colonialism, the pervasive demand for a better material way of life, the thundering impact of science, and the emergence of a vast, new, open society on the international plane—then we must conclude that the United Nations is indeed relevant to these times, that it is very much part and parcel of the contemporary scene. And being relevant, it is in a position to be effective.

Let us come, then, to the question of how effective from our point of view. What's in it for us? How, as the most recent example, does the record of the Seventeenth General Assembly stand the test?

I said a moment ago that the agenda of the Seventeenth General Assembly was a virtual compendium of the ongoing problems of the modern world. Listen to this list of trouble spots and sore spots: the Congo . . . the Gaza strip . . . Southern Rhodesia . . . South West Africa . . . the Portuguese African territories . . . Kashmir . . . Yemen . . . West New Guinea . . . and the Arab refugee camps.

Mark this string of contentious issues: Chinese representation . . . North Korea . . . Hungary . . . colonialism . . . Troika . . . and sovereignty over natural resources.

Consider, if you will, this list of universal concerns: disarmament . . . nuclear testing . . . outer space . . . world food . . . world trade . . . world science . . . and the training of manpower for economic and social development.

All of these issues, in one form or another, came before the

United Nations for some kind of action during the last General Assembly, even if each one did not appear formally on the Assembly's agenda. Many of them are among the most complex, the most intractable, the most ancient troubles of the human race. And many come to the United Nations as a court of last resort, because nobody else has been able to cope with them at all.

Obviously, the United Nations did not "solve" all or even many of these problems; but it worked on them. On a few it took conclusive action; on some it made progress, and on others it did not. But without reading the record item by item and vote by vote, the point to be made is simply this: the United States view was the majority view in over 80 per cent of the forty key votes cast in committees and full Assembly. On several issues we abstained, and on two extreme resolutions recommending sanctions against member states we voted against the majority.

This is the measure of the extent to which our membership in the United Nations served the foreign policy interests of the United States across the spectrum of issues represented by the agenda of the Seventeenth General Assembly.

Meanwhile, the impact of the twin crises in the Caribbean and the Himalayas raised our credit and our credibility; had the opposite effect on the stock of the Soviet Union; improved Western Hemisphere solidarity; activated the members from NATO; and gave pause to those who tend to equate the bona fides of the United States and the Soviet Union.

I am not saying for one moment that the General Assembly, or any other meeting or organ of the United Nations, was the handmaiden of the Department of State. I am not even saying that there were not disappointments or no cause for apprehension; for example, we expect continuing fireworks over the hard-core cases in the remnants of European empires, and we are most gravely concerned at the lack of evidence of financial responsibility on the part of all too many members. But I am saying, most emphatically, that in no case was United States interest damaged, in most cases our objectives were furthered in a positive fashion, and in other cases we have reason to hope for a better result on another day. In short, it was very much in our national interest to be there, paying our considerable share of the cost and exercising our considerable share of the leadership.

The political problems before the General Assembly tend to be those anguished issues which have roots in the past and drag on from year to year, so hardy or so virulent that sometimes our best efforts succeed only in keeping them from going from bad to worse.

But now I should like to discuss two crises which had sudden beginnings, which directly and immediately involved the United Nations, and which now seem to be ended, at least in the form in which they arose. I refer to those most dangerous events which raised the dire threat of great power confrontation, and thus of nuclear war, in the Congo and the Caribbean. The point is to ask in each case whether the role of the United Nations in these crises served the foreign policy interests of the United States.

What were our aims in the Congo affair? Our aims in the Congo are the same as our aims for all of tropical Africa. They are quite simple to state: to help create an area of truly free and independent African states, safe from external aggression or subversion, working out their own destinies in their own way, cooperating with each other and with those who wish to help in their overwhelming task of progressive modernization. In the Congo, as elsewhere, this requires national unity and a reasonable degree of political stability.

Contrasted to this, the collapse of the Congo in its first week of nationhood offered these sudden prospects: national disunity, political chaos, civil disorder, social disintegration and external penetration—prospects made to order for Communist exploitation. And because of this, the ultimate prospect for the Congo was for the forces of the nuclear powers to find themselves face to face in the heart of central Africa in the infancy of independence, about as messy and dangerous a state of affairs as one can imagine.

The story of the struggle of the United Nations, with unflagging support from this country, to bring order out of chaos in the Congo is too well known to members of this committee to review it here. I am all too conscious of every bit and every kind of criticism that has .been leveled against this operation; and it has been of every kind—from honest doubts about the legal basis for United Nations action to purple propaganda and outrageous lies. I also will state that in any historical sense, in this unprecedented, almost fantastic operation, some decisions were not wise, some operations not efficient, some judgments not justified, and a few actions not even excusable. My point is neither to tabulate the accomplishments nor to count the mistakes.

My point is, rather, to look at the results and state that, as of today, civil war has been replaced by national unity, political chaos has been replaced by reasonable prospects for political stability, total disorder has been replaced by order, social disintegration has been replaced by an evolving program for social progress, and the scavengers have been sent home packing. None of this is yet guaranteed to be permanent. But this is what has happened in the Congo; this is what the United States wanted to happen in the Congo; and it could not have happened under any other auspices than that of the United Nations, without the certainty or at least the risk of international war.

It, therefore, is difficult—indeed, it is impossible—to avoid the conclusion that the foreign policy interests of the United States have been served well by the United Nations performance in the Congo crisis—and this, of course, would have been out of the question without our membership and our full support. I know no way of putting a dollar value on the restoration of peace in central Africa.

The United Nations role in the Congo was, of course, an extremely large operational task, by far the largest it has ever undertaken, involving nearly twenty thousand troops from twenty-one nations, supported by a massive airlift, and by hundreds of civilian technicians recruited through a dozen international agencies.

The United Nations role in the Cuban crisis was entirely different. Actually, the United Nations had three roles in the Cuban crisis, two of which were played out while the third was frustrated but nonetheless useful to us. Because the naval quarantine of Cuba was the first dramatic move in that crisis, and because of the critical part played by the Organization of American States, it is easy to forget how the United Nations fitted into the pattern of these supercharged days when the world stood at the edge of the abyss in late October.

You will remember, of course, that the President called into play at one stroke all the available instruments of diplomatic action—United States military power, the Organization of American States, the United Nations and an appeal to public opinion around the world.

The first role of the United Nations was to serve as a world forum where the facts could be laid on the table. When the Security Council met in emergency session, I was able to present the United States case not only to the members of that Council, but to all other members of the United Nations who crowded that tense room, as well as to the press and the microphones and the cameras which carried our story to our own public and to every corner of the world reached by the mass media of today. Our case was right; our case was thoroughly documented; and our case was vastly strengthened as it unfolded before the bar of world opinion in the Security Council of the United Nations —the only bar of universal public opinion there is. Just how much this revelation of Soviet deceit and recklessness shocked the innocent bystanders in the cold war, I can't guess. Nor, of course, can I estimate how much this blow to confidence in Russia's word and influence among the new nations contributed to Mr. Khrushchev's decision to pull out quickly and make the best of a bad mistake.

The second role of the United Nations—or, more precisely, of the Secretary General of the United Nations—was that of third party to the issue. At a critical moment, when the nuclear powers seemed to be set on a collision course, the Secretary General's intervention led to the diversion of the Soviet ships headed for Cuba and interception by our Navy. This was an indispensable first step in the peaceful resolution of the Cuban crisis. The mere existence of an impartial office which could perform such a service in the middle of the night at such a time is no small asset to the human race.

The third role of the United Nations in the Cuban crisis, the one which could not be played out, was that of an international inspector ready and willing to go at once to Cuba to verify the removal of the missiles. As we all know, Castro refused a United Nations presence on Cuban soil—U Thant's visit was in vain, and thus Castro prevented a quicker and cleaner liquidation of the crisis. But the fact is that at the height of this most dangerous period of the postwar world Chairman Khrushchev agreed to—even proposed—an international inspection team under United Nations auspices, a proposal to which we could quickly agree and which became part of the formula for disengagement between the United States and Soviet heads of state. And Castro's refusal of United Nations inspection converted a quarrel between the Soviet Union and the United States into a defiance of the United Nations by Cuba.

Finally—and I won't detain you longer on this subject—the United Nations also provided a site where Mr. McCloy* and I could meet with Mr. Kuznetsov* and the Soviet negotiators for those long weeks to conclude the transaction and bring about the withdrawal of the Soviet bombers.

I should not care to speculate on how or when the Cuban crisis might have been resolved, or whether it could have been resolved, without the United Nations. But I do say that the United Nations played a large part in a complex exercise in diplomatic action which averted the threat of thermonuclear war; and for this I think we can thank our stars.

Now, we have put the record of the United Nations at the Seventeenth General Assembly, during the Congo crisis, and during the Cuban crisis, to the test; and we have seen that, in very large measure, the performance of the United Nations served well the foreign policy interests of the United States. There was, indeed, much in it for us.

But I should prefer, in the end, not to read that record as though it were a scoreboard on which "victories" and "defeats" are recorded. I prefer to avoid the specious habit of treating the course of human affairs, even the massive conflicts in world affairs, like some sporting event which ends when the timekeeper blows his whistle.

The real world of international politics is, as you know, not that simple. We are dealing with fitful tides of history which ebb and flow. We are wrestling often with problems which, when solved in their immediate forms, promptly give rise to new forms and new problems—as witness the case of the Congo today.

---

* John J. McCloy, special U. S. negotiator on the Cuban matter, and Soviet Deputy Foreign Minister Kuznetsov, who negotiated for Russia.

We can, of course, say with assurance that, in this case or that, our policies prevailed and our objectives were gained. We can point to objective proof of progress here and there. We can show that unfriendly moves by X and Y were defeated or diverted, and that in all of these cases the United Nations had a useful part to play.

But to form mature judgments as to the real value of the United Nations to the interests of the United States, it seems to me that we must raise alternatives, that we must ask questions which challenge the imagination to say what might have happened if the United Nations had not been there at all. For example:

Would the Communists have fared better or worse in their efforts to divert the independence movement into a Communist mold—their supreme opportunity to extend power—if the United Nations had not existed?

Would the prospects of peace be better or worse—in Iran, in Greece, in Korea, in Kashmir, in the Middle East, in the Western Pacific, in central Africa—if there had been no United Nations during the past decade and a half?

Would United States foreign policy interests more recently in the Congo and the Caribbean have been served better or worse without a United Nations?

Could the United States put its ideas, its beliefs, its policies before the watching world more—or less—effectively if the United Nations did not exist?

I shall not attempt to speculate on these rather frightening alternatives for, it seems to me, the questions answer themselves.

But I should like to conclude with a few comments about the position of those who favor the United Nations in principle but want to withdraw or restrict our support on those relatively few occasions when the United States finds itself in a minority position.

The basic point here, of course, is that the United States does not own or control the United Nations. It is not a wing of the State Department. We are no more and no less than the most influential of the 110 members. If we were less, we would be failing to exert the influence of freedom's leader; if we were more, we would destroy the effectiveness of the United Nations, which depends precisely on the fact that it is not an arm of the United States or of any other government, but a truly international organization, no better or worse than the agreements which can be reached by the controlling majorities of its members.

Before such agreements are reached, or not reached, debate and negotiation bare differences and reveal similarities which frequently lead to accommodation and compromise. And I would ask: Is this not the heart of the democratic method? Is this not the parliamentary system in action? Is this not our own idea of how we are most likely to make more wise decisions than foolish ones, how the weak are most likely to be protected from the strong, how the will of the majority and the rights of the minority can both find expression without injustice to either?

The answer to these questions is yes. And if we were to pick up our marbles and go home whenever there is a disappointment, we would not only destroy the effectiveness of the United Nations, but would abandon hope that nations can work out their problems most of the time by the same methods by which conflicting interests get resolved within democratic nations and communities. This would deny on the international level the principles, methods and techniques which we swear by on the national and local levels.

Even faith in our kind of institutions would not, however, be enough to justify support for the United Nations if it worked against us. But this dilemma, happily, does not exist, and the record proves it. The fact is that the story of the last General Assembly, when the United States position was the majority position better than four times out of five, is the standard story of succeeding Assemblies over the past seventeen years. The fact is that in seventeen years the Soviet Union has never once—never once—succeeded in building a majority for any proposition of substance against the opposition of the United States. And the fact is that in seventeen years the United States has never felt obliged to exercise its veto in the Security Council to protect its interest, and the Soviet Union has used the veto a hundred times.

That's the record and there is, of course, a fundamental reason for it. The reason should be recalled frequently, for in this fact lies one of our greatest assets in the world today: The fact that the foreign policy interests of the United States are generally in harmony with the foreign policy interests of all nations which want to see a peaceful community of independent states working together, by free choice, to improve the lot of humanity. And since the majority of the nations of the world shares this goal, the majority consistently sides with the United States—or we side with them, depending on your point of view—when the roll is called and the yeas and nays are counted. It's as simple as that.

But let us take a couple of blemishes in the record and the performance of the United Nations and its members, the kind of blemishes that lead some of our people who favor the United Nations in principle to want to restrict it in practice.

First, take a case where the United States could not agree with a majority of the decision-making group in a United Nations agency. A recent case was that of the decision of the United Nations Special Fund to help finance an agricultural research project in Cuba. We objected to that project and still do. Yet the whole story is that out of 288 projects assisted by that fund, in the course of its existence, we approved of 287. So we face a choice: should we retaliate by withholding or limiting our support for an agency which we invented, which has allocated 97 percent of its funds to nations which we ourselves are aiding, and which represents an economical way for the United States to contribute to the Decade of Development, because in one instance out of 288 instances we were unable to persuade a majority that our view was the correct one?

Let me refer also to a situation which seems to agitate some of our people—the fact that the Soviet Union does not make the voluntary contributions which it is well able to make to such programs as technical assistance, the malaria eradication, the world food program and so forth. Their delinquency is deplorable but understandable from their point of view. These programs do not serve Communist ends; on the contrary. So it is hardly surprising that the Soviet Union makes little or no voluntary contributions to agencies whose work cuts straight across their own objectives. But should we support these programs less because they fail to win applause from the Kremlin?

As a matter of fact, I rather suspect that the Soviet Union and other Communist countries will tend to participate—and contribute—somewhat more in the work of these agencies in the years to come. There is some evidence of that already. And I think that the reason is clear. The policy of self-ostracism from the Specialized Agencies has not worked well for the Soviet Union, even though it has made life with them a bit easier for us.

If this in fact happens, it will raise some day-to-day problems for us; but, in my view, it also will raise problems for them and opportunities for us. For while the so-called Communist states operate more-or-less closed societies at home, once they step out into a United Nations forum they enter an open society.

In an open forum, over a period of time, ideology becomes transparent, dogma wears thin and becomes tiresome, and the myth of the magical solution evaporates slowly in the free air of a market place of ideas. There is contention in all this; there is frustration and the stuff of headlines; there is danger that the fearful and the insecure will want to withdraw from the free interplay of conflicting ideas and concepts and terminology, especially if, now and again, things do not go exactly the way we would like them to.

Yet it is we who do best in the open forum, for this is our natural habitat. And if we have the nerve to go ahead, if we have the stomach for the test of the open society, if we have the courage to build even that which is not perfect from our point of view, I can foresee nothing but a more meaningful dialogue coming out of it, a gradual erosion of tension, and finally the dominance of a set of ideas which are better, and better able also to stand the test, than the Marxist ideas as revealed to his successors.

All this would require, on our part, a degree of responsibility, of restraint, of maturity and of political sophistication which never before has been demanded of a democratic public and its elected representatives. It will not be easy and it will not be without temporary disappointments; and I, for one, have no doubt of the outcome, for this, too, would serve and serve well the foreign policy interests of the United States of America.

LET NONE MOCK ITS
WEAKNESS:
SOME THREATS

✌ ✌ *Ever since its founding in 1945, the United Nations has faced serious threats to its continued existence, and new ones occur almost every day. Most of these have been Communist inspired, ranging from the "troika" to that of a "financial veto" or refusal of the Soviet bloc to pay its assessed costs of the UN's peace-keeping operations. Of equal concern to Governor Stevenson as the threats themselves was the attitude of some Americans who, albeit unwittingly, were playing into Moscow's hands by conceding to it the final victory in the cold war. Here, after noting, "This may be no time for words of triumph—but it is most certainly a time for words and deeds of hope," he examines a number of the more serious threats to the United Nations, and points out why Americans have little reason to be discouraged.*

In April, 1945, toward the end of humanity's most terrible war, but before any man had seen the atomic age, the architects of peace met in San Francisco to complete the design of a new dwelling house for the Family of Man.

I was there during those golden weeks. And no one who was will

From an address to the American Association for the United Nations, San Francisco Chapter, October 23, 1961.

ever forget them. It was a beginning. It was the morning—fresh with the hope of a new day.

But now the house is battered. It resounds endlessly with family quarrels. There are cracks in the walls, and inside the cold winds of war and danger and strife from every quarter of the globe rattle the doors and windows. And, as is usual in such cases, quite a number of the tenants are behind on the rent.

But the house is still standing, and I am far from downhearted. We will meet all our problems and in time we will solve them in a way which is tolerable to the community of nations and to our own purposes. But it will be a slow business, and we are not going to score a touchdown on every play.

There is another problem about which I am concerned, however, and which I would like to share with you. That is the problem of being sure that, through all the difficulties which we shall face, America's essential role of leadership in the United Nations will have the indispensable and patient backing of public opinion.

I am not worried about the voices of all-out fanaticism in this country. There are always pitiful little groups of people among us, people with some inner compulsion to hate. To them the true meaning of democracy will forever be a closed book, and in their ears the voice of dissent will always sound like the voice of the enemy. The United Nations has nothing to hope from them.

I am thinking rather of the much broader range of Americans whose instincts are deeply democratic, who have been proud to help their country carry its world-wide burdens, but who now, after these many years of cold war and frustration, are honestly worried lest the United Nations be turned against us and even, perhaps, be delivered into the hands of its Communist enemies. To these Americans let me say with the greatest earnestness:

I share your frustrations but I do not share your fears.

I believe we must be prepared for many troubles.

But as long as we of the United States continue as active leaders in the United Nations, and continue to be faithful to our purposes, I have no fear that the Organization will be turned against us. Still less do I fear that it will ever pass under the domination of Communism, whose philosophy of power and intolerance is utterly alien to the United Nations spirit.

I must say it is not surprising that these fears about the United Nations should arise, considering the amount of alarming misinformation about what happens there. I still meet people, for instance, who insist that the United Nations action in support of a united, independent Congo fitted neatly into the plans of Soviet Communism.

Yet it was this same United Nations action which roused Mr. Khrushchev to such fury and caused him to bang his shoe in the General Assembly and to launch his all-out attack on the Secretary General!

Then I remember seeing in a magazine that with the death of Dag Hammarskjöld the United Nations had passed under the power of none other than Nikita Khrushchev. When I see a report like that, I must admit I blink a little. Can this be the same United Nations where I work, the same place where the members stood fast against Mr. Khrushchev's "troika," and cried out in outrage against Mr. Khrushchev's 50-megaton terror explosion? Evidently this Mr. Khrushchev must be a man who likes to pass resolutions against himself!

I must say I admire the skill of those who, almost every day, concede anew to Moscow the final victory in the cold war. Evidently the United States is completely finished at the close of every working day, but somehow poor Uncle Sam manages to struggle to his feet by morning so that he can be finished off again the next day.

This confusion over who is doing what to whom makes me think of the schoolboy who came home with his face damaged and his clothes torn, and when his mother asked him how the fight had started he said: "It started when the other guy hit me back."

Misapprehensions like these, I think, result partly from misinformation. But there is also something more fundamental which hinders many of us in our attempts to grasp the true meaning of the United Nations—and, indeed, the meaning of our situation in the modern world. I mean that pleasant illusion of omnipotence to which we Americans have clung for so long.

We Americans are not the first to have had this illusion, but I think we will get over it more safely than some of those who have gone before.

The Mongol Khans who exploded out of Central Asia, all across Siberia and to the gates of Vienna—they certainly thought themselves all-powerful, but their huge empire, having lived by the sword, died by the sword even more swiftly than it rose. Hitler, Mussolini, Tojo—all those Genghis Khans in modern dress nourished the same dream and, even more swiftly, met the same end.

The Russian Bolsheviks were not quite so foolish. At first, when Lenin took power in Petrograd in 1917, he thought the workers of the whole world would rise in flaming revolution to support him. The fuses sputtered briefly in Germany and Hungary and then went out. The Bolsheviks tried to set the world on fire, but it failed to ignite.

So Lenin, and then Stalin and Khrushchev after him, settled down to the building of the Soviet state power, and to a long-term strategy of conquest by opportunity. Communism changed from a burning faith into a scavenger of lost revolutions and a camp follower of global war.

Even today that poisonous vision of omnipotence afflicts the Communist rulers. "History is on our side!" they still shout. And in the borrowed name of "history" they do their best to scare the defenders of freedom out of Berlin and every other vulnerable point.

Yet their fanaticism has been tempered by a canny calculation of the possible. Pray God it will remain so, until the poison finally works itself out of their minds!

We Americans, to be sure, had different grounds for thinking ourselves omnipotent. We foreswore conquest by military force, but we made ourselves believe that, when the Second World War was over, our heritage of democratic ideals, by its own magic, would quickly sweep the world. There is no doubt that this illusion helped to sustain us in the war. Certainly it was present at the birth of the United Nations, for which, some of us thought, no exploits of peace would be impossible.

From the first Soviet veto in 1946, blow after blow of reality fell upon this precious illusion. By now it is gone beyond recall. But the danger is that we may now swing the other way, and that we may go from disillusion to despair, from an illusion of omnipotence to a myth of impotence.

Let me illustrate from experience at the United Nations.

It is said that the Soviet Union, by its veto power in the Security Council and by its bullying tactics in the General Assembly, can prevent the United Nations from acting without its consent.

This is not true at all. The fact is that the Soviet Union has not been an effective participant in a single one of the major international operations sponsored by the United Nations.

They do not belong to the World Bank, the Monetary Fund, the Food and Agriculture Organization or the International Civil Aviation Organization.

They take no part in the humanitarian work which the United Nations does for refugees all over the world.

For eight years they stayed away from the World Health Organization, which grew from strength to strength during their boycott.

They contributed little but obstruction to the International Atomic Energy Agency.

As for the world-famous United Nations Technical Assistance Program, and its new partner called the Special Fund, the Soviet contributions have been small, recent and all in nonconvertible rubles.

In the field of United Nations peace and security operations the Soviet performance amounts to a good deal less than zero.

The United Nations action in Korea was taken without them, in spite of them and, in fact, against the aggression which they had sponsored.

In the troubled Middle East they have paid nothing to maintain the Palestine refugees, and nothing to the United Nations Emergency Force.

In the Congo they paid not a ruble to the United Nations efforts; instead, they financed a secession movement in Stanleyville which the United Nations successfully opposed and which collapsed.

All those things, then, have been done by the United Nations, on behalf of the community of nations, without the consent or cooperation of the Soviet Union, and in some cases against its best efforts.

The United Nations *has not been strangled by the veto*—and may it never be!

It is often said that the Soviet Union is inflexible in the United Nations, and that once it has made up its mind all the rest of us have to do the adjusting. This is a long way from the truth. The Soviets do indeed try to convey this illusion of inflexibility, I suppose in the hope that this will improve their bargaining position. But their bluff has been called often and successfully.

After the fall of mainland China the Russians announced that they would boycott the Security Council until the seat of China was turned over to Peking. But in August, 1950, after the Security Council had acted on Korea without them, they came back—and they have stayed ever since.

In 1954 the Soviets announced in the United Nations that the United States proposal for an International Atomic Energy Agency was an imperialist plot to manufacture atomic bombs all over the world, and they would have nothing to do with it. Three years later they joined it.

In 1955 the Soviets said that unless Outer Mongolia was admitted to the United Nations, they would veto all thirteen of the non-Communist applicants. They did, too, but the very next day they reversed themselves and voted to let in twelve. A year later they relented and let in the remaining applicant, Japan.

Now the United Nations has many new and, supposedly, "inexperienced" members.

But they weren't born yesterday.

When Mr. Khrushchev first turned his wrath on Dag Hammarskjöld and put forward his "troika" scheme, the new African members recognized immediately that this was an attack on the United Nations itself, their protector. The Soviets stuck for a solid year to their position, but had practically no support for it.

Finally, we hear it said that the United Nations has failed to fulfill the aims of the Charter, and that we must look elsewhere for a better vehicle of our hopes: to regional organizations; to military alliances; to an entirely new "concert of free nations" or to our worldwide information program; to "the war for the minds of men"; to foreign aid and the improvement of the lot of man; or to the Peace Corps and people-to-people exchanges; to the opening of Soviet society through exchanging people and publications; to our own military defenses; or to our religious faith; or to higher standards of ethics here at home.

But to these I say: Where is the contradiction? Does not every one of these things have its necessary place in the strategy of peace and freedom? The United Nations is not, and has never sought to be, the sole channel for the pursuit of its own purposes. Indeed, it asks of all its members that they obey the Charter in all that they do.

To an open and free society like our own, this plea is addressed to the people as well as to the government.

In the Preamble to the United Nations Charter it is "We, the Peoples of the United Nations" who pledge ourselves to peace, human rights, justice, social and economic progress, tolerance and neighborliness. It is "we the people" who "have resolved to combine our efforts to accomplish these aims."

To no people are these famous words addressed more than to the American people. You, the citizens, through your voluntary efforts to improve our life at home and to make life more abundant abroad and through your taxes and your support of our government in all its responsibilities—you can and must do much to sustain the United Nations and its purposes in the world.

It is written in the Bible that "to whom much is given, of him also much shall be required." I think this applies to us, the American people. For surely much is given to us, and much will be required of us for many years to come.

We must put behind us the illusions born of impatience.

It used to be possible to speak of winning a quick war, but that is out of the question today. We know that the Soviet Union can inflict such destruction on the Atlantic world that survival itself is in doubt. Equally, the United States possesses the ability to destroy much, perhaps all, of what the Russian people have built up with such labor and sacrifice over the past forty years.

This is the ugly vision from which humanity cannot awake because it is not a dream but a reality—a reality into which threats of violence only plunge us deeper still.

So, since we don't wish to die together, we must manage to live together.

We may have had our fill of negotiation already, but there is a lot more to come.

But we must be just as strong to resist the opposite illusion. We shall not win any quick peace by negotiation. For nearly a generation a deep gulf of conflicting aims has split the political landscape of the earth: a gulf between the world of the free and the world of the coerced. It may be many, many years before that gulf is safely closed.

The stern fact is that we are in this struggle for life. As Senator Fulbright has so wisely pointed out, the ones who are "soft" are not those who refuse to rush into a suicidal war, but those who lack the courage to face a grim, lifelong struggle for freedom.

It has been said that in this struggle it is vital to "know your enemy." So it is, both so that we may anticipate and frustrate his attacks and so that, ultimately and gradually, we may learn how to make him our friend.

But the struggle also lays upon us an even more difficult duty of knowledge. It is summed up in the motto of the Greek philosophers: "Know thyself." As never before in our history, we must study ourselves, our values, our institutions, our national style and the goals for which we strive. For the great exertions which we face can only be justified by great goals.

Too often this world struggle has been carelessly caricatured as a mere battle of the giants, an age-long duel in which two nuclear colossi test by threat and counterthreat which shall dominate the globe.

It is no such thing. Power and dominion are not the aim of this country. If they were, if all we could offer were the crushing of Soviet tyranny by a tyranny of our own, then indeed we would have no title whatever to call for sacrifice from a single free man or woman.

But our aims *are* something worthy of sacrifice.

We seek, with all the determination and faith that repeated frustration demands, a complete and completely controlled program of world disarmament.

We seek a multiplication of free and friendly contacts with the Soviet people, until in the fullness of time they and their leaders decide to open their dangerously closed society and to become full members of the community of nations.

We seek world-wide cooperation, regardless of political beliefs, for the relief of human misery; the conquest of the deserts; the development of the riches of the oceans; and the eradication of famine, gross poverty, illiteracy; the peaceful conquest of outer space.

We seek the orderly transition of all subject peoples, whether of old-style colonial masters or of Communist empires, to full political equality and self-government.

And, in the disarmed world we strive for, we seek the logical counterpart of disarmament: the building of the minimum world institutions needed to keep peace among disarmed nations, to settle disputes between them, and to prevent one nation from imposing its will on another by any weapons, be they rifle, club or fist.

These are our goals. If they are not great enough, let us get greater ones; for the exertions demanded of us in this dark uncertain time, and for many a difficult year to come, will be formidable. And the greatest will be the self-restraint, the patience and the perception to perceive and pursue our real interests.

I do not think we dare attempt anything less. The reality in which we live is much stronger, much more unpredictable, much more perilous than any that our prophets or our ideologues ever forecast for us. Which of us foresaw the unlocking of the atom? Which of us foresaw what instant communication all over the globe would do to man and his image of himself?

All these things are new, and unless they are faced with a new spirit and a new courage, they lead in only one direction—to the destruction of humanity itself. Faced with this overriding risk, we must abandon the inherited fears and suspicions of our past and try to see behind each face the troubled soul and searching heart of a man like to ourselves—*"mon semblable, mon frère."*

I believe the cause of freedom and peace has a glorious future in this world. And in that future the United Nations will play a mighty part. Let none of us mock its weakness, for when we do we are mocking ourselves. It is the hope of the world; and our country's pride should be that we stood by the United Nations, the meeting house of the Family of Man, in its time of hardest trial.

LET US LEAVE
RIVALRIES BEHIND:
SOME HOPES

♥♥ *Shortly after he arrived in New York to assume his duties as Ambassador, Governor Stevenson was welcomed to the city at an official luncheon given by Mayor Robert F. Wagner. Fifteen years earlier, he recalled, although not honored at any city banquet, he had also been a new arrival in New York—with the first wave of United Nations staff to set up headquarters and get into business. He then took the occasion to analyze and put into perspective the world of today, offering additional reasons why all peoples—not just Americans —should support the United Nations and forget the rivalries and imperialisms of the old world.*

I believe that what is happening, day by day, at the United Nations is just about the most challenging, the most original, even the most exhilarating work being done by men today.

Let us get the perspective straight. In the second half of this twentieth century, we are living through an historical experience which, in all the annals of man, has proved desperately difficult. This experience is the disintegration of one pattern of imperial power and the establishment of new political facts and relationships and power centers in its place. Whenever such changes occur—the really big

From an address at a luncheon given by the Mayor of New York City, March 2, 1961.

♥ 142

changes which resemble some vast seismic disturbance in the earth's political crust—the inevitable outcome is disorder, catastrophe, civil conflict and war.

Europe lapsed into barbarism after the fall of Rome. Britain's advance into India followed the crumbling and collapse of the Mogul Empire. In China, where man's longest documented record covers the fortunes of his oldest continuous body politic, the rise and fall of imperial dynasties has a rhythm of almost majestic fatality, each new empire rising on the anarchy and ruins of the last and then, in its own turn, falling away.

Times of imperial collapse are always times of trouble. And we are living through the greatest of such disintegrations today. In less than a generation the dominion which Western Europe exercised over most of Asia and Africa until the morrow of the Second World War has all but vanished. All Asia has emerged from colonial or semicolonial control. Africa is in the violent throes of the same process. I doubt if empire on such a scale has ever ended at such breakneck speed. If history is our guide, so rapid and so vast a disintegration must bring the risk of confusion thrice confounded.

And history leaves us in little doubt about the kind of disorder we are likely to endure. We may expect to see new powers jostling to take over the influence and control of the outgoing imperial governments. We may expect to see such efforts sparking local violence and driving it in an outward spiral toward general war. And we may expect, behind local crises and dangers, a general deterioration in international good will, a general increase in distrust and hostility.

Such dangers have marked the collapse of empire before. They mark it now. So the turbulence we see day by day in the world at large, and reflected back to us through the United Nations, is neither surprising nor new. We should and must expect it. And we must get used to it—we who suffer from having had things our way for so long we are shocked and hurt when other people don't share our views or question our motives. We judge ourselves by our motives, others by their actions.

What *is* both surprising and new is what the United Nations is trying to *do* about these risks. Now we come to the wholly new chapter in history, the chapter that gives us at least a marginal hope of escaping the dread fatalities of earlier days. To me, I confess, it is a matter of exhilaration that here, here in America, in the newest of continents and in the midst of perhaps the most far-reaching experiment in free, unimperial government, a new start should be under way in the management of human affairs, a new experiment to defeat and annihilate the set historical patterns and deadlocks of the past.

Here at the United Nations the effort *is* being made to confront the old fatalities of collapsing empires and put in their place wholly new approaches to the dilemmas of our time. It is only when we realize how new they are, how radical, how revolutionary, that we can have any idea of the potential value, the profound historical significance of what is being attempted at the United Nations.

For what we are attempting to do today at the United Nations is to roll back every one of the great historical fatalities which, in the past, have made the ending of empire the most perilous condition for the survival of society. We are trying to end the dreary cycle of imperialisms by which the outgoing masters are quickly replaced by new ones who come quickly in to fill the vacuum of power.

The principle which President Wilson declared has since become one of mankind's greatest aspirations—the self-determination of peoples. In the Western world, in this century, the attempt has been made for the first time in history to outlaw imperialism.

This is new. Like all new things, it is difficult. But at least in the last decade, as we have seen the United Nations grow, we must admit that for millions of God's children a first step toward freedom has been taken—the step which recognizes their right, their inalienable right, to be free.

But then the dangers and the dilemmas press in. We have done something new in proclaiming the right of small peoples not to be run by other, more powerful states. We have decreed and welcomed the end of colonialism. Indeed, it was in these United States that the first practical steps were taken to raise the principle of anticolonialism from a hope to a fact. The shot that echoed round the world from Lexington echoes on to this day.

But have we ensured that our new faith can be fully and irrevocably expressed in works? Hitherto, as I have said, the ending of one imperialism has usually spelled, for the small and the weak, the beginning of a new. Are we doing better today? The principle may be new. Is the practice equally so?

This to me is the most urgent issue at stake in Africa today. Do the new nations, sometimes irresolute, sometimes wobbly, know how much they need us in their period of transition to genuine independence? Or are they blinded by their new nationalism, their hatred of the colonialism of the past, both of which are so skillfully exploited by the propaganda of others who are not trying to help them achieve genuine independence and stability? Was it Alexander Hamilton who said that even to be neutral required a stable government? And Wilson warned us that "Liberty is not itself government. In the wrong hands, in hands unpracticed, undisciplined, it is incompatible with government."

The old colonial system is crumbling and, clearly, only one body can prevent the ancient fatality of simply swapping one control for another. It is the United Nations, consulting closely with its Afro-Asian members, and barring outside intervention from whatever side.

This is our first aim—to put a genuine end to outside imperial control. Our second stems from it—to prevent local disputes from spiraling into general war. Here, again, we do not have to look far back into history to see the kind of tragedy we must at all costs avert.

At the turn of the last century, Turkish imperial power crumbled in the Balkans. Czarist Russia on the one hand, Austria-Hungary on the other pressed in to take its place. In the small, emergent Balkan states, local factions looked to Moscow or Vienna, as in Africa today they may look to Moscow or Paris or Brussels or Washington. The defeat of local Balkan leaders began to take on the aspect of a defeat for the powers which backed them. Two small local wars were contained. Then, in 1914, a bullet killed an archduke, and men stood helplessly by and watched until all the world was engulfed in the horrors of war.

Africa is the Balkans of today. Any outside power seeking to manipulate its griefs and searchings and first fumbling efforts to stand alone risks bringing down on Africa and on the world the dread possibility of nuclear destruction. Is this really what Mr. Khrushchev had in mind when he demanded the withdrawal of the United Nations force and suggested instead that the Congo should become, as the Balkans once were, the cockpit, first of rival factions, then of rival interventions, and finally of a spreading, consuming, horrifying general conflict? I cannot believe that any statesman conscious of the dread brink upon which all humanity stands can seek to widen the crisis.

I know it is not easy to reverse the fatalities of history. We are on a melancholy road, which again and again mankind has trodden flat with legions of men marching to destruction. In the Congo, in Laos, potentially in any area of conflict and civil disturbance, almost nothing is new. The conflicts are old, the rival suspicions and jockeyings for position are old, the brute struggle for power is as old as man himself. And we know where they have always led—to war and death.

But today one thing *is* new. It is the United Nations' effort to attempt to apply peaceful procedures and rational solutions even to the most aggravated and envenomed of political crises. On a dark scene, in a dark time of troubles, New York's guest, the United Nations, is proclaiming by deed as well as word that men can live, not by violence and brute strength, but, at last, by reason and law.

And also I would say to our own people: Support the United Nations with your approbation, your sympathetic attention and your prayers. To the smaller powers, especially the emergent states of Africa, I would repeat that the United Nations is of first interest above all to weaker states, since without it they have no ultimate protection against the force of more powerful and predatory governments.

And to the Soviet Union I would say: There are laws of history more profound and inescapable than the laws dreamed up by Marx and Lenin, laws which belong not to class relationships or stages of economic development, but to the nature and destiny of man himself. Among these laws is the certainty that war follows when new empires thrust into the collapsing ruins of the old. So stay your ambitions. Think twice about your interventions. Allow the new principles of international order—the right of peoples to determine their *own* destiny—to operate in Africa without your pressure from without.

Do not sabotage the only institution which offers an alternative to imperialism. Do not look backward to mankind's evil inheritance of violence. Look forward to a world where the United Nations can be the forum and guardian of peace.

This, I believe, is the hope of the vast majority of mankind. It is above all the hope of the small powers whose only protection lies in the international organization of their security. The Administration of President Kennedy will go to the limits of its strength and ingenuity to work with the general consensus of humanity. It invites all other governments to follow the same path. For let there be no doubt about the alternatives. They are written in words of flame and blood on the walls of the world.

Let us, therefore, leave the rivalries and the imperialisms behind and strive together for the world where nations can be both secure and free.

PART IV

OUR STAKE
IN THE WORLD

A PARABLE FOR STATESMEN:

TO SAVE MANKIND

🌠 🌠 *A meeting of world astronomers caused Governor Stevenson to observe, a bit wistfully: "Your proceedings will be a million light years beyond the comprehension of mere mortals like myself." And then, after expressing envy for astronomy's "single pursuit of truth about the universe," he said: "Would that all of us at the United Nations could follow your example, would that all of us could unite to end cold war and conflict, and concentrate on the arts of peace and the wider enjoyment of the benefits of this age of unparalleled technical progress." This was the setting he gave to his parable for statesmen, a parable that spoke not only of one world in science and the search for truth, but in international life and the search for disarmament, the building of institutions to keep peace and the abolition of poverty and backwardness.*

I have been told that one of the reasons the astronomers of the world cooperate is the fact that there is no one nation from which the entire sphere of the sky can be seen. Perhaps there is in that fact a parable for national statesmen, whose political horizons are all too often limited by national horizons. In the United Nations we have mankind's greatest attempt so far, halting though it is, to widen all our horizons, to cause all men and all nations to accept the fact that

Address to the International Astronomical Union, Berkeley, California, August 15, 1961.

there is but one world, without horizons other than the common horizon of illimitable space—one world not only in science, not only in the search for truth, but in the ordering of their international lives.

But science is more than a search for truth and a noble exercise of the mind. For generations the scientist and his practical cousin, the engineer, have been widening man's grasp of nature with geometrically increasing speed. They have put into the hands of the statesman and the citizen unimaginable powers. And although science itself, and the powers it bestows, are ethically neutral with the cold neutrality of outer space, the ways in which men use those powers carry the greatest consequence for good or for evil.

The same hydrogen fusion process that gives the burning light of the sun and the stars has been in our grasp for a decade, but will we use it for construction or for cataclysm? Earth satellites may soon give us direct and instantaneous communication and television spreading simultaneously around the world, but will we use them for truth or for falsehood, for tolerance or for hatred, for peace or for conflict?

Scientifically and technically the world has already become a single community, yet in our ethical response to this fact, and in our political institutions, we, governments and citizens, are lagging dangerously far behind the scientists.

They have given us dangerous powers, but we have not yet learned to control them. They have given us tools to abolish poverty, but we have not yet mastered them. They have given us means to extend the span of human life, but this may prove a curse, not a blessing, unless we can assure food, survival, and then health and a good life for the bodies and minds of our exploding populations. They have made the world small and interdependent, but we have not built the new institutions to manage it, nor cast off the old institutions which scientific progress has made obsolete.

Every great change wrought by science is foreshadowed years ahead in the laboratory and on the drawing board. But it is not until the new device is fully built and functioning, and has astonished the whole world, that we begin to think of its human and political implications. We are forever running today to catch up tomorrow with what science made necessary yesterday.

This gap must be closed, this disruptive and dangerous lag between scientific discovery and political adaptation to it. I suggest that the natural scientist and the political practitioner must enter into a new communion of early and constant intercommunication, so that the world's institutions can more nearly keep up with the incessant march of science. Unless this is done, the gap will surely widen, for there is no way to slow down the pace of scientific discovery even if we wanted to do it.

There was an age when it was tolerable for outworn institutions and habits of mind to persist for centuries. It took at least three hundred years for the invention of gunpowder, combined with the spreading patterns of commerce, to bring down the proud city walls of medieval Europe. But down they came in the end, and the age of national states, superseding the city-states, had begun.

Today things move more swiftly. Within ten years after man set off his first atomic explosion, the leaders of all the great powers had acknowledged that a nuclear war between any nations would be a catastrophe for *all* nations. There is now an Atomic Energy Agency which is *international*. There are strenuous negotiations for a permanent, reliable, controlled ban on nuclear weapons tests by any nation. There is a groping determination to halt the further spread of nuclear weapons to any nation. Thus atomic energy has already begun to breach some of our national walls. And no doubt the exploration of outer space will breach them further.

Certainly the consequences of space exploration, for good or evil, will be great. Dramatic improvements in weather forecasting and in world-wide communications can be more or less precisely forseen. Science is already acquiring powerful new tools, and what the ultimate benefits to man may be, no one can tell.

We can only guess at such possibilities. But there is no guessing any more as to whether man will undertake the adventure of space exploration. Yesterday's dreams are today's facts. Scientific instruments, then animals, then men, have been hurled into space. There is no turning back; as certainly as the oceans were conquered in the century of Columbus and Magellan, new realms of space will be conquered in our century.

But in what spirit will these conquests of space be carried out, and for what purposes? Our century must answer that awesome question. For wherever man goes, though he travel to another planet, he brings with him the problem of good and evil which is his peculiar heritage. Shall space be explored for war or for peace? For national power or for the good of all men?

These questions are beyond the scope of science, but all of us, as citizens, must help to answer them. If the scientist and the engineer can create a thrust strong enough to defeat the earth's gravitation, and can plan to send groups of men into flight far beyond the earth, then it is up to us in government and diplomacy to develop a comparable "orbital velocity" of our own, great enough to lift *all* mankind beyond the dread gravitation of mistrust and war.

In the years ahead, then, international diplomacy must do far more than put out the recurrent fires of conflict. It must apply itself with massive energy to three great areas of creative effort: to disarmament, to the building of institutions to keep the peace, and to international cooperation for human progress.

All the world agrees that the arms race, especially in nuclear weapons, is anarchic, wasteful and deadly dangerous for humanity. So all agree that we must stop the race, reverse the process and disarm.

Yet it is not done. Why? Because of deep conflicts of purpose, and an even deeper mistrust. But it can be done. It involves principles which are familiar to scientists—freedom of investigation, freedom of inspection and freedom of verification. There must be, in any disarmament program, adequate inspection and verification such that each side can be quite sure, at every stage, that the other is living up to its part of the bargain.

Disarmament has been misconstrued as if it were in some way the enemy of national defense. And the idea of inspection and verification has unfortunately been misconstrued in certain quarters, as if it were in some way the enemy of disarmament. It is not. It is a necessity. The acid test of sincerity is whether one agrees to fully adequate inspection and verification. Only with these can we know that, inside the box marked "Disarmament," we will really find the reality and a peaceful world, and not something ticking away to the destruction of all of us. The same, of course, applies to the banning of nuclear weapons tests, for no permanent ban is possible without adequate inspection and verification. In years of negotiations in Geneva that has always been the key issue. And it still is.

Surely no nation today should, in the name of a selfish sovereignty made obsolete by the interdependence of us all, refuse to permit within its borders that right of adequate inspection and verification, free of veto, which alone can banish mistrust and make possible the achievement of general and complete disarmament and a peaceful world. I am glad to say that the United States has always been willing to grant such right, and I devoutly hope that the Soviet Union may show an equally real desire for disarmament and peace.

The next question is: Who is to do the inspection and verification? What sort of policeman can police the great powers?

Here we find that we cannot take even the first practical step toward general and complete disarmament and a peaceful world unless the nations are willing to build new world institutions which stand above the individual nations and act impartially for the entire human community. What is called for is an international organization within the framework of the United Nations which will see to it that no single nation fails to comply with agreed steps toward general and complete disarmament.

And if we look still further down the road, to the day when national armed forces will be done away with and only internal police units remain, then all the more will the world need institutions of international law and order. Then the United Nations will need its own United Nations Peace Force, capable of deterring or subduing the strongest combinations which might be raised against it.

That is the long-run need, but the short run makes similar demands on us. Events in the Congo have shown how vital it is that the United Nations retain and develop further the capacity to act for peace, to deploy military forces with speed and precision, and thus to uphold the integrity of vulnerable nations in emergencies where direct intervention by a great power would risk disaster. The United Nations is the world's greatest instrument, and the world community must act to uphold it, pay for it, invigorate it and support its able and courageous Secretary General.

All these things are demanded of us to save mankind from violence and war. But the community of nations should be bound together by more affirmative and creative purposes. More and more we must, as a world community, learn to practice the arts of peace cooperatively and together. And, at this fateful moment in history, when man has, so to speak, one foot already in the heavens, surely we must find ways for the powers to cooperate rather than fight in the exploration of outer space.

What good are national rivalries against the backdrop of the solar system? All the world, regardless of ideology, applauds the bravery of the first astronauts. And surely all the world would breathe easier if the conquest of space were looked on henceforward not as a means to the power and glory of particular nations or ideologies, but as one of the great adventures of the whole human race.

"Together let us explore the stars"—so said President Kennedy at his inauguration, appealing especially to the Soviet Union. A few days later he renewed this appeal in these words: "I now invite all nations—including the Soviet Union—to join with us in developing a weather prediction program, in a new communications satellite program, and in preparation for probing the distant planets of Mars and Venus."

Technology will not wait long for an answer. In just a few years there will be rocket boosters, in more than one country, big enough to launch whole teams of men on journeys to the nearest planets. Shall this too be a race for military or psychological advantage at huge and wasteful expense? Or shall it be the occasion for teamwork, ignoring ideological lines? We haven't much time left in which to decide—it is a fork in the road which will soon be passed.

We have many similar choices to make closer to home. The new nations, which have recently become independent, have an almost unlimited need for education, health, industrial development, agricultural improvement, communications and exchanges in the fields of science and culture. Shall more fortunate nations exploit those needs by offering aid only in exchange for political influence? Or shall we help because it is right to help? And shall we prefer more and more the disinterested channels of the United Nations? The path to peace must lie increasingly in the multilateral direction of the United Nations, especially with all the self-restraint and mutual tolerance which it requires.

Such are the specific challenges which face international diplomacy today and which draw still greater urgency under the accelerating pressures of science and technology: Disarmament. The building of institutions to keep the peace, both now and in a future disarmed world. International cooperation in the creative arts of peace, to abolish poverty and backwardness.

We have no choice but to meet these challenges. And, in meeting them, we shall be building together a grand design of peace, a design whose keynote is world community.

If there can be said to be a wave of the future for mankind, I believe it is in that principle of community. No one nation, no empire, no imposed system can dare to speak any more for mankind. All must be willing, if sovereignty is to make any sense in the thermonuclear age, to deny themselves some of the extravagant jungle habits which have accompanied it in times past, and to join their sovereign wills in community institutions, in common community action, and in common obedience to the community's rules.

The rules themselves already exist. They are proclaimed in one of the greatest creative acts of history, the United Nations Charter. We can attempt to restate some of them in the light of our experience since 1945 when that Charter was framed.

The Charter commands every nation not to use or threaten force against the territory of independence of another. But experience requires us to go further, for there are other means of conquest. We have seen nations and peoples subjugated by political subversion and guerrilla warfare. We have seen economic aid used as bait and club to impose political influence and subservience. We could well see the raising of new territorial claims, or even claims of possession, in outer space.

To all these exaggerations of sovereignty we must say: No, no nation, any more, by any means, direct or indirect, shall seek to extend its control at the expense of another.

A second provision of the United Nations Charter calls for international cooperation for human progress—economic, social, cultural and in the field of human rights. Much has been accomplished along those lines, but how much more could be done, both on this earth and in the spaces beyond, if all the nations would willingly pool their capacities and their efforts! The wonderful techniques of material progress should not be perverted to satisfy political or ideological ambitions. The poor and the hungry and the diseased of this world do do not ask for help in the name of one "system" or another. They ask for it in the name of humanity, of the community of mankind, and it is in that name only that they should receive it.

There is a third principle of the United Nations that needs reaffirmation. It is summed up in those splendid words of the Preamble—"to practice tolerance, and live together in peace with one another as good neighbors." And tolerance is the key to peace, for there can be no peace unless there is mutual tolerance as between differing peoples and systems and cultures. Peaceful coexistence should not and cannot involve "burial" by any one of any other.

This world will always be a pluralistic world, made up of disparate beliefs and institutions, ever changing and shifting, and only in a world atmosphere of tolerance and freedom can there take place that varied experimentation and development which alone have produced human progress.

Men of science above all others should value and preach tolerance, for they have only to recall the blight that intolerance cast on Copernicus and Galileo, a blight that held back astronomy for generations, and they know only too well how the orthodoxy of one scientific era becomes the heterodoxy of the next.

The condition of tolerance is openness and the understanding that comes from openness. How can there be tolerance or understanding if great nations continue in secretive isolation from the rest of the world, rearing their children by a closed educational system and in suspicion and fear of sinister foreigners, excluding outside information, periodicals, books and broadcasts, restricting travel and hiding great parts of their territory? Only in openness will that mistrust that poisons the world atmosphere today be dispelled, and only through open societies can there arise that tolerance that will permit all of us to live in confidence and peace with one another.

Amid the darkness of this noontime there are rays of hope that we *will achieve* an open world. It is happening, bit by bit. Recently, for example, I was happy to read the remark of the eminent Soviet astronomer, Professor A. A. Mikhailov, at a meeting in Pasadena on the astronomy of the space age. "Science is international," said Professor Mikhailov. "My hope is for the United States and Russia to share in space projects and in many other fields of human endeavor."

Community, tolerance, openness—those are the words which I would leave with you. And if they are to be made real, we all have one more great duty: to support the United Nations, which is the community's greatest symbol and greatest instrument. It is the world center of tolerance and openness. It is, as long as men are free to differ—which I trust will be forever!—a center of disciplined disagreement. No one power can dominate it, or use it to drive another to the wall. It is the greatest defense of the weak against the bullying of the strong. It is the lightning rod which prevents rampant nationalism from sparking war. And if the world is to be saved from disaster, the United Nations must be built into still more—an institution which can enforce the judgments of the world community against those who threaten or break the peace.

Now, after this exposition of our terrestrial worries, I rather wish that all of us who deal in human affairs could be astronomers and for a while deal but with the remotest celestial bodies! Sir James Jeans called astronomy "the most poetic of the sciences." Perhaps if we all practiced it, we would be filled with the wonder and excitement of discovery, with a sense of elemental majesty and beauty, with our little quarrels in better perspective, and would thus be purged of our pride and prejudice, and all the base motives which complicate and endanger our lives.

At all events, I devoutly hope that all of us in and out of the United Nations will make a new beginning; that we will dare to part with habits and institutions dangerously outworn; and that we will have the courage and determination to construct, soon enough to save mankind, a new world order more nearly worthy of the scientist and the poet, and of the best that man has in him.

A BETTER LIFE:
ECONOMIC DEVELOPMENT

❦ ❦ *In his address to the United Nations General Assembly on September 25, 1961, President Kennedy officially proposed on behalf of the United States that the United Nations designate the 1960's the "Decade of Development." His reason: "Political sovereignty is but a mockery without the means of meeting poverty and illiteracy and disease." The proposal met with unanimous approval. Earlier that year, Governor Stevenson had addressed the thirty-second session of the UN Economic and Social Council in Geneva, Switzerland, and had outlined the United States' views on the need for a concerted program of economic aid to help the lesser developed nations of the world catch up with the wealthier, more industrialized countries. Then, as well as on a number of subsequent occasions, he pointed out that while the political activities of the United Nations received the bulk of publicity, by far the greater part of the UN business, not to mention personnel, was involved in social and economic programs. In the following statement he stresses the urgency to help provide a better life for mankind.*

Economics must always be the servant of society. No amount of steel or cement produced, of oil wells drilled, or acres of wheat harvested is of any consequence except as it fills a human need—unless the steel and cement make decent houses and schools and hospitals,

From a statement to the Thirty-second Session of the Economic and Social Council, Geneva, Switzerland, July 10, 1961.

❦ 161

unless the oil warms and transports man and his goods, unless the wheat means bread and strength for those who hunger.

The most efficient factory cannot justify a city's slums. And economic growth is of little avail if it serves only a fraction of the people. It must serve them all.

The greatest challenge of our century is the aspiration of peoples all over the globe to share the abundant fruits of modern science and technology. The example of the industrially developed nations shows that human beings can lead longer, healthier and richer lives than most of the world's population now enjoy, and that each generation can have the satisfaction of bequeathing new opportunities to its children. At the end of the century we will be judged, all of us, by how well we have met these aspirations.

We must bridge the dangerous chasm between the living standards of the rich and the poor. We must narrow the disparities in the conditions of life between human beings who happen to be born on different parts of the earth.

We seek greater economic equality between nations as well as within nations, not dividing up our present scarcities but sharing in a growing abundance. The world economy must grow in capacity to produce, faster in the less developed regions than in the industrially developed countries, but faster than in the past everywhere. For no one anywhere, any longer, will passively accept the idea that hunger, misery and disease are the immutable destiny of man.

Everyone, everywhere, realizes that in this historic century man has routed the four horsemen of the apocalypse, and that for the first time in human history the ancient evil specters of pestilence and famine have been exorcised. We are crossing a great watershed in history to a time when enough food, shelter and clothing are within the reach of all and new dimensions in human wants and needs are emerging.

It will be no help to the developing countries to slow down the growth of the developed countries. Quite the contrary. For the emerging nations need above all an increased flow of resources from the industrial countries. To be able to provide this aid, and to provide expanding markets for the exports of the less developed economies, the advanced countries will have to progress steadily and rapidly in their capacity to produce.

To meet these and other international responsibilities and to better provide for the wants of our own people, the United States must grow in its own capacity to produce. Therefore, we look to the 1960's as a decade of dynamic and accelerated economic development, demonstrating to all the vigor and vitality of a free economy. And we pledge to do all in our power to make the 1960's a decade of development not only for ourselves, but, we hope, for our fellowmen everywhere.

Our periodic postwar recessions, mild though they have been, have cost us dearly in human disappointment and wasted national opportunities. So the first step in our program for growth is to mobilize the weight of the government's influence to prevent or arrest future interruptions in our economic progress. The idea that the rate of economic growth in a free society does not have to be left to chance, that democratic nations can control their economic destinies, has now become our conviction.

What has happened since 1945 has confounded the pessimists. In no other period of the world's history has there been such a rapid and gratifying recovery from the devastation of war. This recovery has been greatly aided by international cooperation and economic aid. Western Europe and Japan have achieved spectacular results, and we recognize that the record of the Soviet Union, too, is impressive.

In the United States, happily spared the devastation of war and starting from a high level of production and consumption, national production in real terms has increased by more than one-third since the war's end.

If we look further back over the twentieth century, the record of economic and social progress is even more impressive. In the United States per capita income has doubled in the last quarter-century. This growth has been achieved not only through very large investments of new capital but by the growth and improvement of technology, the economies of large-scale production as national and international markets have expanded, and the improvement in the quality of the labor force. It has been achieved while at the same time reducing greatly the hours of work in our factories, mines and farms and providing much more leisure for all of our people.

It has become clear that what happens in research laboratories and in the minds of men can multiply the potentialities of physical factors.

Hours worked, land utilized and capital employed are the elements which, by classical formulas, determine the growth of output. But both the quality and quantity of output have been progressively expanding far beyond what the mere physical combination of these factors would indicate. This we must attribute to intelligence, imagination, inventions, entrepreneurship. Brains have become a real growth industry.

The power of intelligence can manifest itself in every aspect of our lives and in every phase of the development process. We need a concept of social "capital" which goes beyond bricks and mortar and includes investment in education, training and the stock of useful knowledge.

I do not underestimate the need for capital formation. It is true that mere investment without new knowledge and new skills could not have generated the growth in output that we have experienced. But it is equally true that knowledge and skills could not have been productive unless they had been linked to real capital. Indeed, without the prospect of new investment, much of the technological progress would never have occurred at all. If we are serious about accelerated economic growth, we must step up the rate of productive investment. And President Kennedy has made a number of proposals for economic growth based on the need for all three factors: knowledge, brain power, more capital.

Policies designed primarily to stimulate economic growth often turn out to have a desirable incidental effect. Education is a good example. The American tradition values education for its own sake; we led the way in the provision of free public education at all levels of society. But we now feel fairly certain that the resulting improvement in the quality of the labor force has been one of the major factors in our economic growth during the last half-century.

Before I leave the subject of the United States economy, let me say a word about disarmament and arms control. It is no secret that we have been forced to devote a considerable portion of our economy to production for defense. But let me make it perfectly clear that the United States, far from regarding an international armaments agreement as a threat to economic prosperity, would regard such an agreement as an economic opportunity—an opportunity to free our resources from production of instruments of death to the production of the manifold things we need for a better life, for our own citizens and for the citizens of other nations.

This is not to deny that a sudden change in the direction of production tends to be disruptive. This is true for any economy, however organized. But such disruption can be minimized by foresight. The United States is actively studying the economic impact of disarmament and arms control, and is hopefully designing measures to ease the transition. We hope and pray that the day will come when such studies become more than merely an academic exercise, for the United States has no higher priority than genuine disarmament and the building of greater confidence and trust among the great powers who have life and death for the human race in their hands.

The United States is fixing its own economic sights high for the 1960's, but we do not see our goal as a one-nation project. It is a truism that economic development depends primarily on what is done by the country itself. But truisms are also true and we can only help others to help themselves. Our world has become so interdependent, so intertwined, that no country can go forward in isolation. The United States was one of the first to recognize that it is in the interest of all mankind to improve the lot of the less privileged nations, even as we discovered a century ago that to improve the lot of the poor was good for the economy as well as for the soul.

Consequently, when we think of the sixties as a decade of development, we are thinking in terms of a world-wide effort and a general advance, and in working toward this objective, we have sought to refashion our aid program, including increased emphasis to meet the needs of this decade.

Our new program will place primary emphasis on bringing as many countries as possible to the point of *self-sustaining growth* where they no longer need outside assistance. It is not just the goals and the initiatives which will depend primarily on the efforts of the newly developing countries themselves. The greater part of the resources required must also be generated by their own savings and export earnings. On our side, we are prepared to do our utmost to provide that vital margin of help to bridge the gap between their capabilities and their needs.

A study of development during the fifties also makes it clear that private capital has been a most important factor in promoting economic development. Indeed, the country planning economic development without taking into account the great help which foreign private enterprise can provide is like a tennis player who tries to play on one foot.

The resources available from private enterprise, both in terms of capital and know-how, are vastly greater than those available to government. With fairness, good will and good faith on both sides, cooperation between governments and private enterprise, domestic and foreign, can astonish the world with fruitful results for the benefit of people everywhere.

This brings me to another important facet of American economic development policy: Our concern with social justice. We do not have to argue the merits of social justice from the moral standpoint. But the practical economist realizes that it is also essential to any enduring and worthwhile economic development. Neither growth nor political stability can be enduring until all segments of society feel that they have a stake in their country's progress. This is what a distinguished Argentine Minister of Economy had in mind when he used the term "free *social* economy." We have seen it work in the United States; we know it can work elsewhere.

While the United States cannot make decisions for other countries on measures to foster social justice, we plan to offer inducements to make it attractive for any developing country to undertake internal changes in its own best interest. We are determined that the funds provided by the American taxpayers be used, not to enrich the few, but to improve the lot of the many.

Problems of savings, capital formation and external aid are vitally important for the economic growth of the underdeveloped countries. But to dwell on these without reference to the major contribution of international trade would be like casting *Hamlet* without a Prince of Denmark. Trade is the element which binds economies into a closely knitted interdependent world; progress made toward restoring and expanding a healthy multilateral trade has been one of the most encouraging features of the postwar world.

The growth of trade is indispensable to many of the underdeveloped economies which depend so heavily on exports for the materials and equipment so essential for their development. And it is hardly original to say that what happens to commodity prices is a powerful influence for good or bad in raw-material-producing countries, which most of the less developed nations are.

Much effort is currently being directed in the forums of the United Nations and elsewhere to exploring means for dealing with the varied and complex commodity problems which affect the welfare of underdeveloped countries. The possible role of commodity agreements and compensatory financing is receiving particularly close consideration. It is clear, however, that arrangements directed solely to the problem of price instability would not suffice to deal with a major aspect of the current commodity situation, for the fact is that oversupply and overcapacity are the most pressing problems now affecting current commodity markets. This is the single most important cause for the persistent downward pressure upon world commodity prices which has prevented these prices from responding fully to improvement in demand.

Obviously what is required above all in tackling commodity stabilization problems is cooperation between producing and consuming countries. And I want to renew the assurance given by President Kennedy that the United States is prepared to give its wholehearted cooperation in such endeavors.

Here, then, are some of our ideas about the tasks we face in the 1960's. They are by no means original, for we have benefited by the ideas and experiences of other nations. We, in turn, hope that our experience in the United States may contribute to the development of societies which have their own traditions, political concepts and economic goals.

The United States has no ambition to determine the future of the rest of the world. With the liberation of colonial peoples, dozens of new nations claim a voice in the affairs of the world community through their participation in the United Nations and its various agencies. We welcome their emergence on the world scene. We look forward to working with them to maintain and strengthen a world order which no great power can dominate.

As one crisis after another explodes around the globe, we may at times feel discouraged. Yet tyrannical systems have not succeeded in those areas of the world where workable alternatives exist, however different these alternatives may be from what we in the United States call capitalism or private enterprise.

But the crucial necessity is that aid shall be used effectively by governments willing to make economic and social reforms, so that it will benefit not only a few, but the people as a whole. It is necessary, therefore, that our economic efforts and our efforts in the social field should be united in a single grand design for human progress, for "old moulds have to be broken, and that society which does not translate economic progress is doomed."

I shall go further and say that plans for economic development that do not from the very outset take into account social needs must fail to achieve both their economic and human goals.

What good are impressive production figures if the vast majority of a country's population remains ill-clad, ill-housed, ill-fed, sick and illiterate? In a democratic society—in any good society—the only purpose of economic improvement is to provide a better life for all of the people. If our industrial development creates as many problems as it solves, are we improving the lot of the people? If, because of resistance to land reform, the fruits of improved agricultural methods fall into the pockets of a handful of landowners rather than into the empty baskets of the people themselves, why should the United Nations, the Food and Agricultural Organization and other organizations pour time and money into this so-called improvement?

Many countries have learned the wasteful folly of industrial development without social planning. In those satellite shantytowns which surround and deface so many proud cities, all the social evils which economic progress professes to cure, breed and multiply. With no jobs, inadequate shelter, unsanitary living conditions, scanty food and no schools or recreational opportunities, the standard of living and health goes down instead of up. The restraints of family, tribe and village are broken, giving way to the havoc of juvenile delinquency and crime.

Likewise improved agricultural efficiency without social reform often has similar results. Men and women, pushed off the land by machinery, drift into squalid urban centers and, with no provision to receive these newcomers and help them with their staggering new problems, the same old vicious circle is set in motion.

Then there are the stagnant, *status quo* societies where ambition seems buried under centuries of custom and inertia. Here the problems of the *old* shantytowns may be harder to deal with than those of the *new*. They are so much a part of the landscape that they are forgotten, taken for granted. Who cares about the subhuman dwellers who have lived there since the beginning of time? Is it worth trying to improve their lot if the people themselves don't apparently care?

I say it is not only worth it—it is imperative. A number of years ago, the world trend was described in the world situation as "the revolution of rising expectations." Since then the revolution has accelerated beyond anyone's dreams. Its nature, however, hasn't changed, only intensified.

But it isn't factories and roads and dams, in themselves, that people want. These are vastly important, both as symbols and as means to an end. What they really want are homes, food, jobs, decent clothes, an education for their children, a chance at life lived in freedom and dignity.

Land reform, urban development, community development, low-cost housing, education, nutrition, sanitation, hygiene, recreation, social welfare—these are the matters that we should be concerned with if we want our economic revolution to succeed.

For if people have a stake in what they are doing, they will work for it. And many social programs underpin or contribute to economic goals as well—some, such as education or housing, in a direct fashion; others, such as nutrition and sanitation, resulting in improved health indirectly. Insofar as all of these social programs lift the level of living of the people, they improve the chances for sustained economic progress.

So let us not just give lip service to "balanced economic and social development," as we call it; let us remember that the only point of economic development is social development—or, quite simply, a better life for people.

And remember, too, that it is a better life that people all over the world are demanding today with rising insistence. Each year, in millions and tens of millions, with colossal new-found energy, they are marching onto the stage of history; and that is their demand— a better life! No one can march these great hosts of humanity off the stage again. But it is within our power to help determine their future, whether, in their frustration, they will embrace fanaticism and violence, or whether they will be enabled to move in peace toward that better life which this age has brought within the vision of all.

We know that no final solutions should ever be expected in human affairs. We do not preach a counsel of perfection. There will be no point in history at which we shall be able to say that all crises have come to an end, and that we can live peacefully ever after. But all of us can learn to live calmly and constructively with continuing world crises if we persist in the search, to which this Council is dedicated, for new and more effective means of improving the welfare of human beings.

We have just crossed the threshold of a new decade. Let us so chart our course that this decade may be remembered, not as a period of power struggle, but as a decade of great triumphs in the age-old struggle to provide a better life for men everywhere.

THE UPHEAVAL OF A CONTINENT:

AFRICA

W W The transformation of the continent of Africa into a world force is referred to in many of Governor Stevenson's addresses. What follows was not an address in the formal sense but more of a lecture delivered during the course of a seminar. In it he again stresses his theme of aid to developing countries, and offers his basic philosophy on the subject of Africa. It also examines in detail the diverse elements at work in "this avalanche of nationhood."

Pliny, I think, was the Roman who remarked: "Out of Africa, always something new." And never was the aphorism truer than it is today. In the last decade, this ancient continent has brought forth more new nations in less time that at any point in the world's record, and still more are stirring in the womb of history.

This avalanche of nationhood has transformed the continent. And it has transformed the community of nations as well. As I can testify from daily experience, the pattern and direction of politics at the United Nations have been profoundly influenced by the arrival in New York of the African delegations in all their life and color and vivacity. Africa may be in time the last of the continents to begin the perilous

Remarks to an African Seminar at Lake Forest College, Lake Forest, Illinois, April 13, 1962.

W 171

passage to modernity. But few can deny that it is first in variety, exuberance and—today as at the time of Pliny—unpredictable newness.

It is well, too, that vigor and vitality are such marked characteristics of that sometimes rather elusive concept, the "African personality," for I doubt if any continent has ever faced so many and such daunting problems in working for its own modernization. Among these I hardly need mention climate and health.

In the great belt of tropical Africa—and most of the newly independent nations are situated there—the alternation of oppressive heat and torrential rain depresses human energy and, in many areas, creates special problems in agriculture: growing periods for food crops are insufficient, water comes in the most wasteful form of flood and famine, and uncovered soil can be battered into infertility in a season.

Some of the world's most crippling diseases also breed in tropical Africa's lakes and rivers, so the water which should be the greatest force for human development is a menace to life as well. No doubt modern science will master these problems and scourges, but let us not forget the toll they have taken for millennia of Africa's men and women, nor the peculiar and often costly problems they present to the search for better living.

The man-made inheritance of Africa is a dark record, too. Over wide areas, Arab slave traders reduced the peoples of East Africa to mere groups of hunters and hunted. In West Africa, the Western slave trade drained off a high proportion of able-bodied Africans across the Atlantic, while the rivalries and wars of rival slaving kingdoms condemned them to an environment of hostility and stagnation.

Then came colonial control. It established a fair number of quite arbitrary frontiers, especially in West and Central Africa, the boundaries being drawn at the point of encounter between rival European armies. The divisions cut across tribal lines and introduced new cultural barriers—between English speakers and French speakers and Portuguese speakers, for a time even German speakers. Colonialism was not a relatively unifying force as it was in British India or under Dutch rule in Indonesia. The new states have inherited a patchwork quilt of cultures and connections with leaders who cannot speak each other's languages, roads which do not meet at frontiers, communications systems which only work via Paris or London, and a profound mutual ignorance, even on the part of next-door neighbors.

And to these divisions one should add the presence of settlers from Europe who, beginning with the Boers in the seventeenth century, have tended to come in and engross the temperate areas. In the Union, the white minority has nearly 90 percent of the land, in Southern Rhodesia over 50 percent. In a continent in which land is still the basis of life of the bulk of Africans, these transfers have had profound disturbing social and cultural as well as economic effects.

Nor in this swift glance at history can we leave out the economic consequences of the European involvement in Africa. Once the slave trade gave way to legitimate commerce, Africa became an important source of raw materials for the developed Atlantic world. But only in the Union and to a lesser extent in the Congo and Southern Rhodesia did these valuable exports lead to the full transformation of the local economy.

In the South, the processes of modernization have gathered momentum, leading to transformed agriculture, good communications, wider education, the growth of industry and the growth of cities. But the South is not typical. The more normal inheritance of Africa is the colonial-type economy in which modernization is largely concentrated in the export sectors, producing minerals and tropical products—cocoa, coffee, peanuts, palm oil. In return for these exports, manufactured goods from Europe and America are imported and distributed largely by expatriate firms.

Roads and railways drain down to the ports, which are virtually the only great cities. Local food is provided by subsistence farming, and productivity is so low that food imports are going up. There is almost no industry—even in Nigeria the industrial sector provides only just over one percent of gross national product. And education is still not widespread enough to provide trained Africans for all the multifarious needs—in administration, management and teaching—of the modern society.

There is no doubt that the stimulus of Western needs set the processes of economic development in motion in Africa. Where, as in West Africa, the cash crops for export have been produced by African farmers, the direct and indirect stimulus to local income has been very great. But the economies did not develop much beyond this relatively closed circuit of trade with the developed metropolitan powers. And during the general stagnation of the thirties they actually slipped back.

Such, very briefly, is the historical heritage of the new African states. I do not believe it is possible to understand the perplexities of their nation building unless this background is kept clearly in mind. If you want a short summary of the last decade, I would say that the Africans have been striving on every front—political, economic, social —to transcend their inheritance and to do so at treble speed, in spite of all the painful obstacles that their heritage puts in their way.

The first task has clearly been nation building, creating independent states which can carry the burden of sovereignty, maintain a coherent political framework, and register its independent existence in the counsels of the United Nations. However, this is not a very straightforward task, because existing models are difficult to adapt. From the West, from the colonialists themselves, Africa learned to think in terms of the nation-state, master institution of the modern world. But nation-states evolved in Western Europe, where language and frontier more or less coincided. When the same concept was applied in Eastern Europe, the result was a system of states plagued and undermined by linguistic minorities.

In Africa, the natural unit of loyalty and organization is still the tribe, and we must not be surprised if, in state after state, the differences and fears of tribal groups lend a tremor of instability to all political dealings—Yomba against Hausa, Tiv against Fulani, Ashanti versus Fanti, Bamilikes against everyone.

The problem of welding tribes into units or nations or kingdoms, a task Europe struggled with for many centuries, is also complicated by voting issues. Western electorates are based on a certain underlying homogeneity. You vote as a Frenchman, no longer as a Norman or an *"homme du Midi."* But in Africa, tribal voting is the most natural mode. In which case, how do smaller tribes protect them-

selves against larger tribes who may be voted into a permanent ascend-
ancy?

It is largely because of these shaky foundations to modern nation
statehood that I think we should be not too quick to jump to our feet
and cry aloud our blame for African leaders whose rule appears more
authoritarian than we like. For one thing, African training in constitutional government—a process which took a millennium to evolve
in the West—has been almost nonexistent. Colonial rule has been
wholly authoritarian. The governor's will was the ultimate arbiter.

Although valuable concepts of civil and constitutional law grew
up among African lawyers, especially in British and French territories,
and valuable lessons of orderly administration were learned wherever
education gave Africans the chance to advance, political agitation was
still checked by prison sentences or deportation. Full popular consultation began only a decade before independence—in the Congo, the
period was only eighteen months—but in any circumstance, this is
not a long preparation for a form of government which elsewhere
took centuries to develop.

Moreover, our form of government relies so much on consensus and
on compromise that we don't practice it either when the strains of
social change or political upheaval become too great. France solved
her Algerian crisis under a considerable measure of concentrated
power and personal rule. There is, to all intents and purposes, a single-
party government in Northern Ireland. There certainly is in the Deep
South.

While we cannot condone imprisonment without trial or perversions
of justice, wherever they occur, we should not, therefore, be too
much surprised at single-party rule in Africa, nor adopt a "holier
than thou" tone in our criticism. These new states are under strains
which have made us, in our time, accept stronger rule.

To hold the new nation together, therefore, is the first task. The
second is to give it a framework which will not stifle further advance.
A tribe, even a group of small tribes, does not necessarily make up
a modern unity. Many of Africa's new states are hardly viable in their
present form. One thinks of the poor fringe states of the Sahara to

which Paris must still pay a large share of their budgets. One thinks of tiny Togo, representing only a part of the vigorous Ewe tribe, of the sliver of Dahomey, or Ruanda and Urundi, unique in Africa in pressure of population on inadequate resources. Such states—and even larger ones—must be part of wider communities or associations if they are to create the conditions of modern life.

This is, after all, an age of wider units. The world scene is dominated by the giants of America and Russia. Europe is drawing closer together. When African leaders look beyond their frontiers to wider pan-African perspectives, they simply reflect a realization of the scale of operation modern society increasingly demands.

And the vision is more than a mere imitation of existing modes of organization. Africa desperately needs to modify the basis of its traditional, colonial economy. The resources needed to develop a whole continent cannot be earned simply by continuing and expanding the existing pattern of exports. Cocoa already threatens a world surplus. If all the current economic plans of the independent African nations are realized, it should not be long before other surpluses appear—peanuts, palm oil, bananas (on the verge of surplus already), citrus, sugar cane. Science cannot stretch the Western stomach to consume all the products science can produce, and nowhere is research into tropical cash crops more searching and effective than in West Africa.

Export income will continue to be a vital part of Africa's earnings, but it cannot provide a large surplus. On the contrary, prudent planners are now estimating that a 20 percent fall in tropical prices may have to be envisaged over the next five years.

Nor is Africa likely to earn surpluses by exporting cheap manufactures, on the model of developing Asia. Its labor force is not yet skilled enough for the manufactures in fact to be cheap. In any case, Asia has pretty well pre-empted this field. There is left only one alternative—to intensify Africa's *internal* market, to turn to more intensive food-producing farming, to processing local materials, to import substitution, to all the hundred and one ways in which agriculture can be modernized and industry introduced and goods exchanged in the local market.

I see no other way for African advance, and I believe that this *is* the economic reality behind the political dreams of wider African association.

But the development presupposes economic units large enough for this internal development to make good technical sense. Snippets of countries do not develop internal markets. They must be linked to larger ones. And at this point the challenge to Africa's nation builders becomes acute.

The reasons for disintegration are as various as the states themselves. Certainly one reason has been the desire of rich provinces not to contribute their wealth to the support of poorer neighbors. Yet the break-up has been a grave set-back to African unity and growth. One has only to compare the élan and stability of the Nigerian federation with the uncertainties of some of its neighbors, to realize that regional unity, possibly as a prelude to continental unity, is a path that Africa must try, in spite of all its difficulty, to follow.

So far I have referred only to the problems of nation building in all-African states. But I must add two further difficulties—the extra edge of trouble and bitterness added to the African scene by the troubles of the settler communities, and, in and behind all other issues, envenoming and complicating them, the fact of the cold war.

The settler dilemma is familiar. Throughout history, men and women of more evolved techniques and greater material power come in and take up land in a less developed continent. By superior organization, they impose their pattern of life on top of the old society. The Aryans did so in India, the "sons of Han" have done so from one end of China to the other.

Sometimes the local peoples are too primitive to survive the impact. European settlers in North America and Australia virtually wiped out the earlier inhabitants. Sometimes—as in China—the absorption of conqueror and conquered into a single culture occurs.

But there are also areas in which the settler minority neither wipes out nor absorbs the original inhabitants. It simply sets them to work in the new society they, the settlers, direct and control. This, more or less, happened in Latin America. In Africa, it has happened in Algeria, in Kenya, in the Rhodesias, to some extent in the Portuguese territories and, of course, in the Union.

This pattern is almost by definition the most explosive in the modern world. All social lines of cleavage—power, wealth, education—converge at the color line. In a society of helots, this may not matter, since, by definition, the helot has no rights. But Western society is shot through with the concept of rights, above all of equal rights to vote, to be educated, to participate in society.

In Africa, the enormous acceleration of change since the war has meant that the vast African majority, still largely without experience and education, wants the political voting rights which will give it effective power. And those with power now, fearing not only for their own privileges, but also for the consequences of inexperience, fight the advance of popular African representation.

If there is a solution to this dilemma, it is that the leaders of the new African majority should be men of such wisdom and discipline that they can inspire their followers with the same self-control. It is that the guarantees given the settler minority should fully safeguard their rights and give them the chance to go on working for the economic growth of the community.

One hears, instead, frightening talk of a "white" military alliance "to stem the tide of black nationalism." This prospect, bringing with it a total polarization of the continent, is a tragedy we must strain every nerve to avoid.

The more so in that it leads straight to the further polarization of the cold war. I do not know whether Russia has decided to make Africa the scene of a major confrontation with Western influence and interests. On the morrow of independence, all Africa's links, above all the vital link of language, have been with the West. It is not surprising that Russia has sought by offers of economic aid, arms and diplomatic relations to insert its own presence. Nor is it surprising that the Communists tried to fish so aggressively in the troubled waters of the Congo, and that free African states have been ready to travel to Moscow and establish new relationships, almost as a hallmark, a badge of independent statehood.

Does this amount to a shift of loyalties? I doubt it. I doubt, too, whether Russia so far has done much more than exploit obvious points of entry—Guinea's abandonment by France, for instance, or Lumumba's wild searching round for allies against the Belgians. I have little impression of an overwhelming Soviet concentration of effort on Africa. In fact, in Guinea, to mention one example, the Russians either did not or could not mount an overwhelmingly successful effort of aid, and their contact evoked considerable Guinean disillusionment.

But I confess that I would not count on Communist restraint if the polarization between a "white" South and a "black" North were to become the central fact of African politics. The openings for Communist support and infiltration in a long-drawn-out struggle would be legion—arson, sabotage, strikes, boycotts, all these are possible weapons of a movement of African rejection and disobedience financed and supported from abroad.

It is unrealistic to suppose that the Communists would highmindedly give up all opportunities to foster and extend disintegration if such opportunities were handed them on a platter. The lesson of the Congo suggests that chaos is their friend, and they can gain most by implacable conflict between the races. And any such war in the Center and South would create havoc among the "moderates" further north. The pressures toward extremism would be universal.

These, then, are the problems and dilemmas of nation building in Africa in our contemporary world. No one can suppose that the passage to modernization will be easy. On the contrary, it is, I suppose, true to say that the easy tasks in Africa have all been accomplished by now. Decolonization in purely African states is complete. Now they face the vast problems of development and construction. Where decolonization is difficult—in other words, in settler states— the moment of crisis approaches. The next decade in Africa will be much more turbulent and much more dangerous than the last.

What, then, can we, as Americans, do in the troubled days ahead to preserve an element of stability in Africa? It is in Africa's interest. It is in our own interest. But it demands, I believe, more vision and generosity than we have shown so far.

Let me briefly outline, in a form of shorthand, what I consider to be essential features of an American approach to Africa's profound dilemma:

First of all, I would like to see us measure and accept the obligation to give free Africa its essential tool of advance—which is education.

No one who has had the good fortune to visit those parts of Africa where education is already of long standing—I am thinking of southern Ghana or Nigeria or Senegal—can doubt for a moment that a fifty-year tradition of education brings into being trained Africans able to guide their country's destinies. Equally, the Congo, in which preliminary education was splendid and final education all but nil, foundered for lack of this trained leadership. I believe there were something like seventeen college graduates in the Congo when independence came—for a country of fourteen million, in a territory as large as India!

I think, therefore, the aim in education over the next two decades should be to give 50 percent of Africa's children a primary schooling; between 5 and 10 percent should go to secondary school, 2 percent or more to technical training, and 1 percent to new and expanded universities in Africa. These targets refer only to the short run. A broader program would be extemely costly. But it is the core of any significant advance. And it should be embedded in wider programs of assistance:

I would like to see aid to farming, above all to cooperatives, extension services and modernized techniques; local processing is another allied field.

I would like to see aid to infrastructure, designed to foster as far as possible the regional unities Africa so clearly requires.

I would like to see a transport and communications grid opening up contact between the regions.

I would like to see river systems developed as unities, and hydroelectricity shared across the frontiers.

I would like to see us support every African initiative to set up joint development banks or currency zones or common markets, and where —as between a Monrovia grouping and a Casablanca grouping—there are divisions between African states, I would think it the wise course for Western policy to encourage greater unity.

Similarly, I would hope to see our influence used to end the divisions between those African states that are linked to the Common Market and those outside the association. Such ex-colonial divisions should not still be projected from Europe into Africa.

While aid on these lines should help to maintain the stability of independent Africa today, we must also be ready to use the United Nations instrument when, as happened in the Congo, local order breaks down. After all, the alternative to an international intervention would be the reimposition of Western control at the point of Western guns. Africa has got rid of the West too recently to welcome its return, and direct Western intervention, in the Congo or elsewhere, would have invited Soviet intervention, probably with strong African support. This we have brilliantly avoided in the Congo so far, and the pattern is not irrelevent to the future.

I have saved for the last the most important component of nation building in Africa. It is self-help. It is hard work—by Africans. The idea that "freedom" means that everything is free is sweet poison to any languid, lighthearted people. Now that freedom has come, now that the white masters' discipline is no more, the African must discipline himself. Foreign aid is no equivalent for self-help, and that the Lord helps them who help themselves is as true among pagans and Moslems as Christians.

Having worked half a century to maintain our living standards, the Africans now ask a share for themselves. And to get it they have to work for it. To get it, if need be, the African whip will bite more cruelly than the white man's.

We must be clear about our aims—an independent Africa, united, if possible, in a single comity, or at least joining together in viable regions. To this vast emergent area, we must pledge the capital and technical assistance needed to break the closed circuit of the old colonial economy and to build up a large, developed internal market.

It will take time, perhaps fifty years. Education, above all, can perhaps not be achieved in less. But if the time is long, all the more reason to begin now. As Marshal Lyautey said when told a tree would take fifty years to grow: "All the more reason for planting it today."

Yet I know there will be many voices raised to ask why the Western powers should make any special effort or occupy themselves with this great upheaval in a continent not their own. To this I would answer, first, that in terms of general human solidarity, we cannot, we the wealthy West, turn our back on such a mass of human poverty and human aspiration. But I would go further and say that vis-à-vis Africa, the responsibility of the Atlantic powers goes much further than a general moral obligation. The white races have involved themselves by historical decision to go into Africa. By decisions in history, Europeans, like the Arabs, have taken Africans out of Africa. The races have been mixed, not by act of God, but by act of man, and the men who made the decisions made them all too often in brutal and inhuman greed.

I personally cannot read Lincoln's Second Inaugural without wondering whether the justice and retribution of that great address do not apply far beyond the Civil War to all the relations between black and white, to all the debts that must be paid and all the injustices that must be remedied, and all the hate there is to anneal and cancel.

Today we have the resources for a tremendous act of historical justice. I only hope we have the vision and the will.

A LOST SENSE OF MASTERY:
THE ATLANTIC COMMUNITY

❦ ❦ *While Africa was awakening, the Atlantic world was reawakening, and in Governor Stevenson's view, the Atlantic world was also finding a lost sense of mastery. This address, delivered in Rome, was a comparison of the world of the thirties and the world of the sixties. Cautious but optimistic, Governor Stevenson argues that in spite of all the current problems and challenges, the Atlantic world—strengthened in the sixties by the Common Market and its associated institutions—had in its power to bring about "a new birth of freedom." It is a note he also sounds with emphasis in other statements.*

However stern the test of nerves the Soviet Union may choose to present to the West, one thing is certain: The Atlantic world has the reserves and the resolution to face the challenge.

Not only are we united in a common system of defense. Not only have we "brought in the new world to redress the balance of the old." I believe another, profounder change has taken place. We have recovered our sense of destiny, our sense of molding history, our sense of not being simply borne away by a torrent of events we cannot control.

Mr. Khrushchev may boast that history is on his side. The fact is, however, that whatever is new, whatever is fresh and original in the

Excerpts from an address to the Italian Society for International Organization, Rome, Italy, July 26, 1961.
❦ 183

political management of man's affairs in the last two decades has in fact emerged within the Atlantic world. While Russia and China are repeating the most ancient patterns of despotism, aggression and imperialism, the Western nations are seeking on the contrary new patterns of free association between men and peoples.

No doubt, we are only at the beginning of a new phase of dynamic experiment. But already, I suggest, it is restoring to us a lost sense of mastery, and with it a new surge of confidence in the viability of free society, its vast resourcefulness in seeking out the new routes which mankind has to follow if it is to survive.

Perhaps the best way of measuring this new sense of capacity and promise is to compare our present Atlantic posture with the world of the thirties. Then, divided and disorganized, we watched Nazi tyranny carry through its mounting spiral of violence, and we never formed that overwhelming concentration of defensive power which might conceivably have checked Hitler's crazy ambition.

Today, NATO links America to Europe in intimate and unshakable alliance. If Mr. Khrushchev does not understand that the rights of Berlin are a fundamental concern of America as well as of Europe, then it must mean either that language has no meaning for him or that he is as great a gambler as Hitler himself. I do not believe he is, and the fall of that earlier gambler should surely deter him, if he is suffering at this time from the Soviet disease Stalin once defined as "dizziness through success."

In the thirties Western unpreparedness and lack of common defense were doubled by conflicting economic interests. The great depression still cast its blight. Europe struggled to get out of the trough by separate, inward-looking, mutually incompatible policies behind high-built walls, quota systems and inconvertible currencies. Attempts at common action, such as the World Economic Conference, broke up in a mixture of incoherence and irresponsibility, and, on the part of some delegates, even a certain levity. No overriding sense of continuity checked separated interests. The unity that was lacking in defense was repeated in economic policy.

Today, on the contrary, the pattern of policy sketched in at Bretton Woods, developed in our new postwar international institutions and applied triumphantly in the Marshall Plan has created a wholly new mood of consultation and cooperation. Our dilemmas and difficulties are as great as ever. But now we approach them together. And since none is solvable in isolation, the new approach gives us new hope of success.

In the thirties our Western relations with the rest of the world were still those of traditional domination—the explicit domination of colonial control, the covert domination of economic penetration. And the slump of the thirties deprived this domination of its earlier dynamic role as a stimulation of local growth and investment. All through the underdeveloped world, this was a decade of stagnation—stagnation in economic activity, and a sort of dull stagnation, too, in ideas and political inventiveness.

Today we are launched on a new revolution of which we do not see the end. Full political independence, whatever the hazards, is accepted as the Western goal in the developing world, and we are dedicating a wholly new seriousnes and urgency to the task of seeing that the new independence is underpinned with the capital and technical aid needed to make it an economic reality.

And—perhaps the most vital change of all—there is a new mood in the West. Thirty years ago it was not too difficult to believe in the twilight of the brave civilization which had been perhaps the strongest growing point in human history for at least a thousand years. Confidence in free institutions was shaken by their collapse in Europe. The economic system seemed uncontrollable and foundering in irrationality. Nationalism from being a stimulus had become a curse. Sterility and pessimism paralyzed thought, or, by reaction, took it to the violent extremes of right and left. It was of this despairing period that the poet Yeats wrote: "Things fall apart, the centre will not hold." Europe in the thirties was a continent in which the doors were closing and the lights were going out.

I do not deny the perils of the new decade. But I sense everywhere a new mood of hope and mastery. Nations which had rejected free institutions as ineffective and unessential learned in the totalitarian darkness to see their validity as a new revelation.

The economic life of the West is no longer a system mysterious even to its own practitioners. It is the instrument of a fuller, more prosperous life for all. Above all, the possibility of inventiveness and inspiration, the belief that a common purpose can be expressed through Western institutions and that history is an arena of opportunity, not of blind determinism, restores to the Atlantic world a new dimension of excitement and hope.

"The former things" have, in a real measure, passed away. We are faced with what is, in fact, the crowning privilege of free men —the possibility of making, if not all things new—for this belongs to Providence alone—at least some things new, and among them the most vital relations and institutions of our common life.

How has this change come about? Perhaps we must in some degree thank the Communists. Their pressure, their challenge have prevented us from slipping back into the lazy temptations of our own affluence. But I believe this is only a small part of the matter. Hitler challenged us, after all, and we produced no creative response.

No, I believe we have come to a new consensus about the meaning of our civilization and that the new insights it has brought offer the clue to our new performance. Let me take three psychological "breakthroughs" which, I think, we have witnessed in the last decade, each of them central to the new strength and vitality of our Atlantic world.

The first insight fixes the limits of nationalism. We in the West who first created the nation-state are now transcending it. We now see that once science and technology have made the world a single neighborhood, we cannot assume that some hidden hand will harmonize conflicting national interests, or that individual nations can each practice blind self-assertion and still secure the wider good of all.

By trade, by investment, by contact, by influence, we impinge constantly on each other. We must create the framework within which these contacts can be fruitful, not destructive. The blind war of Teuton and Frank, the most terrifying tribal war of history, has had to be ended. In its place, we see the attempt to remake Europe, as much of Europe as can freely act, on the basis of a common social, economic and political life. Such efforts, inconceivable in 1919, have opened up a whole new arena of opportunity in the West. And I hope as an American I can express my pride in the fact that the first great postwar venture in international solidarity, the Marshall Plan, had as one of its specific aims the fostering of unity and the encouragement of a joint attack upon Europe's desperate postwar ills.

A second "breakthrough" in our thinking is concerned, I believe, with the role of government and of private institutions in our economy. We have happily lost the sharp "either-or" of the thirties—the neurotic fear of government action on the right, the obsessive fear of the operations of the market on the left.

That government has the over-all responsibility to ensure the general growth and dynamism of the free economy only a few extremists would now deny. But I notice among all the Socialist parties of Europe a greater readiness to admit that private management is often a handier instrument in the lively and diverse production of wealth than are large government corporations.

This attitude makes possible the successes of our new mixed economy. Italy's example is outstanding, and even incredible to one like myself who was here during the last war and saw the havoc and destruction. In France, under the brilliant leadership of Jean Monnet, government investment strengthened the base of the economy, government forecasts continue to guide and stimulate the business world, and a new generation of managers and entrepreneurs have broken the restrictive traditions of the past and shown, in the Common Market, what the restoration of wide competition in an expanding market can bring about.

We hear boasts of Soviet rates of growth. We forget, I think, that they have been more than equaled in Germany, France and Italy in the last few years.

This expansion of the market could not, of course, have occurred if prosperity had been confined, as in the early days of industrialization, to the propertied few. Other coincidences of public and private economic policies have spread a new well-being throughout our world —the European invention of social insurance, helping to underpin popular consumption, the American revolution of high wages and small profits, creating the popular market for the new mass industries based upon popular consumption.

As Mr. Khrushchev remarked to me in America: "The slaves of

capitalism live well." And the reason is the public and private commitment of our new mixed economy to share as widely as possible the wealth which our advanced technology, properly managed, can pour out.

There are critics, I know, who suggest that this rise in mass consumption reflects a dangerous long-term tendency of wages to outstrip productivity and of inflation to creep or gallop us to disaster. And this fear certainly lent a touch of immobility to some aspects of American economic policies in the past decade.

Here again, however, I believe we have wisdom and flexibility enough in our new Atlantic economy to avoid the danger, and in one member-community this has already been done. In Federal Germany today employment is so high that the unemployment insurance levy has been suspended for the time being. Yet inflation is marginal. The means—responsible trade unions, alert government policy, general economic education, wily management—are not unrepeatable elsewhere. Germany's achievement is just one more of the varied and convincing proofs of economic vitality today in the West.

And from this new capacity to create sustained prosperity and this new realization that nationalism is not enough, I would derive a third great revolution in our thinking—our readiness to see the Family of Man as a community engaged altogether in the common tasks of modernization, and to accept the responsibility of those of us who have already "broken through" to affluence to help with our capital and our skills the peoples who struggle along behind us over the same route.

A few years ago who had heard of the developed "North" assisting the peoples of the largely underdeveloped "South"? It is to my mind the best evidence of our new vitality that concepts which direct our experience in new creative ways now find so wide and so rapid an acceptance in public thinking. We no longer shrink from what is fresh and original. Rather we welcome it because our vigor is now aroused for new opportunities and new tasks.

I do not deny the shadows in the picture. The wealth we have gained is not always used for noble purposes—life before the television screen is hardly the "last, best end of man." Our spreading urbanization creates, all too often, an ugly, stunting way of life. Each can make his own list of modern monstrosities.

My point is not to give the West a final accolade of perfection, but simply to underline the ways in which, I firmly believe, vitality and freedom of action have been restored. I am profoundly convinced that we have turned some dangerous corners in history, emerged from some blind alleys and set our feet once more on roads which can lead us away from stagnation and despair.

Now it is to the future that we must look with our new insights, and ensure that the last ten years are not a brief feverish outbreak of activity before the final dissolution, but, on the contrary, the first act of a great new drama for Western man.

Where should the next steps take us? Our first task is, I suggest, to save the United Nations from the shattering blows of the Communist bloc. And there is, I think, no better way than to finish the work we have begun inside the Atlantic world.

We know that we cannot enlarge and perfect international organization unless the less fortunate and newer states expand and prosper, and thereby develop that immunity to tyrannical solutions which is our great postwar achievement in Western Europe. And we know they cannot do it without our help.

In turn, we cannot expand and prosper without common purposes and common institutions. Our community is full of the partial experiments of unity—common markets, free trade associations, a joint action by central banks, consultations through NATO, the first attempts at common policies on trade and aid through the new Atlantic group for economic development, common action for aid in India and Pakistan through the Western consortium. All these separate activities betray our profound realization that we have to act together.

But we have not accepted and formalized our unity so that it can cease to be a set of expedients and become a great political act with profound historical repercussions. This, then, is our task. The means of attaining it are, I suggest, the further development and strengthening of the Common Market and its associated institutions. Through this process our economic and political evolution, a new dynamism at the heart of the Atlantic Community, exercises the strongest kind of attraction, leading the whole Atlantic area toward the structuring of its political and economic unity.

We must act as a community both with regard to our own international problems and in our efforts to assist other nations facing the overwhelming problems of development. By the pursuit of liberal policies we can do much to ease the dislocations and reorientations made necessary by this growing community, but we should not allow ourselves to be diverted from the great task at hand.

And just as the success and dynamism of the Common Market has proved the chief incentive for Britain to reconsider the issue of entry, I believe that the growing attractions of a thriving market— 200 million strong in Europe—will exercise an overwhelming attraction upon the North American market. One quickly envisions a new community of open trade, investment and opportunity stretching, if you will, from Honolulu to the marches of the Soviet zone. In my view, both Britain and America will gain very greatly from the liveliness of the competition which imaginative management and statesmanlike trade unionism will offer us from Western Europe. And the knitting together of our common life at the economic level will hasten the devising of the new joint political institutions which association between continents now demands.

It is sometimes said, I know, that such a drawing together of the Western powers will leave the uncommitted world fearful and suspicious that what they confront is a new and mightier form of imperialism. And as we succeed we will hear more of this propaganda from the Communists.

But we do not envisage Atlantic unity in selfish isolation. It must be accompanied by a relentless effort to prepare other great areas for local development and then, if they wish, for free association with the Atlantic nucleus. We have learned from the rhythm of history that in the early days of modernization and economic growth total association with other, more developed economies does not necessarily lead to local development.

Europe had to break away from free trade with Britain in the nineteenth century and build up its own industrial structure. America followed the same course. It is only now after decades of local growth that we can come together again as more or less competitive equals, and, in an open market, take new and full advantage of specialization and the division of labor.

The emergent continents will, I believe, follow the same pattern. As modernization and growth build up in Latin America, in Africa, in Asia, we can look forward to new forms of free association. Today their main concern must be for their own advance. Yet we can assist profoundly in the process. Our capital and skills must be sent out to them to the maximum degree at which they can be absorbed. And—perhaps an even more vital point at this stage—our trade policies must also encourage their expansion.

For this reason I welcome the trend in policy in Europe today which suggests that all developing nations, particularly the nations of Africa, should have free access to Europe's widening market, sell their goods there with the minimum of obstacles and yet be encouraged to set up reasonable protection for their own infant enterprises. This may involve readjustment in the West. But in the longer run, flourishing, expanding "Common Markets" in free Asia, in Africa, in Latin America will be better partners in trade—if they wish for partnership —and firmer associates in the building of a better world than countries still dogged by stagnation and falling standards of life.

Thus there is no real contradiction between greater unity in the Atlantic world and unfettered growth elsewhere. On the contrary, each helps the other and all our plans for closer cooperation in the West should include bold policies for the creation of healthy common markets elsewhere.

The whole process has much more than an economic aspect. Our world has to discover the proper instruments of organized unity. We cannot shake ourselves to pieces in the terrible shock of another war.

Our chief need is to discover the minimum institutions under which men may live at peace, and I believe that just as two centuries ago the thirteen colonies were the nucleus of America's continental federation, and a hundred years ago the Risorgimento brought unity to Italy and a German Customs Union preceded a united Germany, so now, by working out in the free world the concrete content of intercontinental cooperation, we can carry on the creative work of Western man in devising at new levels political institutions under which growth, vitality and freedom can all be combined.

The concept of a "more perfect union" cannot be exhausted until its forums embrace all God's children. We must begin where we can —first in the Atlantic arena, and then in building the economic and social foundations of unity in neighboring continents.

And if our building is secure—if we combine national variety with common institutions, if we use judiciously the power of the state and the vitality of industrial initiative—it is at least possible that the new patterns may prove attractive enough to penetrate even the rigidities of the Communist bloc. The tides of history do not run all one way and if we can take our new wave of Atlantic unity and inventiveness at its flood, who knows to what good fortune it may not run in the years ahead?

Perhaps we are so beset with the risks of our day that we almost forget its opportunities. The truth is surely that ours is the first generation of man to lift even by a hairsbreadth the iron weight of necessity. Science, technology and capital, neutral in themselves, are the new instruments in our hands awaiting great tasks and great visions.

Our eyes are raised so little from the aggressive patterns of the past that the first purposive massive use of our resources is still aimed at destruction—eighty to ninety billions of dollars a year are poured into weapons to kill each other, into the arming of men, into research in the warlike uses of our power. Yet this same figure is also the measure of our immense physical elbow room, provided we raise our eyes from a tribal past and look forward to the opportunities of a cooperative future.

I sometimes think that our means have now so far outstripped our aims that we hardly know what to make of our own abundance. For this reason, the aim of building a closer, stronger Atlantic community, associating freely with the emergent continents, has far more than economic significance.

It presents us with a goal bold enough to give direction to our thought and purpose to our superabundant physical resources. It ends the curious, political vacuum in which only the enemies of freedom appear to speak for the future and only the professed materialists speak in the ideal terms of brotherhood and a world made one— by the tyranny of Communism.

These visions, which catch the imagination of the young from one end of the world to the other, need not be the monopoly of the Communist world. The free nations of the West were the ancient cradle of liberal ideas. They can recapture the world's imagination if they show in actual daily effort that their policies are aimed at the unity and welfare of all mankind.

I end where I began. In the last decade, we have recaptured momentum. We have begun to fashion the instruments of a wholly new approach to world affairs. The Atlantic world has left behind the stagnation and frustration of the twenties and thirties. On every side the horizons are opening again, and we are recalled to our old role of pioneers in devising societies ample enough and vital enough to accommodate the energies of free men.

Yet the trumpet still gives an uncertain sound. And we still give an uncertain response. We have not yet gathered up the lessons of the last decade and made them into a grand strategy for the next. The means we have, the ends are still unsure.

We have it in our power to bring about a "new birth of freedom." What we need to mobilize now are our energy and our will.

TWO VIEWS OF HISTORY:
THE AMERICAS

🎗 🎗 *In June of 1961, Governor Stevenson had conducted a nineteen-day diplomatic reconnaissance to Latin America covering much the same ground as he had when a private citizen fifteen months earlier. In asking Governor Stevenson to undertake his 1961 mission in behalf of the Alliance for Progress, President Kennedy had stressed that our cooperation in this hemisphere should not be limited to the economic and social fields, but should extend to all fields manifesting "the diversity of the culture and tradition of our people." The President added: "I think there are few people in the United States better qualified than Adlai Stevenson to examine and discuss these possibilities." In a report issued after his return, Governor Stevenson bluntly enumerated the problems, but said he felt the governments of Latin America now realized they had to translate economic and social reforms into action. The following address, delivered the day after he returned from another diplomatic mission—this one to Europe—again concentrated on the Alliance for Progress and the problems of the Americas that still demanded effort but did not defy solution.*

I am delighted to be here—even though a bit breathlessly.

Yesterday, on Easter Sunday, I was in the Cathedral of Seville in a new community called Europe. This morning I am in an older community called Pan-America—and on Pan-American Day at that.

Address to the Organization of American States on the occasion of Pan-American Day, Washington, D. C., April 15, 1963.

🎗 194

These two communities of free and independent nations, along with others still a-borning, represent the real wave of the future. And there is no better time to point that out than on Pan-American Day.

This is the seventy-third anniversary of the First International Conference of American States, which created the International Union of American Republics. This is the thirtieth anniversary of the Good Neighbor Policy, and it is the fifteenth anniversary of the Charter of the Organization of American States. Less than two years ago we joined in the Declaration of Punte del Este, with its exhilarating promise of things to come; and less than a month ago seven nations joined in the Declaration of Central America, heralding a hopeful trend toward economic integration in that region.

Between 1890 and 1963 there have been many other landmarks—bearing such names as Montevideo, Buenos Aires, Lima, Havana, Rio de Janeiro and Chapultepec—at all of which we moved forward toward the goal of an inter-American community that works as a functioning, healthy community ought to work.

Along the way, the International Union of American Republics has become the Organization of American States. The Council has acquired three dependent organs, six specialized organizations and six more special agencies and commissions. And at long last we established, a few years ago, the much-needed Inter-American Development Bank. So over the years we have erected, bit by bit, the institutional underpinning of an inter-American community.

Just how effective that machinery is in time of peril was demonstrated to all the world last October. At the height of the debate during the first meeting of the United Nations Security Council on the Cuban crisis, I was passed a small slip of paper. It told me—and I quickly told the others—that the Council of the Organization of American States, acting provisionally as the Organ of Consultation under the Rio Treaty, had unanimously condemned the clandestine and provocative installation of Soviet missile bases within the Western Hemisphere and was taking immediate action to bring about a quarantine of Castro's satellite island. I can tell you that in that fleeting moment I rejoiced mightily in the result of our work over the past seventy-two years. And so, some day in the not distant future, will the stricken and subjugated people of our sister nation in the Caribbean.

And if I may digress for a moment here, I should like to say that during my recent journey in Europe and Morocco I received emphatic and universal assurances of support for the Cuban policy we have pursued, both during and since the October crisis. There is particular appreciation of the cool-headed, persevering determination that has characterized the response of the American governments to that crisis and its aftermath.

As President Kennedy has pointed out, there is no instant, easy solution for Communism in Cuba—or anywhere else, I could add. Those who would provoke us into extreme and reckless measures are not serving the best interests of either the United States or the solidarity of our hemisphere—or, for that matter, the long-suffering Cuban people, whose thirst for freedom Castro cannot quench. "In times like the present," as Abraham Lincoln once said at another critical moment, "men should utter nothing for which they would not willingly be responsible through time and in eternity." That is still good advice.

Cuba's freedom will be restored and when it is, it will be our challenging task to make sure that Moscow will never again succeed in converting the tyranny of a Batista into the tyranny of a Castro. And no less will it be our task to make sure that freedom will continue to flourish in this hemisphere long after Castroism has passed into history.

I have one other observation to offer on the Cuban crisis. After our experience with it, it is incomprehensible to me that anyone still thinks of the United Nations and the Organization of American States as alternative instruments of security and peace-keeping. The co-ordinated and complementary use of both instruments was indispensable in the Cuban crisis, which eloquently demonstrated that the regional system and the universal system each have their separate roles in such threats to the peace.

The same point is valid with respect to economic and social affairs as well as to security affairs: The United Nations agencies and the inter-American agencies work hand in glove as one pursues the Decade of Development and the other the Alliance for Progress.

The global agencies and the regional agencies are no more in conflict than are the regional communities of nations in conflict with each other. And I dare say that in the years ahead we shall all be constructing an even wider Western community embracing us all.

Why not? The new Europe can no more look inward than the separate nations which comprise it; nor can the inter-American community. Already the Europeans are showing an increased interest in playing an active and constructive role in the Alliance for Progress, and an awareness of the problems posed by the Common Market for raw-material-producing countries of this hemisphere. The interaction between these communities, once separated and now joined by the Atlantic Ocean, will continue and grow until we see the still wider Western community not as a dream but as an imperative.

In any event, as we look back over the story of the growth of the inter-American community, we can see that Simón Bolívar was right 137 years ago when he first wrote of his vision of an alliance of American states. The Great Liberator, of course, was to be disappointed during his own lifetime; but he took the long view and history has shown how profoundly right he was.

For as we look around at the postwar world, it is clear that the emergence of regional communities of free nations is the historic trend of the twentieth century and a dynamic political movement. The American republics have shown the way; now regionalism is highly advanced in Western Europe; it is stirring in Southeast Asia and in North and Central Africa; and it will come to pass—if slowly— elsewhere. These regional communities are the structural framework of an eventual system of world order within the larger frame of the United Nations.

But even while celebrating the fact of our community it would not be prudent to recall all the virtues and forget all the faults of the past. This would make it seem all too easy when, in fact, it is extraordinarily difficult; for all that holds our community together is free consent. And while this is the best, indeed the only durable, way to build workable communities, it also is the most difficult method of construction.

So it is worth mentioning in passing that in the process of building an inter-American community we have tended too often to consider a conference as a substitute for action. We have been better at writing declarations than in carrying them out. We have been slow, at times, to modernize our doctrines and our institutions. And until the quite recent past my own country has not been entirely innocent of the charge that we tended to take Latin America for granted. And at times we have seemed to be rather more united in what we are *against* than what we are *for*.

Not so today. I like to think that the Charter of Punta del Este was much more than another inter-American declaration of high ideals, much more than just another milestone in the unfolding story of the inter-American community. I like to think that this was the point at which we reached agreement on what we are *for*—and went forth to do something big about it.

But that was twenty months ago. And now we hear complaints that enough has not happened, that progress has been too slow.

I was thinking of this last night as I flew across the Atlantic. Behind me lay a Europe which has some temporary political disabilities—some doubts, some disagreements, which have imposed a pause on the steady and dramatic trend toward widening unity in the postwar European world.

But I was in a Europe which also is prospering as never before, which knows by far the highest standard of living in its history, which is competent, bold and renaissant; so much so that one wonders whether it is relevant any more to refer to it as the Old World, for there is so much that is young and fresh and vital about it.

Perhaps inevitably, as I flew home across the Atlantic, my thoughts drifted back to the Europe of the immediate postwar period. I recalled that it was on another flight over the Atlantic, on the way back from a frustrating Foreign Ministers meeting in Moscow in 1947, that General Marshall first discussed with his staff the need for a major international effort to help Europe get back on its feet after the hammer blows of history's worst war.

I thought back to that Europe of 1947—lying in ruins; a Europe only partly fed, partly clothed, partly housed and partly employed; a Europe half-frozen in the grip of a bitter winter, plagued by an alarming rise in the tuberculosis rate, doing too much of its business on the black market; a Europe struggling hopelessly to solve its economic problems, nation by nation, by imposing more embargoes, more quotas, more duties, more restrictions, more controls; a Europe in desperate need of almost everything and without the foreign exchange with which to buy it.

To many it seemed that Europe was prostrate, deathly sick, and ready to be gathered in by Communism, that eager scavenger of human disasters. To shortsighted people—and there were as many of them as there are now—the situation seemed hopeless. Yet with the blessing of hindsight we see that it was not at all hopeless, that something like a miracle occurred.

But was it really such a miracle? What happened is that a partnership of nations was formed for the great and constructive purpose of restoring Europe to health. The one nation that could afford to contribute the critical margin of external aid agreed to do so—and did. The rest of the partners agreed to put forth their maximum efforts to help themselves and to help each other—and did. A new international organization was created to perform an international job—which it did; and from this experience grew other international organizations until the institutional framework existed for a strong community of nations no longer dependent on anyone.

What's more, a profound revolution in attitudes took place on the European side of the partnership. An obsolete traditionalism which had kept European economies stagnant in the years between the two world wars broke down and gave way to new attitudes. The practice of low-volume, high-cost industrial production gave way to high-volume, low-cost production. Artificially restricted and protected markets gave way to an expanding, competitive mass market. Food production based on peasant farming gave way to food production based on modern agriculture and labor mobility. The concept of low wages and high profits gave way to the idea of management, labor and consumers sharing the fruits of higher productivity. And restrictive trade policies gave way to liberal trade policies.

Above all, the habit of looking inward for solutions yielded to the habit of looking outward beyond national frontiers. As the nations joined together for the purpose of recovery built up their common institutions, one leading to another, they acquired, in the words of one of the pioneers, the "habit of cooperation."

All this did not happen at once, nor did it happen to everyone. But it happened fast enough, and it dominated enough of the thinking of management and labor and governments alike, to add up to a revolutionary break with old attitudes. No wonder recovery was followed by renaissance; no wonder Western Europe is coalescing into a great mass market serviced by a dynamic and growing economy; that a new social mobility is breaking down the barriers of the old social structure; and that Western Europe is finding out what the North American states had discovered earlier—that in unity there is strength. Call it a miracle if you like, but it was a man-made miracle, inspired by high purpose, guided by liberal principles and carried out by hard work.

I am not here to tell you on Pan-American Day that Latin America's problems are just like Europe's problems a decade and a half ago, for they are vastly different; nor that North Atlantic solutions are necessarily inter-American solutions, for we must devise our own solutions.

But I *am* suggesting that common enterprise calls for common institutions, that a functioning community functions through the machinery it has built to service the community. I am suggesting, too, that in Western Europe an objectively hopeless situation was converted into a great success story by the application of physical resources, human energy, international organization and modern ideas.

And I think there may be an analogy in this: the pessimistic view of European prospects in 1947 turned out to be wrong, and I am confident that the pessimistic view of inter-American prospects eventually will turn out to be just as wrong.

This brings us up against the question of how to look at the Alliance for Progress. From what vantage point do we survey and assess the state of our progress? Is it more revealing to take the short view or the long view, the impatient or the patient? My own answer is that we need both points of view, and at one and the same time.

In the long view of history, the growth of the inter-American system, though it is the oldest international political organization in the world, represents a sudden and dramatic surge forward, an historical phenomenon of the very first order, a breakthrough in the technology of social organization. Within less than two centuries of gaining national independence, a mere moment in the long history of man, we have recognized the interdependence of nations and begun to learn to live together and work together in a larger community, to the vast benefit of all.

And not just passively either. For we have, in truth, just joined together in a true alliance for progress. We have committed ourselves deeply and formally to a common crusade against the root cause of political unrest, which is human want and social injustice. We are engaged in nothing less than a massive fight for decent conditions of life for every last man, woman and child in the whole hemisphere, a project which, a short time ago, would have been rightly considered a cruel hoax upon all of us.

So in history's long view, this moment in time is one of forward momentum at a dizzy pace. But in the short view is it yet fast enough for 1963?

Sudden knowledge that poverty no longer is the natural condition for most of mankind has as suddenly banished fatalism and apathy as props for an outmoded social system; impatience is the order of the day for the millions of dispossessed.

At the same time, groups of ruthless men, organized in tiny but disciplined cells and armed with false answers to fair questions, work desperately to turn impatience into chaos, unrest into violence; for violence is the order of the day for Communist agitators in our midst and off our shores.

Meanwhile, democratic governments are caught dangerously in the squeeze between the enormity and complexity of their commitments, on the one hand, and justified impatience, fanned by antidemocratic enemies, on the other.

Add to this the ossified traditionalism which tugs at the brake on social change and you have a fair sketch of our predicament and peril.

Under the circumstances it seems to me to be a matter of some importance for us to somehow embrace both the long view, which reveals the dramatic progress of our times, and the short view, which insists that tomorrow is too late to deal with the hunger of today. Somehow, it seems to me that we must learn to see both the forest and the trees—and simultaneously; that we must act in urgency but think in perspective; that we must acquire a vision which is neither myopic nor hyperopic. And this must be done not by compromising the long and short views but by bringing both within our field of vision.

I am trying to say, I suppose, that we must learn to look upon our progress for what it is but never to be satisfied with it, whatever it is. And this will demand a point of view concocted from equal parts of vision and of realism.

Such a viewpoint would show us that development should be orderly and therefore planned, but we can start at once on elements that would be part of any sensible plan; that sound development programs are essential, but worse than useless unless they are turned quickly from paper to projects in being; that a land reform law cannot be expected to increase the very next harvest, but not many more harvests can be expected unless such a law is passed in the first place, and then carried out.

Such a viewpoint would inform us that large progress is the sum of many small actions; that frustrations are predictable, and so are breakthroughs; that we can manage somehow to wait for the pay-off if there is momentum today, sustained tomorrow.

Such a viewpoint would make clear that twenty months is not a very long time to organize and plan and set things in motion, but that time is nonetheless short and we are in a hurry.

If we can just learn to see the woods and trees simultaneously, we will recognize both that the Alliance for Progress is part of a great progressive trend in human affairs and that its future course will be a year-to-year story of some goals made and others missed, some hopes dashed and others fulfilled.

If we maintain both our pressure and our perspective, we shall see, above all, that our direction is profoundly right and the imperative is to keep going, whatever the obstacles and the shortfalls may be next month or next year.

I would enter only one reservation. If we are to make haste, we must be inventive and adaptable in our plans, our programs and our institutional arrangements; for as I said once before after a trip to Latin America, development is learning by doing.

Yet I have no doubt about our capacity to experiment and create new forms of partnership to further and hasten the Alliance for Progress. And I think we already can detect a new and exciting dimension of our partnership. It lies in the involvement and commitment of an expanding sector of our private society in the common task of creating that medley of institutions upon which any modern society depends. Our land grant colleges and universities, our co-operatives, our credit unions and trade unions, our voluntary agencies and others are now being drawn increasingly into the job—a job in which success will be measured by the growth of an alliance made among governments into a deeper alliance among people. And this is the ultimate dimension of the international community, and the ultimate strength of our system.

Now I know there has been justified handwringing lately over abrupt changes in government in Latin America. Frankly, there have been setbacks, here and there, to the electoral process. But one can be concerned over this, and its effect on democracy, without becoming discouraged. For just as economic advance, as represented by the Alliance for Progress, cannot be measured on a short-term basis, so political advance must be seen in the perspective of time.

So I am persuaded that if we have the stability and the maturity and the endurance to see our Alliance for Progress through setbacks and triumph, through good days and bad, Latin America at the end of this decade will be well down the road which Western Europe took a decade or so ago. And those who are fainthearted about Latin America today will be as wrong as those who were fainthearted about the Europe that once lay prostrate in the ruins of World War II. Miracles will not just happen to us; but miracles have been made by men before—and will be again.

This is my hope, my belief and my prediction for this Pan-American Day, 1963.

THE ROAD TO AN OPEN WORLD:

OUR INTERNATIONAL AIM

🐾 🐾 *Governor Stevenson visited the Soviet Union in 1958. He traveled extensively throughout that country and talked with Premier Khrushchev and other Soviet officials. What he saw and heard convinced him the closed society was at the root of much of the world's troubles. In this address, which has been widely reprinted, he describes life in Russia and offers specific suggestions for signposts on the road to an open world—which, he says, is also the road to peace.*

No nation, however powerful, can subdue all the tides of history to its will. But if we study the tides, and if we have some idea of our own aim, we can try at least, as Jacques Maritain once wrote, "to raise new currents in the flood of circumstance."

What, then, is the international aim of the United States? Are we willing to accept a Communist world empire or, for that matter, a world empire under any power? Certainly not. We don't even want an empire of our own. Nor are we content to live indefinitely armed to the teeth in a bipolar world, trying by a balance of mortal threats to preserve a measure of peace and freedom. That isn't good enough.

No, what I believe we are striving toward, however haltingly, is

Commencement Address at Boston University, Boston, Massachusetts, June 3, 1962.

something much more intricate and much more tolerant than empire, but less dangerous and less highly charged than this present state of cold war. Perhaps the best word for it is *community*.

The obstacles to a real community of nations are many. In the diplomatic struggles at the United Nations, the focus right now is on the colonial and ex-colonial regions, especially Africa. The independence movement has swept a billion people onto the stage of history since the Second World War, and its force is irresistible. Our own efforts, at the United Nations and elsewhere, are aimed at channeling these enormous new energies in directions which will liberate rather than destroy; which will build bridges of cooperation, instead of digging gulfs of mistrust, between continents and regions, between rich and poor, between black and white.

This takes an infinity of patient diplomacy on both sides. It also will take time, decades at best, even if we use the time given to us to the best advantage. But what we hope to produce will be a result noble enough to warrant all the efforts and frustrations: a new international order in which the old empires are replaced not by still another wave of empires, but by a community of the equal and the free and the tolerant.

But beyond this great postcolonial evolution, which is now at the center of the stage, lies another huge challenge: the hostile and still militant power of the Soviet Union. Ultimately the community must deal successfully with that challenge if there is to be real peace in the world.

I have great hope that this problem too, huge as it is, will be solved as the years go by. It will be solved, not by our side seeking to conquer or to dominate the Soviet Union, but by the Soviet Union deciding, in its own interest, in countless small steps from day to day and from year to year, to join the rest of us in building a world of open societies.

In these few minutes, therefore, I would like to reflect with you on just what the open society means for world peace. For this is one of the great issues which will condition our lives for many years to come. I am concerned with the longer run. In the long-time scale of years and decades there are forces at work which make few headlines because they are so huge and we are so close to them that we can scarcely perceive them, any more than the early mariners could perceive the roundness of the world on whose surface they sailed.

It is time for us, then, to climb the mast—or even into the outer heavens!—and study the great globe itself. In such a long perspective I should like to think with you about the biggest country on the face of the globe, the Soviet Union.

Many years ago, in the early days of the Revolution, I spent some time in the Soviet Union. Four years ago I traveled there again and very extensively. I talked with Mr. Khrushchev and many senior officials in Western Russia, in Central Asia, in Eastern Siberia; and although we disagreed a good deal, nobody lost his temper and I was most hospitably received. It is a wonderful, puzzling, frustrating country. The people are warmhearted and hospitable, and filled with devotion and pride in their country. Having known so much suffering in war, they are deeply anxious for peace. Pleased with the improvements in their material lives since Stalin, they are hungry for more.

Wherever I went I was literally overwhelmed by the people's friendliness and curiosity about the United States. Yet, alas, enmity, mistrust and misunderstanding have been the official policy for decades, and the question is how to get through that enmity to establish a real peace.

We know that the only *short* road, by way of nuclear war, is suicidal and is thus closed to both sides. All the other roads are long and arduous. The diplomacy of safeguarded disarmament is one. Germany is another. Peaceful trade is another. Creative cooperation in the United Nations, in aid to emerging nations, in peaceful use of outer space—these roads all lead toward peace.

But our troubles with the Soviet Union far transcend the traditional realm of diplomacy, and it may well be outside that realm—or in a new kind of diplomacy, at any rate—that the best road to their solution will be found. The road I have in mind is one which our diplomacy has only recently begun to reconnoiter: namely, direct relations between the *people* of the Soviet Union and the *peoples* of the outside world, from whom, even today, they remain almost entirely cut off.

This is the road to an Open World. Possibly it will prove the longest road of all; but if we dare to travel it, as I think we must, we may find that the longest way round is the shortest way home.

No small part of the ills of today's world stem from the closed society of the Soviet Union. This closedness—the exclusion of the outer world, the suppression of dissent, the control of personal movements, the secrecy and suspicion—all this goes far back into Czarist Russian history. In the last few years, happily, it has been receding, but so far only a little.

Today that closed society is not only an anachronism; it is a danger to peace when all the peoples of the world, in their rapidly increasing numbers, are being pushed into ever-closer contact by the triumphs of science: global communications, modern air transportation, television by satellite and all the rest. At the same time science has also placed in the hands of the strongest nations, for the first time in history, an almost limitless power of destruction.

And it is at this fateful moment that one of those strongest nations, the Soviet Union, whose people have so much to contribute to the community of mankind, keeps itself sealed off behind an iron curtain; requires its ill-informed citizens to live in daily fear of imaginary enemies; and proclaims that those imaginary enemies will continue to threaten its existence—until the whole world has been remade in the Soviet image. And, of course, by its attempts to remake the world it has made real enemies where none had been before.

Such are the tragic works of closed minds. Russia has no monopoly of them, of course. Every society, I suppose, including ours, has individuals who hunger for conflict, who seem to get a positive joy out of having an enemy to hate and destroy and will doubtless miss the cold war when it finally ends. Indeed, it is a rare individual who has in him none whatever of this warrior urge! But a closed society goes one fatal step further. It elevates the closed mind into an official requirement; it ordains struggle and conflict as the highest and permanent duty of the citizen; and it brands all those whom it cannot control as actual or potential foes.

It is quite a job to keep a closed society closed. Consider the radio-jamming system which the Soviet Government uses to drown out the Russian-language programs of the BBC, the Voice of America, the Vatican radio and so on. This apparatus includes some 2,500 short-wave transmitters, all of them broadcasting nothing but noise. It costs about $100 million a year to run. Soviet authorities say it is worth it to protect the people from all those "lies," but for that price at least twenty thousand Soviet families could travel through the United States or other non-Communist countries, and find out for themselves whether the broadcasts are lies or not!

In Siberia in 1958 my party carried a short-wave radio and heard the jamming wherever we went. The United Nations General Assembly was then meeting in emergency session on the Lebanese crisis, and among the programs on the Voice of America which could not be heard because of Soviet jamming was the main speech in the Assembly of—the Soviet Foreign Minister!

Then there are other devices. One is *Glavlit,* a state agency whose permission is required for the publication in the Soviet Union of any book, pamphlet, newspaper, magazine, movie or television program, whether imported or domestic.

Then finally there is the control over the movement of people. It exists both within the Soviet Union and across its borders. When I went to Eastern Siberia and Kazakstan, I was, by courtesy of the Soviet Government, in a huge area, perhaps 25 percent of the Soviet territory, which is normally closed not only to foreigners but even to Soviet travelers.

As for travel abroad, that is quite beyond the hopes of ordinary people in the Soviet Union. I shall always remember an eager group of young Russians who drew me into friendly conversation on a summer evening in Leningrad; and when it was time to say good night I said, almost as second nature, "Well, come and see us in America."

And one of them, standing there in the northern twilight, answered for all the rest with a single, poignant, memorable word: "How?"

By all these devices the Soviet rulers have made their country into a darkened theater, from which daylight and all the events of the outer world are shut out, and all the play of light and music and action on stage and among the audience is controlled by the director. And just what is the myth which is enacted so dramatically every day in this enormous theater, before 200 million Soviet spectators? It is the mighty struggle of the Soviet people and their Communist allies to build a society throughout the world under the infallible leadership of the Communist party; and the stubborn resistance of a greedy, ruthless enemy called "capitalist imperialism," a shadowy conspiracy which rules the United States, which plots to destroy Communism by war and to enslave the world, but which the common people, led by the Communists, are destined at last to crush.

Facts which support the plot are published in an endless stream. Facts which contradict it are suppressed. It is taught to schoolchildren in their textbooks; to the millions of young men and women in the Young Communist organization; to the soldiers and officers of the huge and powerful Soviet armed forces; and, in fact, to all the Soviet people by every available means, year in and year out.

Now, fortunately, most of the plain people of the Soviet Union don't seem to believe all they have been told for forty-five years. If they did, Americans would not be welcomed so eagerly, even in the midst of official hate campaigns.

But I fear many Russians do tend to accept the image of an America ruled by warlike imperialists. And, accepting this false premise, they justify under the heading of self-defense all the dangers and sacrifices imposed by an aggressive Soviet foreign policy.

If this is in fact the popular attitude in the Soviet Union—and I have found it so in talks with a good many Soviet citizens—we have little reason to be surprised. The people have a deep patriotism and a yearning for peace which make them respond with their emotions to these stories. They have no free press, no freedom to travel, no independent way to check up.

Besides, it is hard for a Russian who has spent all his life under Communism even to begin to comprehend America. He has no experience of an open society like ours, built to tolerate conflicting values, containing countless small, independent centers of influence, making decisions by majority rule but jealous of minority rights. Instead, like his rulers, he tends to picture America as a mirror image of his own system—a dictatorship of an economic class (in our case the rich businessmen) bent on world domination.

Mr. Khrushchev himself spoke for that view of America when he wrote in 1959, in an article published here, that probably many of his American readers "think that the idea of capitalism will ultimately triumph." He cannot seem to believe that for us Americans capitalism is not a total system of life, or a secular religion with which we seek to evangelize the world. We don't even *have* a "system" in the totalitarian sense, because we believe that the human personality requires a margin of freedom to make its own choices, which no total system can ever provide.

Such a view of life is evidently foreign to Mr. Khrushchev and, to a great extent, to the Russian people too.

Yet I believe they will come to it. History, even Russian history, moves on. The violent, fearful Bolshevik Revolution, with all the dark weight of Russian history on its back, obviously felt the need of external foes to frighten the people into action. I believe that the modern Soviet Union will one day feel able to do without that dangerous stimulus. Its people are enjoying more and more security and the good things of life. Its leaders now openly proclaim that no enemy dares attack them. Surely it will do no harm now for the people of the Soviet Union to learn at last that nations can disagree, even about fundamentals, without hoping and working for each other's downfall; that we in the United States do *not* desire their destruction; that we do *not* want to dominate the world; that we *do* want a Russia that is strong and prosperous and at peace with its neighbors, and a wholehearted member of the community of nations.

The Russians have gained much in competence, and in selfconfidence, in recent years. Along with this comes a new tendency to look abroad not so much with suspicion and fear as with frank curiosity. I met this curiosity everywhere, and particularly among the students who before very long will be the nation's leaders. There can be no doubt of their eagerness for contact with the outside world.

Of course there has already been progress in this direction in recent years. Soviet cultural and technical relations with non-Communist countries, including the United States, have grown since Mr. Khrushchev came to power to a point which would have been unthinkable in the last years of Stalin's rule. The United States and the Soviet Union negotiated an exchange agreement in 1958 which was renewed in 1960 and again this year. There have been many useful exchanges, especially both in academic and technical fields and in the performing arts. Other Western countries have done the same.

Under these agreements, for instance, Van Cliburn was cheered to the rafters in the cities of Russia, and the Moiseyev and Ukrainian dancers have been cheered to the rafters in the cities of America. A Soviet exhibition drew big crowds in New York and an American exhibition drew huge crowds in Moscow. American professors have lectured this past year, in Moscow and Leningrad, on American civilization—our literature, our history and our law. And the full text of an interview with President Kennedy was read in *Izvestia* by millions of Russians.

The mood of the young people in Moscow was shown this spring in an article by Igor Moiseyev, the head of the famous dance troupe. He condemned what he called the "disgusting dynamism of rock-and-roll and the twist"—neither of which, of course, took long to reach Moscow. But then he laughed at the Communist puritans who tried to suppress these new dances, and said: "The slogan of modern youth is, 'I want to know everything.' It aspires to independence of thought and opinion."

What a revolutionary trend such a statement suggests! And the visit of Benny Goodman to Russia isn't likely to slow it down much either.

There is a thaw, too, in the exchange of scientific information. In the past few years, Russians have presented important papers at world meetings on atomic science and many other subjects. Now, after a diplomatic launching at the United Nations, there are plans for a permanent "world weather watch"—space satellites managed jointly by the United States and the U.S.S.R., circling the globe and giving every country instantaneous knowledge of the world's weather.

It would seem that the spirit of openness is going to break some altitude records; and one day I think President Kennedy's plea will be answered: "Together let us explore the stars."

The question is, what should be done now? The least we can do, with the future of the world in the balance, is to encourage this delicate growth in every way we know.

—We should redouble our exchange programs and make them fully reciprocal.

—We should end forever such an obsolete practice as the closing off of forbidden zones to foreign travel.

—We should hold more exhibitions on each other's territory—not just in Moscow and New York but in cities from Minsk to Vladivostok, and from Portland, Maine, to Portland, Oregon. And, if I may insert a personal note, I am still waiting and hoping to see the incomparable puppet theaters of the Soviet Union perform in the United States!

—We should adopt a world-wide rule that anybody, anywhere, has a right to read any document issued by the United Nations, and that member governments have a positive duty to facilitate the United Nations information program.

—We should agree that every nation will welcome to the newsstands of its major cities the serious newspapers and magazines of other nations, regardless of politics.

—We should continue to urge the joint TV appearances of President Kennedy and Chairman Khrushchev, about which Mr. Salinger has been negotiating.

—We should extend the free importation of books, without political censorship and without custom duty, to every nation.

—We should multiply international student exchanges.

—We should see that what schoolchildren study about each other's countries is balanced and free from politically inspired hatred and distortion.

—We should let the ordinary citizens of every country, by the thousands and tens of thousands, travel abroad for business or pleasure, and see that there are good hosts to receive them and to help them learn, and to learn from them. And, I believe, we should do all we can to promote mutually profitable trade in those things which improve and adorn the life of the people.

Examples like these can be multiplied. They apply with special relevance to the Soviet Union and the United States, but ultimately they must apply to all countries. There is not a country in the world which cannot improve in this field.

I believe such steps as these are steps toward peace—the peace of the free. At the root of them lies a free society's peaceable view of life—a view which is not terrified by things new and strange; which can be a little bit patient about things it doesn't like; which can disagree, even over fundamentals, without coming to blows, because its deepest beliefs are tempered by a certain humility.

We have had enough of systems of thought which cry: "I alone have the key to truth." We have had enough of movements which set out to prove their godlike understanding by dragging fellow creatures through blood and fire. That belongs to the Thirty Years' War, not to our time. The thermonuclear generation would do better to study the humility of Socrates, who said he was the wisest man in Athens because only he, among all Athenians, knew the depth of his own ignorance.

It would be hard to exaggerate how deeply this great issue of the open society can affect all our destinies. As long as doors remain shut between the powerful nations of the world, the arms race with all its mortal dangers is likely to persist; and the community which the United Nations seeks to embody will remain no better than half-realized. What a price to pay for the pride of ideology!

Sometimes it seems to me, working at the United Nations, that the name of that organization is almost right, but that the verb is in the wrong tense. It should be, if we were precise, the *Uniting* Nations. It was founded to maintain a peace which has never been made. It is not something established and achieved, by means of which we casually attend to little quarrels and difficulties as they arise. It is rather a center of aspiration; a continuous process of wrestling with the seemingly irreconcilable; and a constant straining to break out of those temptingly clear but hopelessly narrow logical systems which drive us apart, into a less clear but far wider and deeper logic of tolerance and brotherhood that can save mankind.

How excruciatingly slow that process seems, and how distant that aspiration! But "man's reach must exceed his grasp, else what's a heaven for?" It is not just the dread of war but the yearning for peace, and the intuition of brotherhood, that can exert the necessary force to move humanity, against all the obstacles of outworn institutions, toward a peace based on tolerance. The movement is glacial in its slowness, but glacial also in its power.

And surely, at some point along the way, it will be necessary for each and all of us—Russians, Americans, Europeans and Latin Americans, Asians and Africans—not only to disarm our armies of dreadful weapons, but to disarm our minds of dreadful fears; to open our frontiers, our schools and our homes to the clean winds of fact and of free and friendly dialogues; and to have done with those exclusive fanatical dogmas which can make whole peoples live in terror of imaginary foes.

Not in order to save one people or one empire or one system, but to save Man himself, we must act on the truth which our experience makes inescapable: that the road to peace in this fearful generation is the road to an open world.

PART V

THE INGREDIENTS
OF FREEDOM

GLENN'S LAW:
OUR NATIONAL VIGOR

✌ ✌ *The feat of Colonel John Glenn in landing his space capsule through the use of hand controls after part of his automatic mechanism had failed, suggested to Governor Stevenson an invaluable lesson for all Americans. His particular concern, as expressed here, is with those who constantly bewail Soviet successes while overlooking its set-backs and the gains of the United States. He also returns to his theme of economic aid for the developing nations of the world, and he urges Americans to show, as had Colonel Glenn, that they—and not unknown forces—were in command of their capsule.*

I believe profoundly that confidence and hope are the natural, historical expression of our great nation's stance in world affairs.

The belief that a new kind of society, without privilege and oppression, could be built on earth inspired our Founding Fathers. Since their day all our greatest leaders have expressed in some way their confidence that something special and something new could be achieved in and by America—a society without slavery; a society without poverty and insecurity; a society which might play its part in leading the nations to a world without war; a wealthy and bountiful community able to extend to all mankind its own principle of "the general welfare."

Address to the Twelfth Annual Conference of National Organizations, American Association for the United Nations, Washington, D. C., March 13, 1962.
✌ 217

These have been great dreams and they have fostered great initiatives. Yet we have not always lived by our best dreams. Some of us, on the contrary, have talked as if mankind were at the mercy of the drift of history, powerless to influence his fate, moving like a sleepwalker to some apocalyptic atomic doom—a mood as far removed from the earlier youth and optimism of our republic as is St. Paul from Jeremiah.

Some of us—alas! among the most vocal—have yielded to still another nightmare, one in which *we* are always doing badly, while our adversaries march from one triumph to the next. From this bad dream come the cries of extreme rightists about an ever-encroaching Communist conspiracy which—if we were to believe them—has not made a single error in forty years.

This picture excludes a whole universe of facts—the fact of unrest in Eastern Europe, the fact of waning Communist belief in Western Europe, the fact of ideological differences between Moscow and Peking. It excludes a whole series of recent Soviet setbacks in the Congo and elsewhere in Africa, and at the United Nations. It excludes the failure of Soviet state capitalism to compete in the production of consumer goods, or to work at all in agriculture.

I suggest that, in lashing out at a vast, overwhelming, irresistible Communist "take-over," the rightists are not only overselling Communism. Worse, they are underselling America—and underselling as well the stubborn will to be free which is Communism's worst obstacle in every continent.

They overlook, too, the fact that never have we, as a nation, shown more confidence and eagerness, a mood, I believe, not so much created as revealed by that astonishing drama at Cape Canaveral when a quiet, unassuming Marine became the first American to ride in outer space and see four sunsets in a single day.

Colonel Glenn and his exploit have many different meanings for us and for our national life; but more than the tumultuous rejoicings and ticker tape parades, he jolted us into a new awareness of confidence and hope.

Let us, therefore, be grateful for that image of Friendship 7, carrying round the earth one of the most buoyant and manly personalities, and one of the clearest, most light-of-day minds, ever "orbited" into the national consciousness. For it has already begun to replace some of the images of unreasoning fear to which we have been treated recently. Let it correct, too, the more widespread miasma of doubt about the ability of Americans in particular, and men in general, to master the incredible forces of nature which human intelligence has unlocked in our time.

To me, there is something superbly symbolic in the fact that an astronaut, sent up as assistant to a series of computers, found that he worked more accurately and more intelligently than they. Inside the capsule, *man* is still in charge.

Let that be called Glenn's Law!

Let us now, with new courage and zest, apply Glenn's Law to this little capsule of the world, spinning through space. Let us do so in the consciousness that America is a great and inventive society, that its occasional tendency to torpor is an essentially uncharacteristic response to the enormous challenges of the contemporary universe.

Communism, like outer space, may be hostile. But it can be lived with and controlled by the same patience, skill, hard work and generous resources that went into Project Mercury. Moreover, like space, it can also be seen as a creative challenge. Would we not have slumbered under the weight of our gimmicks and gadgetry if the cold challenge of outdoing and outthinking the Communist order had not stiffened our backs and our minds?

So, we may conclude, this competitive nation can still compete, and even relish the competition. And I believe Colonel Glenn's space journey points to the kind of victory for which we all hope to strive.

I am sure you have heard talk and criticism recently of the government pursuing a "no-win" policy. Now I am not sure that I altogether understand what the critics have in mind. Do they mean that the Administration is unready to launch a nuclear war to speed the liberation of countries under Communist rule? Or do they mean the United States should send Marines to take over Cuba—and throw away the confidence of most of Latin America?

I do not know. The critics do not spell out what they want, and

so we do not know whether they accept the basic facts of our age—
that in a nuclear war there would be not only "no-win" but no
winners.

From these anxious years our people have been slowly learning a
new truth, and it is this: Democracy has no need of enemies or of
hatred; and the victories it cherishes most are the victories of peace
in which no one suffers defeat and no one nourishes dreams of
vengeance in a future war.

Our orbital flight is such a victory. In it all men are winners. It
has elicited from Mr. Khrushchev the immediate suggestion that
America and Russia should cooperate closely in the further exploration of outer space. As you know, the United States has been trying
for years to promote an international approach by which these vast
new oceans of space would not have to witness the tribal conflicts
of earthbound creatures or be sullied by engines of war. Now with
our orbital flight, we have more chips on the bargaining table with
which to pursue those universal goals.

When we face the dark wall of Soviet hostility and irrationality,
we are a little like scientists faced with the infinitely complex problems
of penetrating the lethal secrets of radiation, or probing the layer
upon layer of mystery that surround both stars and atoms. At times
these scientists must despair. At times they must wonder whether the
small toeholds they have in cosmic research will ever lead on to
wider vistas and broader paths. Small wonder that we, being faced
with Mr. Khrushchev's threats and blandishments and his retreat
from an agreement on atomic testing, find Soviet policy even more
mysterious and hostile than the hazards of space!

How inventive and resourceful they are, those engineers who put
John Glenn, Alan Shepard and Virgil Grissom into space. If a valve
doesn't function, they invent another. If one device disappoints them,
they design a new one. The search for solutions and the certainty
that there *are* solutions continue unrelentingly.

In just such a way we must react to the still more complex task
of creating a viable human order. Frustrated in one place, we must
try another way round. If agreements "leak," new and better ones
must be sought. If we bog down in our efforts to organize joint space

research, all the more reason for trying harder. If the issue of inspection and control proves the toughest nut to crack in disarmament
negotiations, let us work all the harder on that.

But we are hard to discourage. Even though the Russians reject
once again all offers of a reasonable test ban treaty at Geneva, we
are not on that account giving up the search for a breakthrough in
arms control. In fact, we must give to our research in this science of
survival the same ingenuity, and the same scale of resources, that go
into our defense and space research. For remarkable feats of imagination will be needed before we can adequately penetrate the thicket
of technical, diplomatic and psychological mysteries in which the
arms race and the cold war have their being.

We do not know the whole truth about our adversaries, any more
than we know everything about the Van Allen radiation belts. We
know both can be dangerous and treacherous. But we don't stop
seeking a way through. Let our approaches to Russia be made with
the same ultimate confidence, with the same rejection of fatalism,
with the same readiness for work, for disappointment if need be, and
for renewed effort.

To me, one of the primary advantages of such partial "breakthroughs" as a joint geophysical year or a joint program in outer
space is that they give us the chance to begin to attempt the only
final solution to our profound differences with Russia, the solution
that lies in some kind of interpenetration and meeting of minds. If
we can create communities of men—astronauts, scientists, doctors,
geologists, artists, musicians—who have shared tasks of common
discovery, we can at least hope that their discoveries will include
some of the truth about themselves and each other. A Glenn or a
Gagarin, working together in some hazardous yet exhilarating space
project, could scarcely emerge from this experience with all the veils
still drawn down. And if the Soviet closed society opened enough
so that in both societies there came to be men and women who
understand in depth the hopes and fears of their opposite numbers,
we should have opened many windows to the light and set many
candles burning in the gloom of ignorance.

"How beautiful is our earth!" exclaimed Major Gagarin as he

came down from space. And you remember when Colonel Glenn, looking at the same view shouted: "Man, that view is tremendous!" I think those two men have more in common than either has with the ideologists of conquest.

Do not think this is simply Pollyanna talk. Wars start in the blind, angry hearts of men. But it is hard to hate those who toil and hope and discover beside you in a common human venture. The Glenns of our world could be new men in a quite new sense—the new men who, having seen our little planet in a wholly new perspective, will be ready to accept as a profound spiritual insight the unity of mankind.

When I had the good fortune to conduct the astronauts and their families around the United Nations, and to witness the thunderous spontaneous welcome that roared from room to room among all the nations, I had a sense that men such as these belong to a new fellowship which could one day be a great strand in the web of peace. And I believe they felt the same.

Colonel Glenn said, if you recall: "As space science and space technology grow . . . and become more ambitious, we shall be relying more and more on international teamwork . . . we have an infinite amount to learn both from nature and from each other. We devoutly hope that we will be able to learn together and work together in peace."

These are the words of our "new men"—not a narrow arrogance, but a generous vision of the great human family. Let no obstacles, however forbidding, ever blind us to that vision.

This same spirit must animate us in other realms. I am deeply convinced that the tranquillity of the human family in the next three or four decades depends upon bridging the great and growing gap between the wealthy, industrialized, developed Northern Hemisphere and the underdeveloped, poverty-ridden South. After a decade of fairly sustained effort, we are beginning to learn that to move out of the cramped, ignorant, pretechnological conditions of a static tribal or feudal society is fully as difficult as breaking the bounds of space.

All the forces of tradition, all the gravity of ancient habits hold the nations back. Each national "capsule," small or large, has to find its own idiosyncratic way into orbit, and a lot of them are still on the ground. For the process of modernizing nations involves an exceptionally complicated and difficult set of interlocking actions, decisions and discoveries. There will therefore be delays and disappointments.

Some projects, like some rockets, will explode in mid-air. Some will take paths that were not in the plans. Yet failure is often the prelude to success.

In the matter of international assistance, we can say without doubt that we know more than we did. Our techniques are wiser, our sense of what we have to do more sure. Some underdeveloped areas—one thinks of parts of India and parts of West Africa—are beginning to show unmistakable signs of momentum. This is no time to write the program off as a costly failure. We are learning by doing, and results are already beginning to show.

None, however, can show quickly. Changing an economy means, in fact, changing a whole generation of men. I doubt if that can be done in less than two decades. So I would say: Look on the fateful program of modernizing what the French call the "third world"— the world of the poor and dispossessed—as we look on the program for probing the planets. Expect failures. Rejoice in successes. Never doubt the job can be done. Indeed, it must be done if misery is not to turn to despair, and despair to wars, and war to ruin for us all.

So vital is this strategy of development to our country's future security that I never stop being amazed at the way in which this nation, which cheerfully pays fifty billion dollars a year for arms and may pay billions to reach the moon, can begrudge the two billions a year that go to economic development abroad, a program which in human terms must be judged one of the world's greatest adventures.

Yet we still hear the argument that we cannot afford more, that our national resources can't stand it. Yet we are growing richer all the time.

No, the real basis for hesitation about economic aid is not scarce resources, but scarce imagination. There are some citizens whom the prospect of ending the age-old tyrannies of hunger and disease does not stir as does the glamour of space travel or the fear of military defeat. Their dreams—and their nightmares—tend to be those of the rich and the satisfied and the possessors!

Yet how dangerous those dreams are! For the rich are a small minority in this world and their ultimate security can only be found by making common cause with the far different hopes and dreams of the many poor. Only thus can we hope to prevent the despair which Communism exploits and which so imperils our own security. To forget this truth is to be wrong, fatally wrong, about our national strategy.

But it is also wrong at a much profounder level—wrong to leave children to starve who could eat with our help, wrong to let youngsters die when medical skill can save them, wrong to leave men and women without shelter, wrong to accept for others, in the midst of our own abundance, the iron pains of degrading want.

These are moral decisions. We are not bound to such evils by necessity or by scarcity. Our modern technology of abundance gives us the freedom to act—if we so decide. There are no restraints now except the restraints of a blind eye and an unfeeling heart.

I think we should rejoice as we have been given the extra dimension of freedom, for I profoundly believe that at bottom there is here in America a good and generous and moral people.

Yet some of the elements in our way of life, as in all the burgeoning affluent societies of the West, tend to make us allergic to self-denial, to altruism and to difficult endeavor. All around us are voices which rouse the clamor of desires and claims which can stifle our imaginations and douse our sense of pity.

The more we concentrate on our own needs, the less we can measure the needs of others and the more the gap will grow between the overfed, overdressed, overindulged, overdeveloped peoples of the Atlantic world and the starving millions beyond the magic pale.

I would like to end where I began—with the image of Colonel Glenn, Astronaut, Citizen, Dedicated Man. I believe that his courage and humility and high good humor are the qualities we really admire. In a slack age, we can still be moved by the prospect of discipline and dedication. And in an age in which so many people seem to be condemned to wander lost in their own psychological undergrowth, we can still recognize and acclaim a simplicity of doing and being and giving from which great enterprises spring.

We cannot enter with emotion and sympathy into the vast drama of "haves" and "have-nots" unless some image of discipline, I would say even of a certain asceticism, releases us from the pressures of smash and grab, of "me first," of "you've never had it so good." Some sudden new light on the ways in which human beings can live is needed to release us from the obsessions of our "getting and spending," our immense preoccupation with "what there is in it for me," and of what in short-term thrills or benefits I can extract from this day for my very own.

Perhaps there is salvation in the new image of the immense patience and discipline and stripping down of desires and wants that are necessary in the life of those who are fit enough and tough enough to venture out into the new dimension of outer space. Here we can perhaps glimpse some reflection of the kind of discipline and restraint which we all need in some measure if our generation is to achieve great tasks, not only in the upper air but here and now in this bewildered and floundering world.

The sense that something more is required of us than a happy acquiescence in our affluence is, I believe, more widespread than we know. The thousands of young people who volunteer for the rigors and discomforts of the Peace Corps, the uncomplaining reservists, the growing body of students with a passionate concern for world peace or for the end of racial discrimination, the unsung citizens all over this continent whose love and service and neighborly good will are the hidden motive forces of our Republic—all these people will see reflected in the discipline and dedication of Colonel Glenn and his comrades the proof that great deeds demand great preparation, and that no country can hope to master the challenge of our day without a comparable readiness to cut away the trivialities and achieve the freedom which comes from being no longer "passion's slave."

To this kind of greatness we are all called, for even daily life cannot be lived with grace and dignity without some sense of others' needs and of the claims they may make on our sympathy and good will. How much more must the great public life of a whole nation be informed with discipline and vision if its generosity is to shine forth and its courage to lie beyond all shadow of doubt.

I do not believe that in the last decade our Republic has always equaled the brilliant image of youth and energy and regeneration which was once projected to the world when, as a community dedicated to a proposition and an idea, it stirred to life two centuries ago in these United States. Nor do I believe we can fulfill our role in history without a recovery of the original dream.

Therefore I pray that like our young astronauts we soar to the stars in mind as well as body, and recovering that sense of our vocation and dedication without which this people, founded and created in a great vision, will not finally endure.

DREAMS COME TRUE:
GOALS FOR AMERICANS

In his Presidential campaigns, Governor Stevenson had spoken frequently of the New America, an America with purpose and aspiring to fulfill its promise. Here, he once more speaks of that America; and —in a flight of imagination—he tells of some of the things he would like to see if his dreams could be realized. But he does not stop at dreaming, discussing also some of the very real problems of the world that affect the lives of all Americans, and he lists the choices they have before them. His conclusion is both a warning and a challenge.

We Americans are rightly concerned these days with what the admen call our "image" abroad. We spend millions of dollars explaining ourselves and our policies.

The United Nations brings to our shores people from every state under the sun. They come. They see. They judge. And if there is one thing of which I am sure after my time in the maelstrom, it is this: What we say has little impact compared with what we do.

It is our quality that profoundly determines what others think of us. Visiting delegates may delight in the shining skyscrapers at one end of Park Avenue. But they see the crumbling slums at the other end. They admire our great centers of learning, but they do not overlook the two-shift obsolescent city school where poor children learn

Commencement Address at Tufts University, Medford, Massachusetts, June 8, 1962.

227

the habits of delinquency almost with their letters.

In short, brave pretensions and bold speeches are as nothing in the balance compared with the solid facts of decency and amenity, of social justice and pioneering reform. And they also note that, with all our pretensions and failures, there is no more socially responsible and successful society on earth. To keep it that way is the job of America's young.

But we know all this, and I refer to it only because the hope of being the nation our dreams and our wealth can make us depends intimately upon their response.

The privilege—and penalty—of their education is that over the coming decades they will be the pacesetters for political and social thought in their communities. They may not accept this responsibility, but that makes no difference. It is inescapable. For if they decide to set no pace, to forward no new ideas, to dream no dreams, they will still be pacesetters. They will simply have decided that there is to be no pace.

They must, therefore, here and now, in their own minds, make the list of their own priorities, the things they would choose to have or do in our great society, if they knew the resources were available. And I will tell them some of the things I would wish to see in America, if our dreams could be realized and our vision of the good society could be planted solidly in our native earth.

I would begin with education: in high schools imaginative enough to check delinquency and give youngsters a sense of the zest and opportunity of life, in college education available to all who can profit by it, in refresher courses and sabbatical years for teachers, in adult education recalling people at every level of attainment to a deepening of their knowledge.

Next, I dream of cities worth living in.

More and more of our people will live in cities and suburbs. I think of the huddled, blighted centers, the commuter chaos, the shapeless sprawls in which the hot dog stand and the used car lot alternate with the filling station and the drive-in diner; the vanishing of parks and spaces, the outward growth of ramshackle subdivisions destined within ten years to be the slums of tomorrow.

We can do better than this.

I have read of Nanking when it was the capital of the Sung dynasty. It was a great city, yet trees and water followed the streets, fountains and waterfalls refreshed the air, gardens divided the city sectors, and in the evening citizens rowed on the lakes, hearing the sound of bells across the water. They had fewer resources than we have. But beauty, it seems, had a compelling priority it lacks in our abundant society. And they loved and cultivated the arts, not as fringe benefits, but as a central purpose in life.

Here, too, I would like to dream of music and theater in every city, of great festivals of the arts springing up in more and more regions and, above all, of citizens themselves learning to use a growing leisure in making their own art.

Another dream is a vast expansion of our national parks and playgrounds, with services expanded and opportunities increased, both for the gregarious and for the solitary lovers of open life—for the latter-day Thoreau looking for his Walden Pond.

Yet I do not, of course, leave out the attack on poverty as a by-product of better living. It is central to our abundance. Most of those who are poor today in America are so because we are slow to bestir ourselves to end the pockets of destitution—in West Virginia, or New England's mill towns, in big city slums, among migrant workers— where the desperately poor are not floated off the bottom of society by any rising tide of general prosperity.

At this point, no doubt, sober heads are being shaken and voices of ancestral wisdom raised to argue that dreams are all very well, but the fundamental need is to get on with the "real business of life," recognize the "limitation of our resources" and "put first things first" —by which, I think, they usually mean more weapons and more consumer goods.

And this is the thesis I want to challenge today. No one denies that education for excellence, beautiful cities, an open-air world and a society without injustice are in themselves good things. They simply argue that we cannot afford them. This I believe to be profoundly untrue.

I do not believe, in our affluent society, that we are, in more than the very shortest run, short of resources. We simply are not mobilizing enough of them.

Secondly, I believe that the kinds of dreams I have described—which become concrete demands for more schools, more teachers, urban renewal, suburban planning and landscaping—are in fact *the* clue to the next stage of growth in the free economy.

Let us begin with the facts about the American economic system today. While other free nations—Japan, West Germany, Italy and even France—have clocked up rates of growth from 5 percent to 10 and 12 percent a year, and while the Communists claim rates as spectacular, we and the British have jogged along at an average of under 3 percent. This is not catastrophic. Indeed, it isn't much below the historical average. But some things about the curve are disconcerting. Clearly, we are operating below our optimum level.

What has gone wrong?

The difficulty is not on the side of supply. I cannot emphasize too much the availability of resources.

We pay a billion dollars a year to stockpile food. We have vast supplies of metals purchased and stored by government. We dump obsolescent weapons, year after year. Petroleum is in surplus, aluminum is in surplus, steel capacity is in surplus, coal has been cut by half to maintain demand, power may well become surplus in another decade of rapid atomic development. And all through the manufacturing industry we are only beginning to see the consequences of automation.

Labor is surplus as it is. What will it become if most major industries can halve or quarter their working force in the next few years?

We have to face the fact that once economies develop beyond a certain level of sophistication, science and technology place at their disposal so vast an array of techniques and inventions that surplus, not shortage, is much more likely to be their habitual state. And surplus left to itself, and seen as a fact, not as an opportunity, depresses markets, makes men redundant, checks investment and leads on to stagnation. Yet surplus is actually a vast opportunity.

The human race has spent all its yesterdays in a state of chronic and crippling shortage. From harvest to harvest, from hand to mouth —so lived the human family until the twentieth century. And so live still perhaps half of the world's peoples.

If you look at the differences between the rapidly growing economies and ourselves, you will find that the chief factor is the one of demand. Postwar reconstruction started the spurt in Europe and Japan. Now consumer demand is high because these nations are well into the cycle of what the economists call "consumer durables"— cars and dishwashers, television sets and refrigerators.

And these governments also make the maintenance of demand a steady objective of policy, well ahead, incidentally, of surpluses in their budgets. In fact, in France, a technique of stimulating demand has been evolved which countries as various as Britain, Belgium and Spain are thinking of adopting, and Germany and Italy are at least discussing it.

French economists meet with labor and management under the auspices of the planning mechanism established by that innovator of genius, Jean Monnet. There the economists sketch out the consequences—in terms of the need for expansion in steel, power, transport, metallurgy and so forth—of, say, a 5 percent rate of growth. Encouraged by this picture of buoyance, the managers go back and expand their enterprises accordingly. By doing so, of course, they create the demand that sustains a high rate of growth.

I know no more startling demonstration of the fact that demand is not limited by supply. On the contrary, it is supply that is fashioned, shaped and called into being by organized demand.

For the first time in human history, man, Western man, has the power to build society according to his dreams, not his narrow, primeval necessities. He has received, at the hands of science, a new liberation, a new freedom.

But what does this fact look like, stripped for a moment of rhetoric and exhilaration? It means that the creation of acceptable demand is our overriding problem.

We face an economy in oversupply, in surplus, in glut. If we are "to get it moving again," we have to make new experiments on the side of demand, creating new needs and objectives, and it is not yet clear how we are to make them.

Let us suppose that as a community we, like our neighbors the French, accepted a 4 to 5 percent rate of growth as the norm. How should we set about the expansion? I admit that there are some technical obstacles of considerable importance—our balance of payments, for instance, or the pressure of rising wages on costs.

But the difficulty I wish to underline is neither of these. I believe they can be handled. The difficulty I see goes deeper. The issue is, quite simply: What, over the next decade, is going to be the *content* of the demand which will set our economy moving again?

And the reason why even the advanced economies of Western Europe cannot help us here is that, very candidly, much of their present lively expansion comes from the fact that they are going through a cycle of demand which we in America completed in the early 1950's.

The "consumer durables" cycle offers immense stimulus to the whole economy. But what happens when a country has not only the proverbial two chickens in every pot, but two television sets in the parlor?

Now I don't for a moment suggest that every household is in this satisfied state. But enough households are sufficiently modernized for this revolution in household equipment to be no longer the prime stimulus to expansion it is in Europe. We have to discover the *next* great surge in demand, and we have to do it not only for ourselves, but for Europe as well.

At present, there are two items of demand upon which we do not mind, apparently, the lavish expenditure of public money. The first is defense. We are approaching a level of $50 billion a year, and the bills go through Congress with hardly a debate. The next is space research. I suspect that we shall spend $40 billion or so, if not more, over the next decade, and space, being limitless, may well offer limitless opportunities for the stimulus of new demand.

Perhaps I should add one other category—roads. No one minds an $80 billion road program, since clearly mobility has an absolute value in our way of life. But after these categories, any sharp increase in public spending—on education, on health, on urban renewal—runs into the stiffest Congressional opposition, and also arouses a lot of local hostility as well.

Yet of the three highly acceptable forms of public demand, two are, after all, limited. Even with completely balanced forces, could we go beyond $60 billion a year? I doubt it. And one day our major road systems will have been built.

We are left with space. And there, I suspect, the limiting factor will remain trained minds and research.

In the private sector, we pin our hopes on new families and on new products. Our population goes on growing, and in our kind of economy this is a great help. As for products, yes, I suppose space research will breed a large field of by-products. We see them already in satellites for better communications. Perhaps top executives' individualized flying machines and the family helicopter are not far off. Color television should make a new revolution of obsolescence. Pocket TV should come soon, to make sure that not even in fifteen seconds' privacy shall we be obliged to think!

Yet I wonder whether the majority of us need to look for a further stockpile of consumer goods, durable or otherwise. Has not the piling up of things and more things reached a point of reasonable satiety?

I suggest that it is possible that the American people need now to think more of their abilities and their capacities, their sources of inner delight, than of a further accumulation of external wants. It was an American poet, Wallace Stevens, who reminded us: "The world without us would be desolate except for the world within us." Does not our soul now need more attention than our body?

We have, therefore, to face the possibility that the present main stimulants to demand upon which our economy depends—arms, space and other public spending, coupled with the vast pouring out of consumer goods of all kinds—will not push us much above our present rates of growth, and these, unchanged, threaten stagnation and deepening unemployment.

Is there any alternative? And here I turn to the beginnings of this address.

Today, what are our choices? We have abundance. We have an

economy whose health depends upon the creation of new kinds of demand. Can we then argue that better education, fuller health, a determined onslaught on the last outposts of destitution, beautiful cities, dignified suburbs, great art, great recreation, should not appear on the priority list?

We face the strange and stirring truth that our dreams are turning into our necessities. Now that reality is catching up with our dreaming, are you—above all, you, the young—afraid to dream?

I realize, of course, that at this point our visions will be interrupted by loud, ritual cries against "spending," against "statism" and "big government," and while I do not want to engage in this hoary controversy, I would like to make four brief points.

The revenues, even the higher tax revenues needed for more education and urban renewal, form a smaller load on the community in times of buoyant growth than in times of stagnation.

Next, our public spending on nondefense needs today is, in fact, not only smaller, proportionately, than that of most European governments. It is smaller by one-third than our own prewar level.

Next, the public stimulus is in most fields only a small part of the total expansion achieved. Slum clearance enhances private property values. The rebuilding of city centers often ends with private capital carrying three-quarters of the investment—and the gain.

Or, to give another instance, the TVA development created a private tourist industry worth $400 million a year for the area. Better park and wilderness services could do the same.

Or again, where would General Motors be without our road system? In fact, if we starve our public services, we nip off a hundred ways in which enterprising private firms can expand their opportunities.

The chief point I would like to stress is, quite simply, that a proper use of public power and policy, far from being hostile to vigorous private expansion, is essential to it. This is the inescapable lesson of the free system's successes since the Second World War.

The Marshall Plan—a public act—salvaged Europe and restored it to heights of prosperity unknown before. The Monnet Plan—a public act—remade the base of France's faltering private economy. Today, in Europe's bounding expansion, the direction of policy everywhere is toward the closest cooperation between public and private authorities, to check excessive wage and price increases, to oversee long-term rates of investment, and to consider, in the open light of public discussion, the great social priorities of the affluent society.

We, in America, may find soon that not only our relative lack of growth but our seeming indifference to national forethought are losing us our place in the vanguard of free men.

This would be treason to our deepest selves. In a world where vision and decision determine resources, and resources no longer limit vision, it is the boldest dreamers who will move to the vanguard of mankind.

The first society to conquer all its remaining poverty, to give all its citizens the chance of full and diverse education, to build for them greater cities, to save and develop their patrimony of natural beauty, and to launch them on a way of life where work and leisure are creatively intertwined—that society will, by its very being, impose its image on the human spirit.

And if any say to me, "How can we dream such dreams? What utopia are you proposing?" I would answer that it is no longer a dream to think of putting a man on the moon. If we can dream that—and our grandfathers would think us madmen—can we not stir up our imagination to encompass what are in fact less impossible dreams?

What is more difficult, to think of an encampment on the moon or of Harlem rebuilt? Both are now within the reach of our resources. Both now depend upon human decision and human will. I pray that the imagination we unlock for defense and arms and outer space may be unlocked as well for grace and beauty in our daily lives. As an economy, we need it. As a society, we shall perish without it.

It will be tragic indeed if, in this hour of our greatest physical opportunity, we cease to seek the American dream.

WHO IS SPARTA?
WHO IS ATHENS?
AMERICA UNDER PRESSURE

❦ ❦ *Here Governor Stevenson continues his discussion of life in America at a time of historical change. He points to the pressures of the world of today and warns that a greater risk than reaction is that of complacency. And citing the glory of Athens—the prototype of all free societies—in outthinking the discipline of Sparta, he pointedly draws the analogy as he questions: "Who is Sparta, who is Athens? Who has the initiative? Who is making the schemes?"*

The quality of the electorate, the news it will listen to, the leads it will follow, the inconveniences and difficulties it is prepared to face— these are the measure of effective democracy. Even within our system of checks and balances, vigorous and effective government is not impossible. Our republican institutions are now among the oldest continuous political institutions in the world. They could not have survived from a rural, decentralized community to the modern world of cities and industrial concentrations without immense powers of adaptation. These have made it possible for great Presidents to re-shape popular thinking and introduce eras of great reform. They have done this by developing a close dialogue with a responsive public opinion and thus imposing political vision and direction on the chaos

Article for Harper's Magazine, August, 1961.

❦ 236

of separate interests and rival lobbies which make up, inevitably, so much of Congressional politics.

This is as it should be. For interests deserve representation, and the compromises of countervailing power make for healthier social conditions than stifling unity imposed from above by single-party rule. But the national purpose is more than a sum of these compromises, just as the citizen is more than a member of his own lobby. He is neighbor, parent, worshiper and patriot as well. The great social purposes of a community—its security, the quality of its life and education, the beauty of its public monuments, its images of greatness, its communion with past and future—all these must be expressed in the political dialogue, and cannot be if the citizens themselves succumb to what I regard as, historically, the three great distempers of the public mind—reaction, complacency and mediocrity.

Take first the issue of reaction. America is not in temperament essentially conservative. We have no feudal past such as anchors so many communities in unworkable institutions and outdated ideas. We were born in the morning of popular government and national liberation and some of that fresh light still falls on our faces.

We turn most naturally to the future. We live in hope, not fear. All this is true. But it also is true that the challenge presented by Soviet power is a new challenge. It is that of an apparently implacable power pressing in on us from a steadily widening foreign base and threatening, as we see it, all that is most precious in our way of life. This is new to us.

It is not, however, new to others. Between the seventeenth and the early twentieth century, this was precisely the type of pressure that Western nationalism, mercantilism, colonialism and capitalism exercised on Asia, Africa and, in a rather different form, on Latin America. Westerners in those days appeared—to Turks or Arabs or Indians or Chinese—to have the characteristics we see in Communists today. They seemed implacable men convinced of their own mission and superiority. Their power was growing. Their influence was spreading, and with their influence went the destruction of ancient and cherished beauties, institutions and beliefs.

Under this disturbing pressure, which we in the West are only now beginning to appreciate, from experiencing it ourselves, peoples and societies reacted in opposite ways. In India, for example, a long line of philosophers and reformers—from Sir Ram Mohan Roy in the 1820's to Pandit Nehru in our own day—met the Western encroachment with intelligence, balance and a readiness to judge their own traditions constructively in the light of its challenge. On these foundations they built a philosophy and then a movement which were able to reverse British pressure, recreate Indian society and achieve independence in modern terms. But during the same period, other Indian groups took an opposite line. Leaders hankering for old glories and unchanged feudal society brought about the disasters of the Mutiny. Extreme Hindu groups took to terrorism and murder in the name of the traditional gods. On the morrow of independence, such a terrorist killed Gandhi, the father of the nation. From such sterile reaction, no gain came—no nation building, no emancipation, nothing but counterviolence and hate. In short, the way of reaction proved to be the way of destruction.

Now let us look at another instance—this time between nations, not within the same community. When in the nineteenth century, Western pressure in the Far East became irresistible, the Manchu leaders of China refused to recognize the fact. The regime of the Empress Dowager took refuge in an ever deeper conservatism. The modernization of any part of the state was virtually made impossible by the stagnant, backward-looking court. Then rule by eunuchs and assassination, typical of all China's worst periods, continued while the Western powers filched away ports, treaties, territories, customs, concessions, spheres of interest, and turned the proud empire into the sick man of Asia—everyone's butt and everyone's prey.

During the same years, the leaders of Japan looked at Western civilization squarely and, in an intense revolutionary effort, took over from it what was necessary to keep it out. As a result, while China still drifted on, as storm-tossed and rudderless as a junk in a typhoon, Japan rose to modern power in a generation. Once again, the way of sterile reaction brought disaster, while change and adaptation ensured the power to survive.

Or let us take a more recent instance—the response to Communist pressure given by Hitler's Germany. Allegedly to keep the Communists out, Hitler adopted all Communism's most reactionary techniques—the single party, the single ideology, tyranny, total censorship, total police power, government by torture and murder. And the result? After a ruinous war, half of Europe fell under Communist control—a warning against those self-styled defenders of freedom against Communism who care nothing about killing freedom in the process of conducting their "defense."

These are not remote historical analogies. They are relevant to our experience here and now. The central traditions of our country are liberal, generous and forward-looking. But in times of stress our history has continued to throw up groups of irreconcilable reactionaries whose solution to the problems of the age lies in violence, hysteria, distrust and fear-mongering. The Know-Nothings, the Ku-Klux Klan, the McCarthyites, the White Segregationists—all these are recurrent manifestations of the spirit of irrational reaction. I do not know whether our new tensions are breeding, in the John Birch Society, yet another outburst of this destructive and defeatist spirit. But I do know that history gives us only one verdict on the outcome of looking in times of crisis to a fearful and backward conservatism. The outcome is quite simply defeat. Men do not overcome their crises by running away from them backward. No cozy retreats from a challenging future can be looked for in an outgrown past. Times of challenge are times for new frontiers, not last ditches.

Yet reaction is not our chief danger. The greater risk in our present crisis is not that public opinion will react with a blind and backward-looking conservatism, but that it may not react at all. Complacency, not frenzied John Birchery, may be our chief weakness, and it is easy to understand why this is so. We are the wealthiest society in depth that the world has ever seen. More people enjoy more comfort than at any previous time. Yet there is no guarantee that whole communities are any more immune than families or classes from the typical temptations of affluence. Inertia, indifference, exaltation of the pleasure principle, a falling away in curiosity and human sympathy—all these afflict so-called "Café Society." They can afflict general society as well.

Three-quarters of mankind still live in a poverty so grinding, in such pitiful conditions of health and livelihood, that the framework of their brief lives is not very distant from Hobbes' definition: "nasty, brutish, and short." But when Hobbes wrote, the rich minority contrived to overlook the spectacle. In France, the Court played at shepherds and shepherdesses while the peasants ate grass. Today we in America are the rich minority of world society. Are we any less prone than they to while away our most precious gift of time in pursuit of distractions fully as trivial as those of Le Trianon or Le Hameau? Indeed, we have in television an instrument of mass entertainment that does not even demand that we dress up as shepherds ourselves. We can watch other people doing it for us and sink to an even greater passivity of mind and spirit. A nation of viewers, gazing at what FCC Chairman Newton Minow calls the "wasteland" of the television screen, is not likely to widen its sympathies or feel its instincts of justice and compassion deeply stirred. Yet no wealthy group in the modern age has finally resisted the inroads of popular misery and revolt while clinging to all the trivia of a self-indulgent existence. History is neither made nor changed by the complacent and the comfortable. On the contrary, it is made against them and at their expense.

This complacency in our society has its bearing on a third weakness in popular opinion today—the risk of mediocrity. Our tradition was founded and constantly renewed by great leaders responding to a popular demand for great action. Washington and Jefferson guided and canalized the general revolt against colonial rule. Lincoln directed the energies of a mighty nation at war with itself over the great principles of human freedom. Theodore Roosevelt and Woodrow Wilson caught the reforming tide set flowing by popular disgust at the raw, money-grubbing capitalism of our "Robber Baron" epoch. Franklin Roosevelt mobilized popular despair over the depression behind his New Deal, and Harry Truman caught up the expectations and hopes of the immediate postwar years into the superb strategy of the Marshall Plan. In every case a ferment among the people enabled leaders of stature to direct that ferment into new, imaginative and epoch-making acts of policy.

· Against this background, our present predicament is deeply disturbing. The need for great acts of statesmanship is more urgent than ever before. Wherever we look there confronts us a stark crisis, demanding greatness for its resolution. And most of them have nothing directly to do with Communism. They would exist in any case. All that Communism does is, by its extra pressure, to make their resolution more urgent.

In our domestic economy, we have not been able to reconcile the need for economic growth with the desire for price stability. While Western Europe has achieved rates of growth double and treble ours, we have lagged behind with a 2 percent rate that does not fully absorb our rising population. This in turn aggravates the problem of our growing level of built-in unemployment. Bold new measures of replacing and retraining, new restraints on wage increases and speculation, more competition for greater efficiency are clearly needed to reverse these trends.

We add to our population a city the size of Philadelphia every year. These millions will swell the millions already crowding into our vast urban concentrations, there to live with all the discomforts of congestion, commuting and declining civic services, caught between an urban life without community and a nonurban life without access to natural life and beauty. Only heroic measures of urban renewal, metropolitan planning and nationwide conservation can save our national life from foundering in a series of shapeless, soul-less urban sprawls.

The challenge abroad is, if anything, tougher. We have used up the momentum the Marshall Plan gave to bolder Western association. The trade areas we call the Six and the Seven are still divided in Europe. The exchange reserves of the non-Communist countries are inadequate to cover their rising trade. Their capital assistance to developing areas, though considerable, has been undirected and uncoordinated—and often wasted. Their trade policies, particularly in regard to slumping commodity prices, have often undone the work their aid was supposed to accomplish.

· All these facts point toward a unified North Atlantic economy and community, which by freer competition and expanding internal trade would pile up capital for use in the developing world, and by its prosperity attract the trade of other nations. Such a community would also be politically cohesive enough to roll back Soviet pressure in Europe, compete with it successfully in the developing world, and provide within the wider framework of the United Nations a first concrete example of the kind of confederal association under law which the nations of the world must ultimately achieve if they are to avoid the final horrors of atomic war.

These are not remote needs. They are immediate necessities. But how are we to rally public opinion for such great tasks? Our complacency threatens to breed mediocrity of aim—"You never had it so good"; mediocrity of response—"I'm all right, Jack"; mediocrity of vision—our monument, in the poet's phrase, "a thousand lost golf balls." In the past, social discontent was the fuel of the engine of progress. Today, we have never needed creative change more urgently. Yet we were never so lacking in divine discontent.

Of course, we must not restore genuine misery in order to restore general momentum. We must somehow find, in alert, educated, responsible public response, an alternative to the old discontented pressures for change. In every soul, I believe, there lies not only the desire to be left in peace, but also the desire to feel part of a great adventure. It was the glory of Athens, prototype of all free societies, that by the spontaneous will of the citizens, it could outface the might of Persia and outthink the leaden discipline of the Spartans. We carry in our minds echoes of Pericles' great Funeral Oration:

> We admit anyone to our city and do not expel foreigners for fear that they should see too much, because in war we trust to our bravery and daring rather than stratagems and preparations. Our enemies prepare for war by a laborious training from boyhood; we live at our ease, but are no less confident in facing danger. . . . We love the arts, but without lavish display, and the things of the mind, but without becoming soft.

So long as this temper prevailed, Athens proved invulnerable. Its voice remained the voice of confidence, of excellence, of a community attuned to greatness, drawing its reforming energies not from the miseries of past and present, but from a high vision of the future. During its greatest days, it proved once and for all that free societies can show this vitality, that free societies can be the history-making forces in the world.

But today our society is far indeed from a Periclean spontaneity and vitality. Reading further in Thucydides, I found this disturbing comparison of Athenians with Spartans:

> They—the Athenians—are always thinking of new schemes and are quick to make their plans and to carry them out. You—Sparta—are content with what you have and are reluctant to do even what is necessary. They are bold, adventurous, sanguine; you are cautious and trust neither your power nor your judgment.

Today, who is Sparta, who is Athens? Who has the initiative? Who is making the schemes? Who is bold and adventurous? Who is cautious and "reluctant to do even what is necessary"? Have free men become the conservatives and the Communists the adventurers and innovators? Can there be more to Khrushchev's confidence that he will "bury us" than brash self-assertion? Has he captured a sense of history that we in the West have lost?

I hope I know the answer to these questions. I hope that I can say that while free society may have slumbered for a little and rested and drawn breath, it is ready again for great purposes and great tasks, and that its creative imagination, rearoused and refreshed, is equal to all the crisis and challenge of our perilous days.

A CALL TO A NEW BATTLE:
UNFINISHED EMANCIPATION

𝕍 𝕍 *During his two Presidential campaigns, Governor Stevenson prodded the conscience of the nation on the question of civil liberties. The issue occupied him no less after his appointment as United States Representative to the United Nations, and several of his speeches contain the warning that every instance of racial intolerance jeopardizes the position of the United States throughout the world. The speech that follows—delivered on the occasion of the 100th anniversary of the Emancipation Proclamation—is a simple but poignant appraisal of America's unfinished business at home and in the world.*

This day just a hundred years ago, America reached a turning point.

It was five days after Antietam. In the South Mountain defiles and on the fields around Sharpsburg ghastly clumps of dead soldiers lay unburied. The foul weeds of civil war—hatred, fury, cruelty—grew ranker as the lists of slain and wounded filled the bulletin boards, and the hospital trains crept North and South between lines of harrowed watchers. In Europe, leaders pondered intervention; some ready to take harsh advantage of the New World's agony; some like Gladstone racked with anxiety to stop the slaughter.

Remarks at the Emancipation Proclamation Ceremonies, Lincoln Memorial, Washington, D.C., September 22, 1962.

Then came the flash, the lightning stroke that enables men to see the changes wrought by the storm. A haggard President told his cabinet and his Maker that if the foe was driven from Union soil, he would declare the slaves "forever free." Within hours headlines all over this land clamored with the word "Emancipation!" Within days every slave had heard the news. Within weeks people all over the world were hailing the redemption of young America's promise.

Like all title deeds of human progress, the Proclamation of Emancipation meant more than it said. Morally, it meant that American civilization and human bondage were irrevocably incompatible. And a panoply of larger freedoms was bound up in that first small step. For the Proclamation touched not the fate of Americans alone; it gave courage to the oppressed from the Thames to the Ganges; it inaugurated a new age of world-wide reforms. It was an application of the basic tenets of the nation, tenets which gave promise, said Lincoln, that "in due time the weight would be lifted from the shoulders of all men."

Since we admit so readily our gratitude and our debt to other nations for their enrichment of our national fabric, I hope it will not seem immodest to others that Americans take such pride in the momentous milestone we commemorate today nor in the globe-circling spread of our spirit of national independence and individual freedom. During the past two centuries the two have walked hand in hand. Beside national independence in 1776 stood the goal of individual freedom; beside the preservation of the Union in 1862 stood the same great idea, planted there by the most beloved of American leaders.

And today, just a century later, freedom is again at stake. This time the whole world-wide society of men is perilously divided on the issue. National independence has swept the earth like wildfire, but individual freedom is still the great unfinished business of the world today. Once more we doubt whether the human experiment can survive half slave and half free. Once more we feel, as men did in Lincoln's day, that the future of mankind itself depends upon the outcome of the struggle in which we are engaged.

In this context, with this urgency, with these fears, it would be easy enough to slip into the path of cloudy rhetoric. I could paint you a picture of this world struggle in which our adversaries would be pitch black and we, "the land of the free and the home of the brave," would be lily white.

Such speeches are not too difficult to concoct. But since today we celebrate not only the act of Emancipation, but also the Great Emancipator who sits brooding behind me, it is well to point out that Lincoln, throughout all the agonies and defeats, and the breathtaking triumphs of the Civil War, never made such a speech. Never did he define his cause, this overwhelming cause of freedom, in terms of white and black, good and bad, excellence and evil. Abraham Lincoln never stooped to the cheap rhetoric of the patriotic occasion. Instead, he continued, obstinately and greatly, to see human affairs and human emotions in all their complexity and ambiguity, and to refuse the snap judgments into which self-righteousness can so easily lead us all. If ever a leader lived by the Biblical injunction, "Judge not, lest ye be judged," it was Lincoln. For him, truth was the groundwork of freedom, and you could no more build victory upon delusion than you could sustain society in slavery. And this is reason enough for his saintly rank among world statesmen.

So if today we wish to honor both the act of emancipation and the man who framed it, we have to follow in the same dedication to truth, and the same abhorrence for pretension and self-deceit. We know that we uphold the cause of freedom. Equally we know that we risk betraying it if we have any illusions about our failures and insufficiencies.

If the issue between North and South sometimes seemed ambiguous to Lincoln; if, as in the Second Inaugural, he recognized the equal complicity of Northerners organizing the slave trade and Southerners profiting by the results, so, too, today we must approach the theme of freedom in the world context with some of Lincoln's modesty and accuracy.

Are we the pure-souled defenders of freedom when Negro citizens are anywhere denied the right to vote, or to equal education, or to equal opportunity? Can we be surprised if, abroad, friends with sadness and enemies with delight observe the inequalities and injustices which still mar our American image?

In his day, Lincoln was bitterly attacked for this unwillingness to take the straight partisan line, to claim all virtue for the North, all evil for the South, to praise himself and his cause, to damn all his adversaries. His sense that issues might be relative and ambiguous roused men of rougher certitude to furies of denunciation, and Lincoln was accused of weakness, even of treachery, because he could not go along with the single-minded jingoism of much of the propaganda of his day.

So today, there is a danger that those who do not see things in the stark contrasts of black and white will be denounced as feeble and even treacherous. It is, therefore, worthwhile recalling that Lincoln's sense of the complexity of all great historical issues did not hold him back for one hour from "doing the right" as God gave him to see the right, or deter him from emancipating the slaves and fighting a great war to its finish to ensure that the Union would be preserved and the Emancipation honored.

So today, our sense of our own failures and weaknesses in the struggle for freedom does not mean, for one instant, any faltering in the sacrifices which are necessary to ensure that the Western democracies and the unaligned peoples of the world have the shield against aggression that they need, and the aid necessary to uphold it. That we make no claim to final righteousness will help us to keep open all the paths to negotiation and fruitful compromise. It does not, any more than it did for Lincoln, make us compromise with violence, aggression or fraud. We shall stand all the firmer for not standing in a false light. Our defense of freedom will be all the stronger for being based, not on illusions, but upon the truth about ourselves and our world. Freedom must be rooted in reality or it will crumble as errors are revealed and faith is shaken. Only the truth can make us free.

The immortal document that the Great Emancipator read to his advisers just one hundred years ago closed one era of American history and opened another. It freed the Negro from his age-old bondage; it freed the white people of the South from an outworn and crippling institution; it freed the Republic from the darkest stain upon its record. It gave freedom a mighty impulse throughout the globe. And it will surround the homely features of President Lincoln with an unfading halo.

But it marked a beginning, not an end; it was a call to a new battle, a battle which rages around us in every part of the world in this new time of testing.

Truth was never the enemy of liberty, and it is no coincidence that the greatest statesman of liberty, the greatest champion freedom has ever known, was also the man who claimed least infallibility for himself and for his cause. We can be humble as he was humble, knowing that the cause of freedom is greater than its defenders, and can triumph in spite of all their shortcomings.

In this spirit, we dare declare that the concern and dedication of our Union is the freedom of all mankind. With this candor, we can claim to be Lincoln's heirs in the unfinished work of emancipation.

THE ESSENCE OF DEMOCRACY:

ITS PROSPECTS AROUND THE WORLD

❦ ❦ Governor Stevenson remarked before he began the following address that Dr. Robert Hutchins, President of the Center for Democratic Institutions of the Fund for the Republic, had lured him to its tenth annual convocation with the assurance that it would surpass in importance the Constitutional Convention. He had been skeptical, he added, but now looking around the room he wasn't so sure Dr. Hutchins had not been right. His discomfort, too, he said, had not been relieved by the subject assigned to him: "The Prospects for Democracy Around the World." After asking, "Have you no little questions?" he proceeded to give the following answer.

I understand you have been dissecting democracy morning, afternoon and evening for two days. I wonder if the time hasn't come to leave the poor thing alone to recuperate!

As an ex-politician and a practicing diplomat—although many would doubtless dissent from both of these claims—let me say that when it comes to faith in democracy, I refuse to take a back seat even for my distinguished predecessors on this platform. Because I believe in democracy and freedom, and I believe in their ultimate triumph with the fundamentalist fervor of a survivor of Valley Forge

Address at the Tenth Annual Convocation, Center for the Study of Democratic Institutions, Fund for the Republic, New York City, January 22, 1963.

❦ 249

or a Presidential campaign—not to mention two! As Macauley said of Lord Brougham, or vice versa, "I wish I was as sure of anything as he is of everything." Well, the one thing I'm sure of is that constitutional democracy is that form of government which best fulfills the nature of man. Moreover, my faith, I remind you, has survived some rather disillusioning experiences.

That's why I'm glad to be here among people of like convictions who are trying so hard to make freedom and democracy working realities. And that's why I toil in the tangled vineyards of the United Nations, where the leaders of the whole world are trying to practice parliamentary democracy on a global scale.

Bernard Shaw said that democracy was a device that ensures we shall be governed no better than we deserve. The Center for the Study of Democratic Institutions, as I understand it, can be thought of, then, as a kind of national insurance plan, a way of making certain that we will deserve better and better.

For years Robert Hutchins talked about the need for a democratic version of the Platonic Academy, to deal with new questions of freedom and justice as they emerged on the changing horizon of our times. Finally, with the establishment of the Center, his dream came true. Now, I gather from a few delicate hints that the time has come to think about an endowment policy for this insurance plan, and I am pleased to lend my endorsement to what the Center has already done and promises to do in the years ahead. For busy, battered bureaucrat though I be, I am a staunch believer in the leisure of the theory class.

Ten years ago last July, as Governor of Illinois, I welcomed the Democratic National Convention to Chicago. And I hope you will forgive me for resurrecting some of my words.

"This is not the time for superficial solutions and everlasting elocution," I said in 1952, "nor for frantic boast and foolish word. . . . Self-criticism is the secret weapon of democracy. . . . We dare not just look back on great yesterdays. We must look forward to great tomorrows. What counts now is not just what we are *against,* but what we are *for. Who* leads us is less important than *what* leads us— what convictions, what courage, what faith."

I should like to think that these words apply to the Center for the Study of Democratic Institutions and the work that goes on there. For we have all learned that modern technology can strengthen the despot's hand and the dictator's grasp, and for that reason, if no other, we know that democracy is more necessary now than it ever was.

Of course, democracy is not self-executing. We have to make it work, and to make it work we have to understand it. Sober thought and fearless criticism are impossible without critical thinkers and thinking critics. Such persons must be given the opportunity to come together, to see new facts in the light of old principles, to evaluate old principles in the light of new facts, and by deliberation, debate and dialogue to hammer out the consensus that makes democracy possible. And this, as we all know well, though some of us forget from time to time, requires intellectual independence, impenitent speculation and freedom from political pressure. In a word, it requires centers of the kind found on Eucalyptus Hill in Santa Barbara.

And I hope the day may come when such centers are multiplied the world over. For democracy's need for wisdom will remain as perennial as its need for liberty. Not only external vigilance but unending self-examination must be the perennial price of liberty, because the work of self-government never ceases. The work of an institution like the Center, therefore, is similar to the work of the church in this regard—it will be required as long as final salvation eludes us, which will be until the end of time.

The study of democratic institutions—how to create them, how to sustain them, how to preserve them—will be necessary as long as men continue to seek faith in themselves, continue to harbor hope in their own capacity for progress, and cherish the charity that unites them in a common cause.

And with a world undergoing such rapid change in geography, politics and economics, the need to adapt our old and venerated institutions to the changes is urgent.

Ten years ago, Robert Oppenheimer said: "In an important sense, this world of ours is a new world, in which the unity of knowledge, the nature of human communities, the order of society, the order of ideas, the very notions of society and culture have changed, and will not return to what they have been in the past. . . . The world alters as we walk in it, so that the years of man's life measure not some small growth or rearrangement or moderation of what he learned in childhood, but a great upheaval."

I suppose whether democracy can prevail in the great upheaval of our time is a valid question. Certainly, after 150 years of uninterrupted expansion of the idea of government by consent of the governed, it has recently met with mounting and formidable challenges all over the world from Fascist, Nazi, Communist authoritarians, and a variety of dictatorships. And we have good reason to know how clumsy, slow, inefficient and costly it is compared to the celerity, certainty and secrecy of absolutism.

But the important thing is that it *has* survived. The important thing is that even the absolutists masquerade as democrats; even the military and quasi-military dictatorships strive in the name of democracy to manage the public business. And all of them say that authoritarianism is only a necessary transition to democracy.

Why? Because it is the most popular form of government yet devised; because it is, as it always has been, not only the prize of the steadfast and the courageous, but the privilege of those who are better off; because, in short, as Jefferson said, it is "the only form of government which is not eternally at open or secret war with the rights of the people."

I have, therefore, no doubt that, distant as it may be for many people, it will ultimately prevail, that it will rewin lost ground, that it will expand its dominion, that it can withstand the wild winds that are blowing through the world if—and I repeat if—we who are its custodians continually re-examine and adapt its principles to the changing needs of our changing times.

Years ago, Reinhold Niebuhr observed that "man's capacity for justice makes democracy possible; but man's inclination to injustice makes democracy necessary."

And I suppose that most of us, if we were asked to name the most profound issues at stake in the world today, would say the issues of freedom and democracy. We would say that the Western world, for all its errors and shortcomings, has for centuries tried to evolve a society in which the individual has enough legal, social and political elbow room to be not the puppet of the community, but his own autonomous self.

And we would say that the enemies of freedom, whatever the magnificent ends they propose—the brotherhood of man, the kingdom of saints, "from each according to his ability, to each according to his needs"—miss just this essential point: that man is greater than the social purposes to which he can be put. He must not be kicked about even with the most high-minded objectives. He is not a means or an instrument. He is an end in himself.

This, I take it, is the essence of what we mean by democracy—not so much voting systems or parliamentary systems or economic or legal systems (though they all enter in) as an irrevocable and final dedication to the dignity of man. In this sense, democracy is perhaps mankind's most audacious experiment. This dignity and equality of the human person could hardly be further removed from the existential facts of human existence. There is precious little dignity or equality in our natural state.

Most human beings have to spend their lives in utter vulnerability. All are murderable and torturable, and survive only through the restraint shown by more powerful neighbors. All are born unequal, in terms of capacity or strength. All are born to the inherent frailty of the human condition, naked and helpless, vulnerable all through life to the will of others, limited by ignorance, limited by physical weakness, limited by fear, limited by the phobias that fear engenders.

For nearly three thousand years now, the political and social genius of what we can permissibly call "Western man" has struggled with these brute facts of our unsatisfactory existence. Ever since the Hebrews discovered personal moral responsibility and the Greeks discovered the autonomy of the citizen, the effort has been made—with setbacks and defeats, with dark ages and interregnums and any number of irrelevant adventures on the side—to create a social order in which weak, fallible, obstinate, silly, magnificent man can maintain his dignity and exercise his free and responsible choice.

The task has never been easy. Each step has been a groping in the dark—the dark of violence and brute power and overweening arrogance. Yet we have learned some of the preconditions and expedients of freedom. And we have incorporated them in societies and institutions. What we seek to defend today against new critics and new adversaries is essentially a great body of *experience,* not theories or untried ideals, but a solid mass of lived-through facts. First in time came the great medieval discovery that the king must be subject to the law.

Equality before the law has been expanded and safeguarded by consultation and representation—in other words, the vote. This is not simply a device for peacefully changing government, although it is that, too. It is not only a means of allowing the wearer to say where the shoe pinches. It is, in addition, a means of offsetting the natural inequalities which grow up in any society, however organized, as a result of the unequal endowment of people.

The head of, say, General Electric, has more means of influencing society than a small-town electrician. Against the advantages of brains and money, the vote is the only advantage the small man has. His voice, or vote, added to millions of other voices, offsets the accumulated power of society's entrenched positions.

But equality before the law and at the ballot box are only strands in the seamless robe in which all our liberties are woven together. Carelessly unravel one and the robe itself may come apart.

Another is enough social and economic opportunity for each man, even the poorest, to hold his dignity intact. The widest access to education and training, equal opportunity for talent to find its niche, security of income and work, the chances of health—all these belong to a social order of responsible and respected citizens. We no longer define democracy solely in political terms. The great effort of this century has been to work out its economic and social implications.

If we take these three main strands of democracy—equality before the law, constitutional, representative government, and social and economic opportunity—it is clear that they face, as evolving free society has always faced, new challenges in our own day. It is profoundly concerned with the extension of the concept of democracy—

extension in depth, for we now believe that no human being, however lowly his occupation or poor his resources, can be excluded from the dignity of man—extension in space, for the whole world is now a community and we have to find ways in which the idea of a truly human society can be realized on a planetary scale. The two processes, going forward simultaneously in every part of the globe, make up the vast revolutionary ferment of our day.

What we have to attempt today is the building of intercontinental forms of free community—certainly the most testing experiment of all those made so far by free men. Yet our past achievements give us the right to hope for future success.

One form of association already exists between virtually all the nations of this globe and, whatever work we may accomplish on a regional basis, progress at the United Nations in the direction of a free society of equals must be part of our effort to extend the principle of liberty as the essential working principle of mankind.

How are we to set about this task? There is one method which, I most profoundly hope, we shall avoid, and that is the method of self-righteous exhortation. We have, I fear, sometimes displayed an unattractive tendency to lecture new governments on their constitutional shortcomings and to point, sometimes openly, sometimes implicitly, to the superior performance of the West.

We can admit that free government *is* a Western invention—by all odds, its finest political achievement. But there are several things we must remember as well. We must remember that it took about eight centuries to develop these patterns of life in our own culture. We must remember that our form of democracy is the most subtle and sophisticated form of government in the world; other, more primitive, still developing peoples cannot be expected to master it overnight. But move toward it they will; and such institutions as the United Nations help to train their leadership in our ways. Moreover, new states always face appalling problems of readjustment and we must be smart enough to recognize when and how these alien leaderships move our way.

If now we see in Africa single-party rule dominated by one leader, with changing policies and political choice severely restricted, we should not hold up our hands in horror, but remember that this is not far from our politics of two centuries ago.

Where we have every right to express our alarm is in the breakdown of constitutional protection by the law. The danger lies not so much in parliamentary failure as in judicial failure. Yet even here our alarm should be expressed in modest terms. In eighteenth-century England, a man could be hanged for stealing a sheep, and horrible ships took convicts to Australia for no more than petty larceny. Nor was Europe's recent Fascism precisely a law-abiding mode of government.

No—the way ahead does not lie through sermonizing carried on by people whose own eyes are too full of beams to judge clearly the others' motes. It lies rather in a sustained effort to work out, within the United Nations and in partnerships with other nations, the chief lines of advance toward a more coherent and viable world community, with freedom as its working principle and constitutionalism as its political habit. No one is likely to underestimate the appalling complexities of the task. But the outlook must have seemed as daunting to the lawyers struggling against Stuart despotism or the Founding Fathers attempting to turn federalism into a workable system.

The task is indeed "piled high with difficulty." We should attempt it, therefore, with all the more vigor and clarity, and I would suggest that the three criteria I stressed in domestic democracy are relevant, too, to the global democracy we painfully must try to build.

Today, the first of all tasks is to restrain the nation-state from taking law into its own hands—in other words, from using force to assert its will—or, in the final word, from making war.

From domestic society, we know the only way to banish lawless violence and fratricidal strife is by accepting rules of peaceful change and adjustment, and building an impartial police force to enforce the peaceful solutions that are agreed. This I take to be a task of the United Nations. However, no world body can yet take on the tasks of global peace. Some of our vast modern states are still, like the medieval barons, too powerful to be controlled in their feudal fastnesses.

But perhaps we have reached a first stage of restraint on arbitrary power. Troubled areas—Palestine, the Congo, Laos—are policed, not by rivals whose rivalry would lead to war, but by an external and impartial third force.

Could we not extend the principle? Could we not aim at the policing by the United Nations of more and more areas in which the rival interests of powerful states threaten to clash? Global systems of restraint may still evade us. But history suggests we can start from the particular instance and then extend the principle, and every area withdrawn from the naked arbitrament of force is an area saved for the constitutional working of a sane human society.

Does the second principle I have picked out—the procedure of equal voting—apply to the building of a free world society? The critics say the new states, holding the balance of power by means of their combined vote, drive the United Nations on toward ferocious extremes of anticolonialism and attempt to impose other imprudent policies on the Great Powers which must disrupt the whole organization. Meanwhile, the great foot the bill.

There is much to be said on this score. For the moment, let me only say that in world society, the small nation, like the small man in domestic society, is most likely to be vulnerable. His equal voice, his capacity to unite it with other small voices, is a measure of protection against his inequality. We see the need for this countervailing power inside our states. So let us not be too quick to denounce it in the world at large.

There is a further reason for being cautious and patient about the workings inside the United Nations of the potential ex-colonial majority. If we turn to the third principle of democracy—equality of esteem, equal dignity, equal access to the social and economic possibilities of society—we find that the disproportions which distort true community inside our states are present in world society, too. This Afro-Asian bloc—a misnomer, for, save on the colonial issue, there is no bloc—represents most of the world's most truly underprivileged peoples. If they cling to their United Nations status, it is because, as citizens of our planet, they have not yet much else to cling to. Pushed to the first outskirts of modernity by Western investment and trade, emancipated before they had received either the training or the powers of wealth creation needed for a modern society, they are caught between two worlds—the powerful, affluent, expanding world of the developed "North" and the traditional, pretechnological, largely poor world of the underdeveloped "South."

This division in world society is a great obstacle to the expansion of the confidence and community the world needs for a truly human society. And it threatens to become worse if such experiments as the European Common Market or the Atlantic Community prove to be, vis-à-vis the less fortunate parts of the world, a rich man's club, exclusive in its commerce, its investments, its arrangements and its interests. The gap exists. We must not make it worse.

What can we do? I would like to suggest that we, the wealthiest, most fortunate of all the developed states of the "North," have two lines to follow, both of them essential if we in this generation are to make our full contribution to the advance of world democracy.

I know there is much dissatisfaction about aid, much feeling that it is wasted and never achieves a "breakthrough," and dribbles away down thousands of unspecified drains and ratholes. Yet just so did the Victorians talk about tax money devoted to lifting the standards of the very poor in early industrial society. There were the "good poor" who said "Please" and "Thank you" and touched their forelocks. Then there were the "bad poor" who kept coal in the bathtub. But over a couple of generations, it was the raising of all this unfortunate mass of humanity that turned Western society into the first social order in history in which everyone could expect something of an equal chance.

After ten years, we are only at the beginning of the experiment of international aid. We are learning greatly. We see the relevance of some policies, the supreme obstacles offered by others. We discriminate more. We are learning to be better givers.

Our second task is harder. It is harder for us than for any other member of the world's wealthy elite. It is to see that the last vestiges of discrimination inside our own society are speedily abolished. It is no use talking of ourselves as the vanguard of freedom and democracy while any of our fellow Americans can be treated like a James Meredith at the University of Mississippi.

Must we not, as lovers of freedom and as—too often—self-styled prophets of the free way of life, sometimes lapse into a shamed silence when we even have to talk about social injustice, let alone deal with it—one hundred years after the Emancipation Proclamation?

I must end as I began. The essence of democracy is the dignity of man. We shall create a free world order on no other basis. If we attack Communism—as we must—for its contempt for political dignity, we must attack as unrelentingly lapses in social dignity.

It sometimes seems to me today as though through all the great issues of the day—the anticolonial revulsion, the political contest with Communism, the unification of Europe, the clamor of poorer lands for advance—there runs the underlying desire for some lasting realization of the dignity of man—man with a measure of political autonomy, man with the economic elbow room to live above the torturing doubts of food and work, man with the dignity to look his neighbor in the face and see a friend.

Isolate the problems, measure their magnitude, measure our progress in dealing with them, and you have my answer to your little question—"The prospects for democracy around the world."

In these remarks I have quoted some moderns. I should like to close with a few words from an ancient. Plutarch wrote: "Only those persons who live in obedience to reason are worthy to be accounted free. Only they live as they will who have learned what they ought to will."

If you have no engraving over your door in Santa Barbara, Mr. Hutchins, that quotation might not be half bad.

THE PRINCIPLES OF PATRIOTISM:

LOVE OF COUNTRY

❦ ❦ During his Presidential campaign of 1952, Governor Stevenson offered a memorable definition of patriotism and what it meant to him. Here again, speaking with emphasis, he gives his personal philosophy on love of country and tells why it is hard to be a patriot —the right kind of patriot. His remarks were made in accepting the tenth annual Patriotism Award of the Senior Class of Notre Dame, which had cited him, in part, "as an unselfish and courageous philosopher-statesman, as the very embodiment in contemporary society of the ideals of freedom and justice which our founding fathers treasured and desired to come to pass through the generations."

I am most grateful to the members of the Senior Class for choosing me as the recipient of the Notre Dame Patriotism Award. It is a great compliment, and it is also nice to win an election—especially when you haven't won one for a long time, and especially when the prize brings with it not headaches, but the headiness of pride and satisfaction.

This is a Catholic institution, but its doors are open to all, in keeping with the American tradition of respect and tolerance for all religions and races. And now, at long last, the doors of the White

Address in acceptance of Tenth Annual Patriotism Award of the Senior Class of Notre Dame, South Bend, Indiana, February 18, 1963.

❦ 260

House itself have opened to a Catholic, a remarkable and gifted President, with whom that precious American tradition of tolerance has taken a long leap forward.

For bigotry and freedom are incompatible. If freedom is not to be self-destructive, it must be tolerant. It must be mature enough to face the dual nature of all human relationships—part conflict, part community—and it must always stress community and tolerance as the higher principle. This is an old, revered truth spoken by the Apostle Paul, reminding his flock in Galatia that, in their Christian fellowship, "there is neither Jew nor Greek," and today we could add Baptist or Methodist, Negro or White. Even Unitarian, I hope.

Did you know, incidentally, that the year Notre Dame was founded was also the year that an anesthetic was first used—sulphuric ether gas? I think it has been administered to me more than once in my public life by politicians, writers and even magazines. And in due course many of you won't escape it. I can suggest an antidote I discovered a long time ago in the schoolboy notebook of the great patriot we honor today, George Washington: "Labor to keep alive in your breast that little spark of celestial fire—conscience." I commend it to you, this spark of celestial fire. With it falsehood is routed; with it we can survive our Valley Forges; with it patriotism becomes a shield, not a weapon.

And, as you've honored me for patriotism, perhaps I should tell you what I think about that much abused word. Ten years ago I said to an American Legion Convention that "What it means to me is a sense of national responsibility which will enable America to remain master of her power—to walk with it in serenity and wisdom, with self-respect and the respect of all mankind; a patriotism that puts country ahead of self; a patriotism which is not short, frenzied outbursts of emotion, but the tranquil and steady dedication of a lifetime. The dedication of a lifetime—these are words that are easy to utter, but this is a mighty assignment. For it is often easier to fight for principles than to live up to them."

It is not easy to be a patriot these days—not because it is difficult to love one's country. The difficulty lies not with the love, but with loving one's country in the right way.

The love itself is profound and instinctive, rooted in our childhood discovery of all the infinite delights of being alive—for me, the vast skies, the spring green of the corn, the fall colors and winter snow of the Illinois prairie; for all of us, the shining Christmas trees, the colored mesas and bright flowers of the desert, the rocky shores and pounding seas "way down East," the aspens showering autumn gold on the slopes of the Rockies.

It doesn't matter what your picture is. For all of us, it is "home," the place where we spent the endless, dream-filled days of childhood, the place that still nourishes our secret, life-giving imagination, the place we love as we love bread, as we love pure water, as we love the earliest image of maternal care, as we love life itself. No, it is not difficult to love our country. In doing so, we love what has largely made us what we are. The difficulty is, as I have said, to love it in the right way.

I think the complexity of modern technological society makes the loving difficult for everybody, as I shall try to show. But I want to start with us here in America, because we have some quite special problems, which come not from our complex present, but from our historical inheritance.

Some states emerge from some pre-existing tribal unity, some grow up within an already established culture, and some are forged by conquest, victor and vanquished settling down to a new synthesis.

None of these routes was followed by America. Our people have come from every "tribal" group, they have largely had to create their own civilization as they went along to absorb a continent. They have never been conquered or had any sort of synthesis imposed upon them. Their community had, in fact, a unique beginning; it was from the moment of its birth a land "dedicated to a proposition"—that men are born equal; that government is a government of laws, not men, and exists to serve them; that "life, liberty and the pursuit of happiness" are man's inalienable right.

But consider the consequences of this astonishing start. We are Americans because we belong to a certain ideal, visionary type of political and social order. We can't point back to a long, shared civilization. It is true, most of us have Europe and the West behind us.

But not all—and, anyway, it is a concept of the West that we create rather than inherit. And no one is standing on our necks keeping us down and together.

The result is a community, surely, whose instinctive rooted, inherited, taken-for-granted unity is much less than is normal in the world and whose intellectual, ideal, created and worked-at unity has to be all the more dynamic. If we are not dedicated to our fundamental propositions, then the natural cement in our society may not be enough to take the strain.

I would agree that there are substitutes. When a President said that "The business of America is business," he told us something about the degree to which a standard of living can do stand-in duty for a way of life. But the question, "What manner of people are we?" cannot be everlastingly answered in terms of two-car families or split-level homes.

And if the gods of the market give no answers, neither, for us, do the gods of the tribe. We come back to our propositions. America is much more than a geographical fact. It is a political and moral fact, the first community in which men set out in principle to institutionalize freedom, responsible government and human equality. And we love it for this audacity! How easy it is, contemplating this vision, to see in it, as Jefferson or Lincoln saw in it, "the last, best hope of man." To be a nation founded on an ideal in one sense makes our love of country a more vital and dynamic force than any instinctive pieties of blood and soil.

But it also demands a more complex and discriminating love. Will the fabric hold if the ideal fades? If the effort to realize our citizens' birthright of freedom and equality is not constantly renewed, on what can we fall back? As a going concern, we can no doubt survive many shocks and shames. It was Adam Smith who remarked that "There is a great deal of ruin in every state." But can we survive, as a great, dynamic, confident and growing community, if the essentially liberal thrust of our origins is forgotten, if we equate liberty with passive noninterference, if we exclude large minorities from our standards of equality, if income becomes a substitute for idealism, consumption for dedication, privilege for neighborly good will?

Well, you may say, "Why be so concerned? After all, one of the most forceful elements of our free society is precisely our discontent with our own shortcomings. Haven't you yourself said that 'Self-criticism is our secret weapon'? Because we are free, because we are not the victims of censorship and manipulated news, because no dictatorial government imposes on us its version of the truth, we are at liberty to speak up against our shortcomings. We don't confuse silence with success. We know that 'Between the idea and the reality falls the shadow,' and we are determined to chase away that shadow in the uncompromising light of truth."

But *are* we? It is at this point that our patriotism, our love of country, has to be a discriminating, not a blind, force. All too often, voices are raised in the name of some superpatriotism, to still all criticism and to denounce honest divergencies as the next thing to treason. Thank God, we have risen up from the pit of McCarthy's time, when honest men could lose their jobs for questioning whether there were 381 known Communists in the State Department. But the intolerant spirit which equates responsible criticism with "selling the country short" or "being soft on Communism" or "undermining the American way of life" is still abroad.

You will meet it—no doubt you have met it already—and I can give you no comfort in suggesting there is an easy way out and around this type of criticism. Our position today *is* equivocal. We *are* in one sense a very conservative people, for no nation in history has had so much to conserve. Suggestions that everything is not perfect and that things must be changed *do* arouse the suspicion that something *I* cherish and *I* value may be modified. Even Aristotle complained that "Everyone thinks chiefly of his own, hardly ever of the public, interest." And our instinct is to preserve what we have, and then to give the instinct a colored wrapping of patriotism.

This is in part what the great Dr. Johnson meant when he said: "Patriotism is the last refuge of scoundrels." To defend every abuse, every self-interest, every encrusted position of privilege in the name of love of country, when in fact it is only love of the *status quo,* that indeed is the lie in the soul to which any conservative society is prone.

We do not escape it, but with us, an extra edge of hypocrisy attaches to the confusion, for, once again, I repeat, our basic "social contract," our basic reason for being a state, is our attempt to build a dynamic and equal society of free men. Societies based on blood ties can perhaps safely confuse conservatism and patriotism. People with long backward-looking traditions can perhaps do so. Countries under the heel of dictators must do so. But if the world's first experiment in the open society uses patriotism as a cloak for inaction or reaction, then it will cease to be open and then, as a social organism, it will lose its fundamental reason for existence.

Do not, therefore, regard the critics as questionable patriots. What were Washington and Jefferson and Adams but profound critics of the colonial *status quo?* Our society can stand a large dose of constructive criticism just because it is so solid and has so much to conserve. It is only if keen and lively minds constantly compare the ideal and the reality and see the shadow—the shadow of self-righteousness, the shadows of slums and poverty, the shadow of delinquent children, the shadow of suburban sprawls, the shadow of racial discrimination, the shadow of interminable strikes—it is only then that the shadows can be dispelled and the unique brightness of our national experiment can be seen and loved.

The patriots are those who love America enough to wish to see her as a model to mankind. They love her, of course, as she is, but they want the beloved to be more lovable. This is not treachery. This, as every parent, every teacher, every friend must know, is the truest and noblest affection. No patriots so defaced America as those who, in the name of Americanism, launched a witch hunt which became a byword around the world. We have survived it. We shall survive John Birchism and all the rest of the super-patriots, but only at the price of perpetual and truly patriotic vigilance.

This discriminating and vigilant patriotism is all the more necessary because the world at large is one in which a simple, direct, inward-looking nationalism is not enough. Let me give you only two instances of the intricacies of our modern interdependence.

We face in Communist hostility and expansionism a formidable force, whether Mr. Khrushchev and Mr. Mao Tse-tung pull together or apart. Their disagreement so far only turns on the point whether capitalism should be peacefully or violently buried. They are both for the funeral. So long as this fundamental objective remains, we must regard the Communist bloc as a whole with extreme wariness.

Even if the Communists are divided and confused everywhere, even if they have scored of late none of the victories in Africa, East Asia and the Middle East our doomsayers predicted, still the Communist bloc is aggressive and powerful and determined to grow more so. Taken individually, the European states are all outnumbered. Even America has only a margin of superiority over the tough, austere Soviet Union. Even if the Russian forces in Cuba are not going to conquer the Americas, still their presence in this hemisphere endangers the peace.

We have sensibly concluded in the NATO Alliance that our separate sovereignties and nationalisms must be transcended in a common, overwhelming union of deterrent strength. Together our weight keeps the balance of power firmly down on our side, and it removes from each state the temptation of playing off one state against another and weakening the over-all power in order to strengthen its own. This is the first reason for transcending narrow nationalism.

The second follows from our economic interdependence. The Atlantic world has taken 70 percent of world trade and absorbed 70 percent of its own investments for the last seventy years. We are an interwoven international economy. Bank rates in Britain affect investments in New York. Restrictions here affect carpet makers in Belgium. French farmers affect everybody. We can only avoid the failure of our interwar mismanagement of this community if we pursue joint policies. Those my friend Jean Monnet has outlined are on the essential list: expansion of demand, currency stability, investment overseas, trade with the developing nations, reserves for world trade. Without joint policies here, we could easily slip back to the debacle of the period between the great civil wars of Europe of 1914 and 1939.

In this context, separate, divisive nationalism is not patriotism. It cannot be patriotism to enlarge a country's illusory sense of potency and influence and reduce its security and economic viability. True patriotism demands that in some essential categories purely national solutions be left behind in the interest of the nation itself. It is this effort to transcend narrow nationalism that marked the supremely successful Marshall Plan. It marks the great enterprise of European unification after so many tribal wars. It could mark the building of an Atlantic partnership as a secure nucleus of world order.

So our vision must be of the open society fulfilling itself in an open world. This we can love. This gives our country its universal validity. This is a patriotism which sets no limits to the capacity of our country to act as the organizing principle of wider and wider associations, until in some way, not yet foreseen, we can embrace the Family of Man.

And here our patriotism encounters its last ambiguity. There are misguided patriots who feel we pay too much attention to other nations, that we are somehow enfeebled by respecting world opinion. Well, let me remind you that "a decent respect for the opinions of mankind" was the very first order of business when the Republic was created; that the Declaration of Independence was written, not to proclaim our separation, but to explain it and win other nations to our cause. The Founding Fathers did not think it was "soft" or "un-American" to respect the opinions of others, and I want to put it to you that today for a man to love his country truly, he must also know how to love mankind. The change springs from many causes. The two appalling wars of this century, culminating in the atom bomb, have taught all men the impossibility of war. Horace may have said, "It is sweet and fitting to die for one's country." But to be snuffed out in the one brief blast of an atomic explosion bears no relation to the courage and clarity of the old limited ideal.

Nor is this a simple shrinking from annihilation. It is something much deeper—a growing sense of our solidarity as a human species on a planet made one and vulnerable by our science and technology. That cry of John Donne, "Send not to ask for whom the bell tolls," echoes round the world, reaching, I believe, deeper and deeper levels of consciousness.

For, on this shrunken globe, men can no longer live as strangers. Men can war against each other as hostile neighbors, as we are determined not to do; or they can coexist in frigid isolation, as we are doing. But our prayer is that men everywhere will learn, finally, to live as brothers, to respect each other's differences, to heal each other's wounds, to promote each other's progress, and to benefit from each other's knowledge. If the evangelical virtue of charity can be translated into political terms, aren't these our goals?

Aristotle said that the end of politics must be the good of man. Man's greatest good and greatest present need is, then, to establish world peace. Without it, the democratic enterprise—one might even say, the human enterprise—will be utterly, fatally doomed. I need not belabor that point. It is clear to all of us that war under modern conditions is bereft of even that dubious logic it may have had in the past. With the development of modern technology, the "victory" in war has become a mockery. What victory—victory for what or for whom?

Perhaps younger people are especially sensitive to this growing conviction that nowadays all wars are civil wars and all killing is fratricide. The movement takes many forms—multilateral diplomacy through the United Nations, the search for world peace through world law, the universal desire for nuclear disarmament, the sense of sacrifice and service of the Peace Corps, the growing revulsion against Jim Crowism, the belief that dignity rests in man as such, and that all must be treated as ends, not means.

But whatever its form, I believe that, far from being in any sense an enemy to patriotism, it is a new expression of the pietas and respect for life from which all true love springs. We can truly begin to perceive the meaning of our great propositions—of liberty and equality—if we see them as part of the patrimony of all men. We shall not love our corner of the planet less for loving the planet too, and resisting with all our skill and passion the dangers that would reduce it to smoldering ashes.

And, if I may for a moment speak to you all as members of a great Catholic University, I hope you will not mind my saying that of all the leaders in the world at this moment seeking to give guidance and counsel to the human race, I know of none who so radiates a sense of paternal regard for all God's children as Pope John XXIII. Again and again he returns to this concept of "the human family"—

"the sons of God," "the brotherhood of all mankind." Whether he is inviting all men of good will to pray for spiritual unity or pleading with all wealthy nations to acknowledge their physical obligations to the less fortunate, one feels that before his eyes the vast restless species of mankind appears indeed as a true family—troublesome, no doubt, confused, bewildered, easily misled, easily cast down, but one which must be loved and sustained, and treasured as parents love their family and patriots their land. He adds, in short, the extra dimension of a universal patriotism and makes the brotherhood of man not a cliché, but a living, burning truth.

I can, therefore, wish no more for your profound patriotism as Americans than that you will add to it a new dedication to the world-wide brotherhood of which you are a part and that, together with your love of America, there will grow a wider love which seeks to transform our earthly city, with all its races and peoples, all its creeds and aspirations, into Saint Augustine's "Heavenly city where truth reigns, love is the law, and whose extent is eternity."

PART VI

MISCELLANY

A NEW DEAL FOR DAD

I have come here today not so much to accept an award as to strike a much needed blow for fatherhood in America.

There was a time when father amounted to something in the United States. He was held with some esteem in the community; he had some authority in his own household; his views were sometimes taken seriously by his children; and even his wife paid heed to him from time to time.

In recent years, however, especially since World War II, father has come upon sorry times. He is the butt of the comic strips; he is the boob of the radio and TV serials; and the favorite stooge of all our professional comedians.

In short, life with father seems to have degenerated into a continuous sequence of disrespect or tolerance at best. It appears that the poor fellow is unable to hang a picture or hit a nail without some mishap; no radio or clock will ever work again after he fixes it; he can't boil water or even barbecue a steak, at least not without burning it.

Every time the so-called head of the household attempts to assert himself or express his opinions, the whole family is convulsed with indulgent if not scornful laughter.

Personally, I think all this has gone far enough, and father certainly needs his Day! So all of us fathers should be grateful to you for contriving this brief hour of recognition. I am honored that you have chosen me, a father and a grandfather.

I do not think we would want father restored to his nineteenth-

Remarks to the National Father's Day Committee, New York City, May 25, 1961.

century role of absolute monarch,. but, even though we don't want him to be the autocrat of the breakfast table, I think we might consider giving him at least a polite seat at the table.

After forty or fifty years of life, after hard experience in the world of affairs, after education both in college and in the school of hard knocks, and after sweating away at earning a living for the whole family, it is conceivable that father could have learned a thing or two, and the rest of the family could listen to him with profit once in a while for the honor of raising a plaintive voice on behalf of so many. We might even have some better-behaved children if they did listen to him now and then. But of course I except my own children. I have to—or I might not survive Father's Day!

In all candor, I cannot say that I know for sure just how seriously my own children listen to me, but, God bless them, they at least pretend they do.

So all things considered, I have this suggestion to offer: Instead of a Father's Day, maybe we should try a Father's Year for a change. In any case, whatever we call it, let's have a New Deal for Dad!

Now it has been said that paternity is a career imposed on you one fine morning without any inquiry as to your fitness for it. That is why there are so many fathers who have children but so few children who have fathers.

Is there truth or cynicism in this remark? A bit of both, I imagine, but far too much of the former for my taste.

It is an all too visible truth that fatherhood is no longer the sacred duty it was once held to be. There are, today, far too many absentee fathers, fathers in name only. Paradoxically, and this is an insight into the nature of contemporary society, they are, in many cases, men whose ability, sense of responsibility and moral integrity outside the home are of the first order.

Apologists for these errant progenitors (in most instances, offenders themselves) have called up a multitude of rationalizations in their defense—two world wars in less than half a century, the pressures of modern urban life, business before pleasure, country before self and other tired old saws.

What nonsense. There is absolutely no excuse for a parent to abdicate his most important duty—the proper raising of his children. No father should be allowed to get away with the cowardly logic which concludes that his only job in the family is to pay for the bacon.

His role is much more grandiose than that. If it is to be properly fulfilled, he should be, in his realm, a man of many faces—an artist, a philosopher, a statesman and, above all, a prolific dispenser of good sense and justice.

But it is vitally important, especially in the early years, that his children see in father a working model of the social order in which, not so many years hence, they will be expected to play a dynamic part.

How can we, the parents, hope to secure a just and rational society if we neglect the development of those very instruments, our children, most necessary for its implementation? What good does it do to conceive grand moral, social or political plans for a better world if the children who will have to live them out fail to see their importance?

I know there are utopians who believe that human progress is inevitable, a divine trajectory irreversible in its upward motion. Let me just point out to them that in the last few thousand years we have blazed what I consider to be a trail of questionable glory—from Abraham and Isaac to Dennis the Menace.

I fear that no logic, no optimism can controvert the irrefutable equation that a father brings to his son what his son brings to the world. For sure, leaders in the Soviet Union believe this. In Russia, children are barely out of diapers before the full attention of the stage is focused squarely upon them. They are prodded, led and coaxed through the intricate social, moral and political byways of the system into which they were born. By the time they reach maturity their values are crystallized and they know their duties as responsible Soviet citizens.

In a democracy—in America—the state does not presume to be the father of the man. That responsibility is left to our schools, our churches and, most of all, to our parents.

On the contrary, to our way of thinking, it is the individual who is destined to become the father of the state. And to succeed in his parenthood, he must himself be well trained.

In a very real sense, a father's relations with his children should be a microcosmic reflection of their relations with the society in which they live. Through his actions a father must teach his children the intrinsic meaning of the democratic concept—freedom with restraint and the nature of integrity.

Several years ago, at a "Father-and-Son Team of the Year" ceremony held by the National Father's Day Committee, the father was the first to speak and said:

> I claim no credit for my son being what he is . . . people make their own intellectual and moral characters. If he was helped in making his by me . . . it was he who decided to accept the help. The decision in such matters is finally with ourselves. To say that responsibility begins at home should mean, I think, that it begins—and ends, too—in the individual. Sooner or later he must help himself. There are no alibis.

The son then spoke of his father:

> He has been able to move me, to laughter and to tears, for as long as I can remember, both in public and in private—and that's of the greatest importance. For my father has been to me both a public and a private man.
>
> But my experience has reminded me of something that he taught me—not consciously, I'm sure, but as an example. For the extraordinary thing about my father is that his public face and his private face have been the same. He has been the same man to the world as he has been to his family. And that is harder than it sounds.
>
> It is the very definition of integrity, I suppose.

In modern society everyone faces in some degree the problem of making his public face the same as his private face.

How far any individual succeeds in this effort—which is indeed harder than it sounds—may be taken as a rough measure of "public ethics" for our time and place. Thus in an era of growing artificiality of tinsel and packaging and makeup, and "falsies" of mind and body, the highest compliment that can be paid to a public man is paradoxically that he is made of the same stuff all the way through, inside and out. The more public responsibility he carries, the more important it is to have a private face that can without embarrassment be displayed in public.

I hope no one asks my sons how I've performed in that respect.

WHY IS ROBERT FROST
OUR BARD?

Poets from Vergil and Dante to Frost himself have paid tributes to statesmen in their own stock in trade.

But what is to be done when the roles are reversed? What can I, a dealer in international politics, do for our renowned poetic guest? What is *my* stock in trade? Perhaps I can make him a present of a problem—such as the cold war; or disarmament; or the rule of law. And I have many more in the inventory.

But I can tell you, in part at least, what the public servant has to give to the poet—the defense of the society in which the man like Robert Frost will still have, in his own words, "the freedom of my material—the condition of body and mind now and then to summon aptly from the vast chaos of all I have lived through."

That is all a poet needs from society; the rest, the power to reveal truth and clarify paradox, he has inside himself.

We feel a special affection for Robert Frost because he loves his work. So he could write that: "Like a piece of ice on a hot stove, the poem must ride on its own melting." Or this:

> Only where love and need are one,
> And the work is play for mortal stakes,
> Is the deed ever really done
> For Heaven and the future's sakes.

There are many reasons why we admire Robert Frost, in whom the American people have found their archetypal poet, their singer, their seer—in short, their bard.

Address at a dinner honoring Robert Frost, Washington, D.C., March 26, 1962.
🐾 277

Fortunately, Mr. Frost concurs with at least part of our judgment. In a quatrain—clearly aimed at lawyers and politicians such as I have been—he says:

> So if you find you must repent
> From side to side in argument,
> At least don't use your mind too hard,
> But trust my instinct—I'm a bard.

But if one goes further and asks, "Why is Robert Frost our bard?" then I suggest that in our democratic community, each must be allowed to speak for himself. I have no authority at all to tell you why so many million other Americans like Robert Frost. But I can tell you why I do.

He once defined a poem as he would define love. "It begins," he says, "in delight and ends in wisdom." And I am grateful to him for describing with such precision the reason why, for me, his poetry lives and speaks. You hardly need to read two pages before you encounter the first of these delights—the sudden brilliant image of mankind's "outer weather"—that natural environment of tree and bird and stone which his words make more vivid than even our senses can—"the whirr of sober birds," "cottages in a row, up to their shining eyes in snow," the "whelming east wind . . . like the seas' return." We smell, we taste, our eyes are freshened and renewed, we see better because the poet has seen for us.

And he is the poet of our "inner weather," too. No living poet describes more dispassionately and compassionately the sea changes of the human heart, or has more sly humor to debunk the pretensions and pomposities we mistake for living.

Sometimes it is a casual aside:

> A small bird flew before me. . . .
> He thought I was after him for a feather—
> The white one in his tail; like one who takes
> Everything said as personal to himself.

Sometimes it is a sort of gentle self-mockery:

> I choose to be a plain New Hampshire farmer
> With an income of cash of say a thousand

(From say a publisher in New York City).
It's restful to arrive at a decision,
And restful just to think about New Hampshire.
—At present I am living in Vermont.

Sometimes the light tone and the punch line covers a sad and serious thought:

I turned to speak to God
About the world's despair.
But to make matters worse,
I found God wasn't there.

God turned to speak to me
(Don't anybody laugh),
God found *I* wasn't there—
At least not over half.

But humor—and beauty—do not alone make a bard. He begins in delight. He ends in wisdom. A lot of things, it seems, pass for wisdom these days—flag waving, superpatriotism, frenetic business confidence of the don't-sell-the-country-short variety, conformity, anticonformity, the power of postive thinking. We'll find nothing like that in Robert Frost. His wisdom does not shirk the risk of suffering and injustice and disaster. It measures it. Indeed, not many poets have expressed the anguish more directly.

A voice said, Look me in the stars
And tell me truly, men of earth,
If all the soul-and-body scars
Were not too much to pay for birth.

It is just because there is no naïve optimism, and the abyss is recognized for what it is—the possibility of ultimate despair—that Robert Frost's constant extolling of a quiet, unsensational but dogged courage is more than a conventional theme. It is an inspiration and a force.

I, for one, do not believe that these are days of halcyon weather for America or for the world. We need poets who help us to gird ourselves for endurance, and who walk with us on dark roads where the end is not in sight.

And if you asked me to name of all poems one poem which enshrines for me the spirit in which as a nation we should confront our troubled future, I would quote you these familiar lines:

> The woods are lovely, dark and deep,
> But I have promises to keep
> And miles to go before I sleep,
> And miles to go before I sleep.

We have promises to keep—promises of steadfastness, dedication and vision. And there are miles to go before we can rest from these promises.

We need a poet to remind us of the weight of our destiny. We are blessed that we have such a poet in Robert Frost.

FIFTY PERCENT
OF OUR BRAINS

Nietzsche said that women were God's second mistake. And Radcliffe is my third mistake.

I made a commencement address at Vassar College one time and wisely concluded that I would never make that mistake again. But I did. The next time it was Smith; and once more I resolved never to face all those disconcerting, lovely young faces again. And here I am, as uncomfortable as I look, making the same mistake for a third time—and of all places at Radcliffe, which to a Princetonian is such a luminous and pretty part of Harvard.

I've been wondering *why* I make this foolhardy mistake again and again. Perhaps, like the ancient Greeks, I am so desperate for learning that I even turn to lecturing to acquire it. Or is it, as Dr. Johnson wrote, that one of the last things we men are willing to give up, even in advanced age, is the supposition that we have something to say of interest to the opposite sex? But, of course, it's neither. I'm just an old man who can't say no—to President Bunting and certain charming young ladies of my acquaintance.

In previous appearances at women's colleges, my solemn remarks were addressed to women specifically—about the place of educated women in our society; about bringing up children in a neurotic world; about the conflict between the office desk and the kitchen sink. After listening to my highly instructive addresses I came to the enlightened conclusion that women would not be truly emancipated until commencement speakers ignored the fact that they were women,

Commencement Address at Radcliffe College, Cambridge, Massachusetts, June 12, 1963.

and directed their remarks to graduating students who happened to be women and not to women who happened to be graduating.

So, like most of my decisions, I shall of course ignore it and talk to you as women.

I proceed at once, then, to the central question. The question is whether the wonderfully diverse and gifted assemblage of humans on this earth really know how to operate a civilization. Survival is still an open question—not because of environmental hazards, but because of the workings of the human mind. And day by day the problem grows more complex.

However, there is something even more difficult—something even more essential—than comprehending the great complexities. And that is comprehending the great simplicities.

Let me mention only a few. The first is that human ingenuity has shot far ahead of human responsibility. The destructive intelligence has far outstripped the moral imagination.

Another simplicity is that this world exists for people before it exists for anything else—whether we are talking about ideologies or politics or economics. It exists for people ahead of nations, notions, machines, schemes, or systems.

Therefore, this world must be made safe for people. And it must be made fit for people.

And a third simplicity is that each of us is born with a capacity for growth—not just physical growth but growth of the ability to think, to create works of beauty, to live freely and wondrously, and to add to the lives of others.

And that is where you come in. For nowadays trained intelligence is the nation's best weapon in the battle for a world fit for people and safe for people. We can no longer be content—in the old Ivy League–Oxbridge tradition—to educate a few supremely well. We have to educate every citizen capable of intellectual development. We have to cherish and expand every "erg" of brain power.

Our gravest social evils now spring from the neglect of training and opportunity. One thinks of the immature adolescents in our big cities, often from colored families, who are flung skill-less on a labor market which is hungry only for skills. Our greatest social opportunities—in every field of research and discovery—spring from the scale of the investment we are prepared to make in minds. Some economists are ready to argue that perhaps 60 percent of our gains in output and productivity over the last fifty years can be traced back not to physical capital—in plant and tools—but to mental investment to quick brains and visionary imagination.

But I believe the need for trained minds extends far beyond the limits of economic life. The forces of science and technology have made the world one, abolished space, given us instant communication, brought the world's leaders into our homes and showed us all the cultures of our shrinking globe co-existing with our own in a familiarity we might not have felt for even the next county a hundred years back.

In such a transformed environment, we cannot rely on tradition or habit or what has been called the "conventional wisdom." We can rely on only the rational response of trained minds—minds that can discern facts and judge outcomes, minds sufficiently informed of the lessons of the past to know when, say, an analogy from Thucydides makes sense in the modern context and when it does not, minds disinterested enough to distinguish between a prejudice and a principle, minds steady enough to weigh risks and imaginative enough to take them. Genius consists in anticipating events and knowing how to accelerate or prevent them.

At any time of great social upheaval—and no age has undergone such changes as our own—profound emotions, above all the emotion of fear, are unleashed. There always seems to be so much to lose when changes are proposed—even though more will be lost if the changes are not accomplished.

In the summer before the French Revolution, all of France was gripped by a deep malaise, an underlying panic to which contemporaries gave the name of *la grande Peur*—the great Fear. In our country, where vast social transformations, especially in the relations between the races, have to be achieved, you will find, too, a fringe of hate and fear—an appeal to panic, ignorance and suspicion.

Again, I ask, with what can we combat these panic reactions except with steady intelligence in command of the facts, with the moderation that comes from knowledge, with the freedom that springs from objectivity? Today, as always, it is the truth that makes us free. But how, in this confused and confusing world, can we recognize the truth and adhere to it unless we have the tools for truthseeking—a critical faculty, a certain humility in face of the facts, the coolness and disinterest which comes from habits of study, concentration, and judgment? A mind clear of cant, a mind that "is not passion's slave," is *not* the natural state of our grasping egos; it is something we have to achieve, and it is something which is the proudest aim of education to produce.

So, I repeat, for all who love the human city and wish to see its commerce proceed in dignity and peace, commencement day is or should be a day of rejoicing. And indeed, as I look about, I do rejoice. For Radcliffe is about to launch another task force of intelligent and disciplined good will. And we can take comfort from the fact that one of the truly revolutionary consequences of modern science is that the great majority of you here today will be alive and effective some fifty years hence—yielding a steady return in terms of good sense, good work and calm and rational influence.

When, on commencement day, a man looks forward to his unfolding future, he is unlikely to see, as it were built into it, any marked discontinuity. He will change jobs and places, no doubt, but probably remain broadly within his chosen calling, advancing in it with what skill and industry he has, establishing his family and his reputation, and hopefully ending as chairman of the board. Of course, there are exceptions. I, for one, can guarantee that there are few discontinuities as marked as those of politics and public affairs. Starting from scratch over and over is the lot of most of us.

But for most women there is a large and obvious "discontinuity" to be faced—by most of you, I suspect, fairly soon—and that is to be married and raise a family. Then—in our servantless society—will follow some years in which the life of the mind will co-exist, with some difficulty, with the life of the diaper and the kitchen sink. From the kind of work pursued in the Greek ideal of the academy, you proceed to the work which in the Greek definition is the work of the slave. For the Greeks, the servile quality of domestic work lay precisely in its recurrent rhythm—meal after meal, bed-making after bed-making, washing day after washing day.

Is this, then, the parabola of your future—from scholar to slave? The contrast is too savage, no doubt, but the dilemma is one on which we must reflect.

Let us put into the balance first all the obvious, unquestionable joys and rewards of family life—love, companionship, the excitement of unfolding young minds, the satisfactions of dreary work well done. And in our democratic society where politics are in large measure a "do-it-yourself" job, much community action depends upon voluntary work and many housewives will be able to make their contribution as educated citizens, too.

So, I don't suggest in our free, open society that woman's home is her prison. On the contrary, it will be for many of you the proud center of a rich and satisfying life.

And yet my doubts persist. It is partly a social concern. Fifty percent of our brains are locked up on the female side. (Perhaps your estimate is even higher!) Can we afford to waste a large percentage of this intellectual power? Can we afford not to use it in the sciences, in the professions?

It is also an individual problem. Many women *are* content with the domestic role. But some are not. And since, with women as with men, brain power comes not as an evenly distributed mental quota but often in large patchy concentrations, it is frequently where the talents are highest that the frustration is greatest, too. Social and individual waste reach a peak when the young woman who has it in her to be, say, a brilliant atomic physicist, or a pioneering sociologist, or an historian of formidable insight finds herself in front of the dishes and the diapers. The case may be exceptional. But surely in a free society we must never let the tyranny of the normal trample down the supreme contribution of the unique.

Another problem, as I have said, is that today a woman of forty is still young. She has thirty years or more of active life ahead of her. Is there not here again a factor of waste if, after ten or twenty years of housework, reentry into active professional, civic or academic life is not available?

In a world still very largely run by men, you will not find many ready-made answers to these questions—even though they are urgent for you and should be urgent for all of us. Men, clearly, have had some difficulty in making up their minds about women and their role: Freud remarked that after thirty years of research into the feminine soul, he still could not answer the great question: What do women want? Some philosophers dismiss you as a "second sex," inferior, says Schopenhauer, in every respect to the first. Lord Chesterfield was not alone in thinking women "only children of a larger growth." And we all know the restricted sphere of influence Bismarck allotted you in children, kitchen and church. But I like best Maeterlinck's observation—that woman is mysterious—like everyone else!

You have, of course, had noble defenders too—Plato, John Stuart Mill, Erasmus, Darwin, Shelley. One of the most unequivocal recent statements in favor of removing all irrational restraints upon your capacities came from that remarkable man, Pope John XXIII.

Certainly our Western tradition has never denied you souls—as did the ancient world—or made your total segregation an essential foundation of the social order. But contemporary reactions to the role of women in our society remain ambiguous, and, as a result, women often lack a clear, confident picture of their status and even their identity, and for some this uncertainty reaches a tragic pitch of frustration.

Nor do some of the impersonal forces in our society help to clarify the issue. When were women so bombarded with the suggestion that their success depends upon the right mascara on the eyelash and the right beguiling whiff of irresistible perfume? The aspect of glamour, of allure, of conquest screams at you from a million color ads and television screens. Influenced by these hosts of persuaders, you could come to believe that your rating as a woman, as a wife, as a mother depended on the sheen of your hair, the softness of your hands, your ability to do fifty hot, vexing, repetitive jobs, and emerge looking like Jackie Kennedy or Princess Grace.

I remember one of those masterly Thurber drawings portraying his furiously funny view of the war between the sexes. A shapeless Thurber male leans aggressively over the back of a sofa at a startled and equally shapeless Thurber female. "Where," he hisses at her, "where did you get those great brown eyes and that tiny mind?" Can you have such perpetual insistence upon those aspects of women which are determined by her sex, and not diminish in some degree her other attributes—intellectual power, executive ability, common sense, mature wisdom?

Her image can be molded in other ways, too. "A woman preaching," said the great Johnson, "is like a dog on its hind legs. It is not that she does it well. The remarkable thing is that she does it at all." It is frustrating, it is humiliating, it can be destructive of ease and confidence if women have to feel like dogs on their hind legs whenever they leave the domestic haven to which so much of the folk thought of our society assigns them.

None of all this should, however, discourage you. Many great social transformations have occurred *against* the grain of accepted thought and practice, and if society is slow to realize how much it loses by this potential stifling and inhibiting of half its brain power, there is a good deal that can be done to speed up the recognition. Radcliffe is the sponsor of one such approach in your Institute for Independent Study, at which women receive fellowships to enable them to carry on their scholastic and professional interests part-time to prepare themselves for greater participation in the post-domestic years.

I would hope to see every university in America provided with similar institutes.

In devising institutes for retraining, in fashioning tax patterns which encourage both continuous and post-domestic professional life, in reconsidering problems of responsibility and promotion, we have to use genuine social inventiveness, and with institutes such as yours— and with others of similar intent—an initiative of first class importance has been taken.

Society could help more than it does to give its women citizens the fullest sense of participation. Yet I believe that for men and women alike the fundamental liberations, the genuine experiences of equality, depend not only upon the opportunities—or disabilities— society offers, but also on the reactions and beliefs of the human beings involved. Confusion of roles, problems of identity have their origins in divided and uncertain minds, and there are ways, I think, in which all of us, as members of this strange, varied, immensely talented yet sometimes delinquent human family, can confront the future with some hope of making better sense of the years ahead.

In what I have to say now—(do not be perturbed, this *is* the peroration)—I confess that I have been profoundly influenced by a great and noble woman whose friendship was one of the exhilarating rewards of a public career in which the rewards were not, shall we say, the most notable feature. Since Eleanor Roosevelt's death last year, I have reflected often on what made up the peculiar quality of her greatness. And I can only conclude that it was her absolute disinterestedness. She did everything because it was worth doing. She did nothing because it would help to enhance her own role. Of that she seemed to be unconscious. Work was there. Work had to be done. And it would require all her energy and concentration. But the fact that Eleanor Roosevelt was doing it interested her not at all.

I have never known her equal for objectivity, for unbiased judgment, for a sort of divine fairness and simplicity which sprang from the fact that she never felt her own interests or status or reputation to be involved in her activities.

I recall the beguiling statement of an eighteenth-century lady, who wrote that she did not find the garden of the Doge of Venice so remarkable as the fact that she was sitting in it. For Eleanor Roosevelt, what she did, what her role might be, how people thought of her, her image, her repute—all this meant nothing. The work to be done meant all.

So this is the thought that I would leave with you as you start to play all the various parts which life will bring you—do them all if you can for the sake of the work, do them as little as possible for the sake of yourself. Resist those obsessive commercial voices. Be indifferent—if possible—to any limited view of your part in society. See your life as a whole, with times, no doubt, of concentrated domesticity, with times beyond when you will have leisure and energy and experience for work.

All these forms of work and dedication will be fruitful, will support your self-respect and give you tranquility, if they are done with self-forgetfulness because they are good in themselves. None of them, on the contrary, will release you if you are imprisoned in a narrow, inward-looking self and see them as means of self expression, self fulfillment, and heaven knows what other confusions of purpose and integrity.

That this mood of detachment is more difficult for women than for men in our society I do not doubt. If people constantly exclaim that you as a woman are doing this or that, your role, not the work in hand, can appear the main objective. But never doubt one thing. The more the work is done for its own sake, the more it imposes its own respect. The more objective and disinterested your efforts, the more rapidly shall we all—men and women alike—reach that condition for which a famous English woman pleaded so eloquently when she wrote: "Let us consider women in the grand light of human creatures, who in common with men are placed on earth to unfold their faculties."

May every one of you stand beside us males, not as the classical helpmeet one step behind, but shoulder to shoulder, "in the grand light of human creatures."

HER JOURNEYS ARE OVER

One week ago this afternoon, in the Rose Garden at Hyde Park, Eleanor Roosevelt came home for the last time. Her journeys are over. The remembrance now begins.

In gathering here to honor her, we engage in a self-serving act. It is we who are trying, by this ceremony of tribute, to deny the fact that we have lost her, and, at least, to prolong the farewell. And —possibly—to say some of the things we dared not say in her presence, because she would have turned aside such testimonial with impatience and gently asked us to get on with some of the more serious business of the meeting.

A grief perhaps not equaled since the death of her husband seventeen years ago is the world's best tribute to one of the great figures of our age, a woman whose lucid and luminous faith testified always for sanity in an insane time and for hope in a time of obscure hope, a woman who spoke for the good toward which man aspires in a world which has seen too much of the evil of which man is capable.

She lived seventy-eight years, most of the time in tireless activity as if she knew that only a frail fragment of the things that cry out to be done could be done in the lifetime of even the most fortunate. One has the melancholy sense that when she knew death was at hand, she was contemplating not what she achieved, but what she had not quite managed to do. And I know she wanted to go when there was no more strength to do.

Eulogy at Memorial Service for Mrs. Eleanor Roosevelt, at Cathedral of St. John the Divine, New York City, November 17, 1962.

Yet how much she had done—how much still unchronicled! We dare not try to tabulate the lives she salvaged, the battles, known and unrecorded, she fought, the afflicted she comforted, the hovels she brightened, the faces and places, near and far, that were given some new radiance, some sound of music, by her endeavors. What other single human being has touched and transformed the existence of so many others? What better measure is there of the impact of anyone's life?

There was no sick soul too wounded to engage her mercy. There was no signal of human distress which she did not view as a personal summons. There was no affront to human dignity from which she fled because the timid cried "danger." And the number of occasions on which her intervention turned despair into victory we may never know.

Her life was crowded, restless, fearless. Perhaps she pitied most not those whom she aided in the struggle, but the more fortunate who were preoccupied with themselves and cursed with the self-deceptions of private success. She walked in the slums and ghettos of the world, not on a tour of inspection, nor as a condescending patron, but as one who could not feel complacent while others were hungry, and who could not find contentment while others were in distress. This was not sacrifice; this, for Mrs. Roosevelt, was the only meaningful way of life.

These were not conventional missions of mercy. What rendered this unforgettable woman so extraordinary was not merely her response to suffering; it was her comprehension of the complexity of the human condition.

Not long before she died, she wrote that "Within all of us there are two sides. One reaches for the stars, the other descends to the level of beasts." It was, I think, this discernment that made her so unfailingly tolerant of friends who faltered, and led her so often to remind the smug and the complacent that "There but for the grace of God . . ."

But we dare not regard her as just a benign incarnation of good works. For she was not only a great woman and a great humanitarian, but a great democrat. I use the word with a small "d"—

though it was, of course, equally true that she was a great Democrat with a capital "D." When I say that she was a great small-d
democrat, I mean that she had a lively and astute understanding of
the nature of the democratic process. She was a master political
strategist with a fine sense of humor. And, as she said, she loved a
good fight.

She was a realist. Her compassion did not become sentimentality.
She understood that progress was a long labor of compromise. She
mistrusted absolutism in all its forms—the absolutism of the world
and even more the absolutism of the deed. She never supposed
that all of the problems of life could be cured in a day or a year or a
lifetime. Her pungent and salty understanding of human behavior
kept her always in intimate contact with reality. I think this was a
primary source of her strength, because she never thought that the
loss of a battle meant the loss of a war, nor did she suppose that a
compromise which produced only part of the objective sought was
an act of corruption or of treachery. She knew that no formula
of words, no combination of deeds, could abolish the troubles of
life overnight and usher in the millennium.

The miracle, I have tried to suggest, is how much tangible good
she really did; how much realism and reason were mingled with
her instinctive compassion; how her contempt for the perquisites of
power ultimately won her the esteem of so many of the powerful;
and how, at her death, there was a universality of grief that transcended all the harsh boundaries of political, racial and religious
strife and, for a moment at least, united men in a vision of what
their world might be.

We do not claim the right to enshrine another mortal, and this
least of all would Mrs. Roosevelt have desired. She would have
wanted it said, I believe, that she well knew the pressures of pride
and vanity, the sting of bitterness and defeat, the gray days of
national peril and personal anguish. But she clung to the confident
expectation that men could fashion their own tomorrows if they
could only learn that yesterday can be neither relived nor revised.

Many who have spoken of her in these last few days have used a word to which we all assent, because it speaks a part of what we feel. They have called her " a lady," a "great lady," "the first lady of the world." But the word "lady," though it says much about Eleanor Roosevelt, does not say all. To be incapable of self-concern is not a negative virtue; it is the other side of a coin that has a positive face—the most positive, I think, of all the faces. And to enhance the humanity of others is not a kind of humility; it is a kind of pride—the noblest of all the forms of pride. No man or woman can respect other men and women who does not respect life. And to respect life is to love it. Eleanor Roosevelt loved life—and that, perhaps, is the most meaningful thing that can be said about her, for it says so much beside.

It takes courage to love life. Loving it demands imagination and perception and the kind of patience women are more apt to have than men—the bravest and most understanding women. And loving it takes something more beside—it takes a gift for life, a gift for love.

Eleanor Roosevelt's childhood was unhappy—miserably unhappy, she sometimes said. But it was Eleanor Roosevelt who also said that "One must never, for whatever reason, turn his back on life." She did not mean that duty should compel us. She meant that life should. "Life," she said, "was meant to be lived." A simple statement. An obvious statement. But a statement that by its obviousness and its simplicity challenges the most intricate of all the philosophies of despair.

Many of the admonitions she bequeathed us are neither new thoughts nor novel concepts. Her ideas were, in many respects, old-fashioned—as old as the Sermon on the Mount, as the reminder that it is more blessed to give than to receive. In the words of St. Francis that she loved so well: "For it is in the giving that we receive."

She imparted to the familiar language—nay, what too many have come to treat as the clichés—of Christianity a new poignancy and vibrance. She did so not by reciting them, but by proving that it is possible to live them. It is this above all that rendered her unique in her century. It was said of her contemptuously at times that she was a do-gooder, a charge leveled with similar derision against another public figure 1,962 years ago.

We who are assembled here are of various religious and political faiths, and perhaps different conceptions of man's destiny in the universe. It is not an irreverence, I trust, to say that the immortality Mrs. Roosevelt would have valued most would be found in the deeds and visions her life inspired in others, and in the proof that they would be faithful to the spirit of any tribute conducted in her name.

And now one can almost hear Mrs. Roosevelt saying that the speaker has already talked too long. So we must say farewell. We are always saying farewell in this world, always standing at the edge of loss attempting to retrieve some memory, some human meaning, from the silence, something which was precious and is gone.

Often, although we know the absence well enough, we cannot name it or describe it even. What left the world when Lincoln died? Speaker after speaker in those aching days tried to tell his family or his neighbors or his congregation. But no one found the words, not even Whitman. "When Lilacs Last in the Dooryard Bloomed" can break the heart, but not with Lincoln's greatness, only with his loss. What the words could never capture was the man himself. His deeds were known; every schoolchild knew them. But it was not his deeds the country mourned; it was the man—the mastery of life which made the greatness of the man.

It is always so. On that April day when Franklin Roosevelt died, it was not a President we wept for. It was a man. In Archibald MacLeish's words:

> Fagged out, worn down, sick
> With the weight of his own bones,
> the task finished,
> The war won, the victory assured.
> The glory left behind him for
> the others,
> (And the wheels roll up through
> the night in the sweet land

In the cool air in the spring
between the lanterns).

It is so now. What we have lost in Eleanor Roosevelt is not her life. She lived that out to the full. What we have lost, what we wish to recall for ourselves, to remember, is what she was herself. And who can name it? But she left "a name to shine on the entablatures of truth, forever."

We pray that she has found peace, and a glimpse of sunset. But today we weep for ourselves. We are lonelier; someone has gone from one's own life who was like the certainty of refuge; and someone has gone from the world who was like a certainty of honor.

Format by Gayle A. Jaeger
Set in Linotype Times Roman
Composed, printed and bound by The Haddon Craftsmen, Inc.
HARPER & ROW, PUBLISHERS, INCORPORATED